DRIVING TOWARD CLARITY

BRIAN WESTBYE

NOTEBOOK
PUBLISHING

First published in 2023 by Notebook Publishing, an imprint of Notebook Group Limited, 11 Arden House, Deepdale Business Park, Bakewell, Derbyshire, DE45 1GT.

www.onyxpublishing.com
ISBN: 9781913206505

A CIP catalogue record for this book is available from the British Library.

Typeset by Notebook Publishing of Notebook Group Limited.

This book is dedicated to all who dream big and keep going, in spite of it all.

There are two kinds of travelers. There is the kind who goes to see what there is to see and sees it, and the kind who has an image in his head and goes out to accomplish it. The first visitor has an easier time, but I think the second visitor sees more. He is constantly comparing what he sees to what he wants, so he sees with his mind, and maybe even with his heart, or tries to. If his peripheral vision gets diminished—so that he quite literally sometimes can't see what's coming at him from the suburbs of the place he looks at—his struggle to adjust the country he looks at to the country he has inside him at least keeps him looking. It sometimes blurs, and sometimes sharpens, his eye. My head was filled with pictures of Paris, mostly in black and white, and I wanted to be in them.

—Adam Gopnik, *Paris to the Moon*

If you come to a fork in the road, take it.

—Yogi Berra

I never really said all the things I said.

—Yogi Berra

FOREWORD

SPRING 2019

This is not a Route 66 book, nor is this a midlife crisis book.

Granted, Route 66, depression and anxiety, and midlife ennui factor heavily into this book, but hundreds of forests have been felled in the service of paeans to both The Great American Road Trip and The Great American Midlife Crisis, all written by scribes far more qualified than I, and I have no business adding to that repertoire. No: this book is really about finding yourself broken down on the side of the road, totally lost and a little afraid, and trying to make sense of the landscape; trying to find and hold onto familiar landmarks so you can find your way back to clarity. Getting lost and finding your way back is a universal theme in many works (I, for one, recommend getting completely, hopelessly lost frequently), and whether you're a Mother Road enthusiast or a fellow depression warrior, I hope you'll ride along with me for a spell.

I drove many miles over the course of this narrative, and there's a great story at each stop on the way.

This is the story of *ourselves*.

For the last decade (plus), I have been existing, but I haven't been *living*. Not like I should be, anyway. Instead, I have unintentionally let depression and anxiety take over, and I need to do something major to take my life back; to rediscover my joys and passions; to share my tale, and maybe inspire someone else to roll the bones and hit the gas.

Basically, I need to find my calling.

Don't get me wrong, life is not, nor should it be, a constant gas—a never-ending party—nor a never-ending escape hatch. Life must inevitably contain more mundane day-to-day patterns and rituals and going-through-the-motions moments than Big Adventures. But it's the Big Adventures (and the planning that leads to them and the lessons learned from them) that make life great. The Big Adventures provide the snapshots and stories we take home and carry with us. When you know what it's like to have authentic New Mexican Chile sauce from a mom-and-pop dive in an Albuquerque strip mall, the PB&J you're choking down in the office somehow begins to taste a whole lot better. And when you've seen the sun hanging low over a swath of Missouri farmland, getting stuck in traffic during your evening commute in Maine suddenly isn't so bad. And *you need the Big Adventures to know these things*, because these are the things that give our day-to-day fresh context and perspective; the things that smooth out the rough edges and inspire us to do things differently.

I am, in early 2019, forty-six years old, and I'm in the throes of a midlife crisis. My life right now is about stagnancy... and I'm not cool with that. Hence, it's time for me to allow myself to be open to Big Adventure and to take the lessons I will learn along Route 66 to heart. It's time for me to throw myself into a foreign America and to let the snapshots and stories I collect along the way guide the rest of my life. It's time to take a chance and do something big.

It's time to do things differently on Route 66.

But why now? Why Route 66?

Let's address those questions one at a time.

First: why now?

I fully believe in being open to the moment, ready to catch whatever curveball life throws in or out of our strike zone. I believe that life falls out of the sky and into our laps, and if we're smart about it, we can recognize these gifts and make the most of them: an article in a random magazine at the dentist's office piques our curiosity; a sunset in a strange town tugs on our heartstrings; a snippet of conversation on a diner stool in the middle of nowhere resonates for the rest of our days. And I want to make myself available for these out-of-the-blue moments that change everything. The rest of my life may well depend on it.

Second: why Route 66?

Because I love America, Americana, American roots, and American experiences. And Route 66 is the Great American Touchstone; a cultural talisman whose import spreads far beyond its 2,278 physical miles. It is the road of dreams; the road that leads to a better place—or so we think. It is the inspirer of songs, the carrier of Joads, the gateway to... Something Else, Somewhere Else. Millions have been inspired by this stretch of American macadam for nearly a century, and I want to see why. I want to get lost in a foreign American land and to find my way back. I want to see, taste, and smell an America that I didn't know before, and I want to bring those sensory experiences back home, to my own life. I want to see the topography change before my eyes. I want to wake up in one state and pack it in for the night in another state—another world.

Route 66 is the dream road, and with a bit of gas money, that dream is within reach.

I've had plenty of American experiences, but I've never had *these* American experiences, even though I've always wanted to. I am the traveler in that Adam Gopnik quote—the one who has an image in his head and goes out to accomplish it: I have long had images of what Route 66, and that America, would be like, and I want to see whether those images reflect reality. Confirm or deny, and then recontextualize my images accordingly.

I know Chicago, and I love her, but I've never seen Downstate Illinois. I've never been to St. Louis. I've never seen the Gateway Arch; the Ozarks. Ironically (or maybe not, being the spawn of eighties pop culture that I am), my cherished images of the Midwest largely originate from John Hughes films and TV commercials: the brilliant winter sunset as Neil and Dell drive their burnt wreck of a car from St. Louis to Chicago in *Planes, Trains And Automobiles*; the Currier and Ives snowscape that greets the Polka Kings of the Midwest on their drive in *Home Alone*; the joy of Christmas in Chicago in *National Lampoon's Christmas Vacation*... all Cinematic American wonderlands. Ed McMahon's "Holiday Greetings from Budweiser!" commercials. The Midwest, in my mind's eye, is elderly farmhands with Vitalis-slicked hair wearing Dickies and talking about the price of sorghum at the general store, with Jack Buck calling a Cardinals game on KMOX on the store transistor in the background; the sound of a lonesome train whistle and crows flying across fields of corn stubble; hearth and home, kith and kin.

Texas, to me, is vastness and heat; endless plains of scrub-grass, cattle, and Stetsons, everything bigger than life; *Flintstones* brontosaurus-size steaks and Shiner Bock by the trough-full. A "how-dee" and a hoedown, swing your partner. The stars at night, big and bright.

The southwest is mesas and steppes the colors and magnitude of which I can't fathom; fresh tortillas made by hand from decades of motor memory, the smell of roasting peppers everywhere; the sound of coyotes and dreamcatchers in a rusted-out '49 Ford and gentle Native American chanting.

The Mojave is unending dust, the road a shimmering ribbon, the mountains seemingly unreachable on the cusp of the swallowing horizon, adorned with cacti and palm trees. It is filled with a sense of unease that settles into the last stretch as you hope to God you can just make it over the hills, to the promised land...

I've long had these images in my head, and I want to see if I'm right. And maybe the reality will be even better than I've imagined.

The reason I give all of this background is, this has all set me up for where I am now: forty-six and a bit freaked out by life. Specifically, I am battling with my demons. Hello, depression and anxiety, my old friends.

I have lived with depression and anxiety and OCD my whole life. I'm drastically better than I was in my twenties, when the demons had such a stranglehold on me that I could hardly get out of bed and the thought of being around people brought on far too much agony to bear, but I know I'll never be fully free of them. As I always say, I'm battling, but I'm battling.

I've spent years on the couch, indulged in my share of recreational self-medication, and probably kept several major pharmaceutical corporations in business.

I've conquered all this, and managed to arrive at a

place of stability and serenity.

I live with (I always say "live with" rather than "struggle with" or "suffer from"—a small way of reframing things that gives me more control over my own narrative) depression, anxiety, mild OCD, and HSP (Highly Sensitive Person trait). In my twenties, before I was diagnosed, those four forces had me in an utter chokehold: my depression kept me incapacitated for long stretches of time, and my anxiety, OCD, and HSP held me captive to my own brain.

HSP means I think and feel deeply. For most people, seeing a story of a car fatality between two strangers might make them sad for a few minutes, and then they move on. For me, I think about the people involved and the people left behind in great depth. Somebody has lost a mother. A daughter. A sister. A wife. A father. A son. A brother. A husband. What are they going through? Was the accident quick and painless, or did the victims suffer? I think deeply on these things. I also can't do violent movies because I *feel*, on a very real visceral level, the pain and terror of someone being slashed or shot in a convenience store.

Understandably, I kinda don't like that feeling.

HSP also means I'm hyperaware of my senses and get overwhelmed easily, such as in crowded rooms or social situations. So, if you see me making frequent trips to the loo or somewhere else private, I'm just finding my air pockets and getting a few minutes alone to regroup and recenter.

HSP also means I intuit and tap into the moods of

others—so if I'm in a room with ten people and one is going through something rough, I instantly tap into that vibe and want to help.

Worst of all, HSP means that I overthink everything. I have the greatest friends and family in the world, and all I ever want is to take care of them all and save the world, even though I can't. I reach out to friends even if I don't have to—and then I worry that I've reached out too much. I crack a joke—and then I worry whether it was taken the wrong way. I take a comment at face value—and spiral into a worry cycle, fearing that everyone sees me in the same negative light I suddenly see myself in. I commit the most minor social *faux pas*, and I am instantly convinced that this is a fatal error; that the person I transgressed against will never forgive me and I will *never* recover.

I hang myself on the cross day in, day out, and the pain and shame I experience becomes an all-consuming fog, shrouding my every waking moment.

Meanwhile, the other person has forgotten my minor fuckup by lunch—yet there I am weeks or months later, still kicking myself for ruining everything.

Honestly, I don't know how I was functional for large stretches of my twenties. Often, I wasn't.

To summarize: I overthink and I overshare and over-apologize.

People have moved away from me because of my HSP, and that is an incredibly painful hit to take. All I ever want to do is care for people and bring them together, so knowing that I have made someone uncomfortable or think I'm a neurotic freak who they don't want to be around is a horrible thing to come to terms with. Even still, I get it, and I accept it. I may not be able to undo it, but I can recognize it and try like hell to not do whatever it was that pushed them away this time. And I'm getting better at this, with practice (and some hard lessons).

The thing about depression is that when you're in the worst of it, you don't see how bad it is. You sense it, but until you pull out of it, you're in too deep to see how overblown it truly is; how all the things you panic about and overshare and over-apologize for aren't *worth* oversharing and over-apologizing for. When you're in the midst of it, it's a constant reinforcing echo chamber: one neurosis dies down, and then another neurosis flares up. It's like dropping a match in a forest: a tiny patch of needles flames up, you stomp on it, and then another patch flames up. Pretty soon, the whole goddamn forest is ablaze, and all you can do is uselessly throw your Dixie cup of water at it.

You do your best. It's all you can do.

Now that I'm pulling back from this depression, however, I can see how bad it got and how much I overcompensated when in the throes of it. This is a horrible realization, and all I can do is battle the shame and try to be gentle with myself. (This is the Buddhist concept of *maitri*, unconditional friendliness toward ourselves. I'm working on it.) Happily, I can say that I'm now drastically better at pulling myself back from these spirals—yet in the aftermath of my falling in this hole over these last few years (the damage done and the black depression that has followed), it's been bad again. And that's not living.

I have lived with some shit that many people could never handle—and I've battled and (mostly) won. This has come from being honest with myself and getting to work on what I want to change about myself. It has come from having a fierce self-preservation streak and the gifted ability to step back and say, "No, this is fucked up. We're not doing this anymore." And it has come from my having such a great support network in place.

I've struggled and I've survived.

In the words of Lou Gehrig: "Today, I consider myself the luckiest man on the face of the earth."

Writing these chapters has been a rather intense experience, and it has both heightened and diminished the midlife crisis I've been alluding to and experiencing. I see more clearly now who I am and how I got here. And while I don't quite see where I'm going yet, this has been a great start. Because now, I see me with vivid clarity...

I see a kid with a lust for life (thanks, Iggy) and a shit-ton of talent and potential... and hints of Occasionally Suspect Mental Wiring. I see a kid with lots of early love and nurturing from his (extended) family and a gift for holding onto moments and feelings. I see a kid that dreamed big and didn't even entertain talking himself out of his goals.

I see a kid that had his mundane world ransacked by a sudden move and became shellshocked when he had to start over at five schools in two states across four years—five new beginnings where, at each stop, he started as a pariah. I see a kid who never felt like he fit in and struggled to find friends, normalcy, trust, and kindness. I see a kid with no sense of roots; no sense of place.

I also see a kid who overcame these struggles, finding a voice through his guitar; I see a young man championing his gifts and succeeding in a small pond; I see a young man thriving in his environment and chasing his dreams—and then becoming disillusioned with his new environment and putting the dreams aside. I see a young man seeing his old demons rising and growing in power, in turn swallowing his abilities to hold onto youth and joy and inspiration; to adapt and grow and, ultimately, to function. And I see a young man struggling under the weight of the old status quo, floundering and terrified.

I also see a man who ultimately revisited and fulfilled his dreams—and then put the dreams on hold once again for the sake of practicality and accordingly settled into a great (if artistically unfulfilling) life. I see a man whose world came to a sudden, sickening end, and who was unexpectedly granted the chance to revisit the old world and reinvent it. And I see a man who's going for this reinvention at full speed.

I see a man with a fierce self-preservation streak; a

man who is realizing his strengths and choosing to grow beyond; to silence the demons and relive the dreams. He's getting off the mat and coming back for more. He is De Niro in *Raging Bull*: "You never got me down, Ray!"

And I see myself as I currently am, as I write this in 2019, pre-Route 66: forty-six and newly ensconced in a great job... while still aspiring to move beyond (into a life of self-sufficient creative endeavor) and to finally reach my potential. I see myself burning to become my own self—my own boss—and to tell the tale that comes from it and inspire others.

I see now that I've always been fiercely protective of the kid that I was, always trying to help him out and keep him around. I see all the little dumb things I do today to (as I see now) conjure, protect, and encourage my six-year-old self, and I marvel again at my ability to hold onto the important stuff and cultivate it; to let it inform myself and my future. And I realize more and more that I'm doing okay every day and will continue to do better and better.

I see myself at six, sixteen, twenty-six, thirty-six, and forty-six, and realize that it's all the same: I'm the same individual with the same dreams and the same abilities. I may not have realized these things when I was younger, but I do now. And now, at forty-six, I realize that I can revisit myself at all my ages and integrate all those phases of my life into where I am now; channel myself at any point in my life and re-evaluate what was important then and what's important now.

I see that it's *all* important now. It's *all* who I am.

I'm a bit fucked up, and a bit okay—and now, I'm ready to be all okay (or as okay as I can be) and to try to be the best I can be. I see that I can challenge myself and achieve great new heights.

Do I really think that driving Route 66 specifically will cure this midlife crisis? Truly, I have no idea, but I don't think it'll hurt. Besides, I'm viewing this trip as a chance to put myself in my own preconceived images of many places in America—and not only my own images of Ariston Café in Litchfield, IL, the Ozarks, Tulsa, Tucumcari, the Mojave, and Dodger Stadium, but also in the snapshots of myself that I've envisioned; the *me* that I want to embody when I find myself in these places. I know where I'm at now, and can clearly see and understand where I've been and why I've been there—so now, I want to see the *connections:* how did me at six inform me at forty-six? My logic is, maybe if I retrace my life while tracing this new route, I'll be able to rediscover myself.

I've been thinking a lot about the drives from Maine to Brooklyn we took to visit my grandmother when I was younger (we'll discuss this later!) and how meaningful the little things, like a tunnel or a water tower, were. I've been thinking of the three-day drive from Florida to Maine in 1986, when I was fourteen and we moved back north, and how my gut was nearly bursting with excitement at the thought of going *home*. I've been thinking of the thrill of the college road trips I made with my brother and friend from Maine to Philadelphia and New York for baseball games and general youth hijinks. I've been thinking of driving from Seattle to Boston in a ten-foot Ryder with my bride-to-be and how monumental it was to see the entire country in one journey: one Big Adventure. And it's become clear to me: I've taken some amazing road trips, but never a great *solo* road trip. And what would be a great solo road trip? The Great American Road Trip, Route 66. What better road to get lost and rediscover myself on?

I hope my story will resonate with you and will inspire and encourage you to keep fighting; to keep getting off the mat. Because I'm just like you.

I've battled depression and anxiety my whole life, and for the last few years, I've been in the deepest, darkest depression I've ever experienced—and I have used every bit of my waning strength to pull myself out of it.

I know that too many of you know what that is like.

We are living in a time of great fractions and fissures, and we seem to be more distant from one another than ever before—but we all have so much more in common than we realize. We all struggle, we all hurt, and we all overcome. We all live, laugh, love, and want to make a difference. And we all *dream*. We dream of making our lives and ourselves better, and we've all seen our dreams crushed along the way.

I'm no different.

We dream of belonging; of connecting; of finding our community. And I consider all of you to be my community—all of you who have battled depression or anxiety; all of you who have dreamed big; all of you who have seen your dreams wither; all of you who have gotten off the mat and put the gloves back on. And all of you who have dreamed of Route 66 and what you might find along the way.

Life is so much better when we connect with each other, and I want to connect with you. That is part of what this book is all about.

And I hope you'll come along for the ride.

Let's go.

CHAPTER 1

A MAN AND HIS MIDLIFE CRISIS

I DON'T INTEND FOR THIS to be a maudlin, self-pitying wankfest.

Okay, so yes, at forty-six, in early 2019, I was having another midlife crisis (my first was when I was twenty-six; a quarterlife crisis, maybe?), only this time around, I was much more grounded—but God, this still fucking *sucked*.

Over the past decade, I'd seen the death of at least ten friends and former classmates. Some succumbed to long illnesses; some suffered heart attacks; some were killed in car accidents; some spent their short lives burning the candle brightly at both ends; some were taken by cancer. The latter has visited my friends and my family, and cancer lingers in the background still, a dark whisper beneath the placid surface.

Death is inevitable, and its presence is with me daily.

Despite my life of sometimes-fabulous excess, however, I was fine. My cholesterol was a bit elevated, as was my blood pressure, but I was on meds for those, and my diet was generally good. Even after years of chain-smoking, my lungs got a pass with every physical, and my doc's finger let me know in no uncertain terms at my physicals that my prostate was in good shape.

Still, I was forty-six—almost past the fifty-yard line of life—and of the age where it all starts to go downhill (or so they say). I was realizing more and more daily that the clock *was* ticking, and I'd goddamn well better make the most of what I had left.

And so, I decided I was going to do so on Route 66.

Turning forty had been easy. *Being* forty-something was proving a bit tougher.

Even still, I *think* I'm aging fairly well. I don't sit around bemoaning my age and checking the clock every five minutes to see when it's going to run out. I don't automatically think that every ache and pain is imminent doom. (Okay, I'm really a total hypochondriac, but I'm a *secret* hypochondriac, at least.) Age is just a number—truly—and overall, I felt younger than I ever had in my life. My twenties sucked, my thirties were great, and now, midway through my forties, so far, so good. No complaints.

Well, maybe a few. Most notably, this midlife crisis that I couldn't figure out—that is, whether it qualified as normal, or teetered into abnormal territory. (Ain't that always the million-dollar question!) Whichever it was, I'd been feeling it.

Basically, I was now at the age where I was constantly wondering if I *was*, in fact, aging fairly well. At least I wasn't embarrassing myself by acting ten years younger than I was. I was mostly bald, but wasn't hiding from it with a mountain man beard, a mullet, or a Dick Van Patten combover. I was an off-the-rack Kohl's kind of guy, so I wasn't fooling anybody by frequenting the Slim Fit collections at Macy's. I wasn't up onstage doing splits and trying to rock out with my occasional trick back, and I had no desire to para-ski the Alps, base-jump the Eiffel Tower, or even dive for a ball five feet out of my range.

All set, thanks.

And yet all too often lately, I'd been thinking of the scene in *The Great Outdoors* where Uncle Roman (Dan Ackroyd) muses while trimming his nose hairs, "Why do Chet's [John Candy's] kids look at him like he's Zeus, and my kids look at me like I'm a rack of yard tools at Sears?" (Yes, this scene usually played out in my head while I was trimming my own nose and ear hairs.)

I was relatively comfortable in middle age, but I was also now comfortably *in* middle age, and often, I felt like a window display: collecting dust and cobwebs while the rest of the world hurtled by.

So, I was, as of spring 2019, a somewhat-dumpy mid-forties domestic who didn't see anyone and almost never went out (except in his boxers to grab the Sunday *NY Times* off the lawn). And I was in the throes of a midlife crisis.

I was also a failed corporate drone. I don't belong in your corporate cube: I belong to the creative class; with the *philosophes* yearning to breathe free. It took me years to allow myself to accept this, but now, it's a very obvious part of my personality. I am, shall we say, a late bloomer—but a bloomer, nonetheless.

Most of my twenties was a blur of temp jobs and unemployment (we'll get to that later), but by the time I hit my late twenties, I realized it was time to grow up. And to an extent, I did: from February 2003 through to February 2015, I was a production coordinator for a major grocery chain, producing weekly ad flyers, shelf tags, and in-store signage for 200 stores in five states. For 12 years, I spent my days working eight 'til four-thirty examining images of pork butts and beef shanks, making sure that a thirty-pack of Bud Light was $17.99 in Albany and $18.99 in Poughkeepsie, and verifying that Florida Oranges were $0.79/lb in Augusta and $.89/lb in Bangor—all with the correct image and UPC for billing purposes.

It was a good job, and I was happy to have it, but Christ, what a soul-suck. I'm not a negative person, but being in a negative environment will bring anyone down and make them think the worst of themselves; of their present; of their future; of their potential.

That's what this job did to me for 12 years.

At this job, I worked with a collection of characters. They included [observations taken at the time, hence the present tense]:

The Mood

The Mood has been with the company for decades and knows everyone and everything that goes on. They are constantly digging for and spreading gossip. When not pushing back on perfectly reasonable requests or walking away mid-conversation for a "personal call", The Mood is observed reading Drudge Report, shopping at Amazon, or going to the mall. (Note: they are called "The Mood" because if The Mood is in a mood, you'll feel like you messed on their rug for the rest of the day.) The Mood smells like Marlboros and pancake syrup every morning.

Snorts

Snorts has the worst sinuses in the world. You know the sound of a branch hitting the blades of a woodchipper? Imagine hearing that *multiple times* every few minutes. *Huunk. Huunk. Huunk.*

Snorts spends the first 45 minutes of the workday snorting and gabbing with The Mood. Fancies himself a real yukster, with lines like, "You came in today! Why?" His A-material repertoire is limited to two Friday-specific jokes and derivations thereof, however. These are: a) "Hey, you look a little tired! Why don't you take the next two days off?" and b) "Hey, don't look so down! Monday will be here again before you know it!" Both lines are repeated, with derivations, multiple times each Friday. *Each and every Friday.* Derivations can include, but are not limited to: a) "Take the next two days off! You'll feel better!" and b) "Man, it really sucks being Friday! Oh well, Monday will be here again before you know it!"

These lines are always the introduction to Anecdote Time. Anecdotes include, but are not limited to: a) the times he drove on the Autobahn while stationed in Germany; b) the time he dropped the bottle of Schnapps he brought *back* from Germany and thought about licking the floor; and c) the routes programmed into his GPS to get to the kids' high school sports tournaments in Massachusetts (93 through Tewksbury, bypassing I-495, is an oft-remembered stroke of genius).

Giggles

Giggles is a man in his fifties. Giggles giggles like a schoolgirl. Giggles giggles at every other thing anybody says, and Giggles giggles at every other thing *he* says. Often, Giggles cracks himself up to the point where his giggles are accompanied by clapping and/or stomping. An example of this occurred when he speculated that the CEO of the recently bankrupt Hostess bakery, with his golden-parachute bonus, would be "rolling in the dough".

Giggles is fond of Hawaiian shirts and leaves a cloud of product in his wake. Giggles often makes theatrical productions of his visits, including such moves as "doff-chapeau-and-bow" or "stick-finger-in-mouth-and-pull-trigger". These productions have included unsolicited (I assure you) shoulder rubs. Giggles' theatrics often cause him to, yes, giggle.

Working with Giggles is like working with Poppin' Fresh, only Poppin' Fresh's giggles are limited.

The Loud One

The Loud One has—you guessed it—a very loud voice; loud and booming. After years of smokes, she somewhat resembles a wood carving of an owl. And after years of smokes, she has a loud, booming voice. She uses this voice often—and it's usually used to voice grievances. Example: she once made a $25 payment on her Macy's card even though her minimum payment was five dollars—but because she made this $25 payment five days after the grace period for payments (which was five days after the payment due date), The Loud One was hit with a $25 late fee. "But I friggin' made a $25 payment on a... frickin'... five dollar minimum payment!" Yes, deadlines be damned. Another example: "Jeez, I've got to friggin' get out of here and drive... frickin'... all the way across town for my daughter's softball game and sit in the friggin' cold..."

During the runup to Bush's invasion of Iraq, The Loud One was often heard loudly championing the White House cafeteria's change from "French Fries" to "Freedom Fries" and slagging off any country not in the "Coalition of the Willing", such as Belgium. I was tempted to suggest that since our grocery chain is owned by a Belgian company, she should demonstrate her patriotism and quit, but, of course, this would have flown ten miles over her head.

The Loud One is also fond of her electronic correspondence acumen: "I'm gonna send them a friggin' nastygram, 'cause they don't... frickin'... get it..."

The Velvet Smog

The Velvet Smog also has leather skin from years of smoking. The Velvet Smog is a much sunnier version of The Loud One and laughs frequently—and by "laughs", I mean cackles. And this cackle inevitably turns into a hacking nicotine fit in which one can hear 50 years' worth of tar whooshing out of her lungs. The Velvet Smog talks on the phone frequently, pacing in a tight circle and cackling often.

The Guy Who Never Washes

I've seen The Guy Who Never Washes piss, flush, and walk out more times than I can count. I've never once so much seen him splash water on his hands, let alone touch soap. I see him in the hall or in the cafeteria, and I can practically see a halo of germs and pestilence and sickness and death around his mitts. The Guy Who Never Washes is the reason God cries.

The Guy Who Drinks Nothing But Mountain Dew

I got into the office at 7:30AM once, and The Guy Who

Drinks Nothing But Mountain Dew was already on his third Dew of the day. He once went on a rant because his Chinese dinner had vegetables that he had to pick out and because it took him four tubs of duck sauce to cover the taste of broccoli. He was once given six Mallow Cups and consumed them all before lunch. My friend Jessica says, "Sugar-betes is going to give that wazoo a cold leg in no time."

I feel kind of terrible presenting these characterizations now, and, on a barstool in faraway Gallup, New Mexico, I will feel even worse about it. But that's to come later. My point is, I spent 12 years driving one hour each way to this job so I could work with these characters, getting my soul sucked like a hoover vac daily in the process. That said, I was a good corporate shill, and I was really good at my job: I did everything that was asked of me, never once saying, "That's not in my job description." This included traveling to our North Carolina office to set up and train our sister department for our sister chain.

12 years of solid performance, 12 years of being a go-to resource for my teammates, and 12 years of solid reviews... and no promotions despite my efforts. No reason to believe that I would ever have another life.

That is to say, I spent *11 years and 364 days* driving one hour each way so I could work with these characters and be a good corporate shill.

The 364th day of my 11th year on the job went a little

something like this...

Monday, February 23, 2015, started as a day like any other. It was the day of my performance review—the day before my 12th anniversary of starting work there. I was to go from three to four weeks of vacation. Woo hoo!

My boss, a spawn of nepotism, had just had his second kid the Friday before, so I thought it was a bit strange to see him in—but whatever.

The review was scheduled for 11AM. At nine-thirty, boss asked if I had a second.

Nice! Getting my review done early!

We took an extended walk, and the whole time, he seemed fidgety and kept asking if I'd visited my camp lately. (I'd already stated many times that our recently purchased Maine lakefront camp was summer-only.) Finally, we arrived at a conference room, and there, after 11 years and 364 days of tireless work, I was informed that I was being terminated for "falsifying records".

Um, what?

What sort of criminal enterprise had I been running to be "falsifying records"?

The answer: I'd missed a timeclock punch and hadn't got the chance to correct the mistake due to ad deadlines.

Oh. Okay.

So, at forty-two years old and after 11 years and 364 days of faithful service, I was suddenly perp-walked out of the building—out of work—and faced with the not-so-insignificant question of, what the *fuck* am I going to do with the rest of my life?

I filed a grievance the next day, of course. On my termination letter, the boxes "First Counseling", "Second Counseling", and "Final Counseling" were unchecked and, curiously, blank of notes.

The thing is, missed timeclock punches happened all the time, to myself and to the rest of my colleagues, and when it happened, you'd be informed by the payroll department, fill out the adjustment form, have your boss sign it, and turn it in. Not even remotely a big deal—and certainly not enough to be *fired* over. If I were a suspicious type, I might've thought that there was something going on beyond a missed timeclock punch!

Of course, I pointed this out in my grievance letter. I also pointed out the fact that in nearly 12 years, I'd never once been counseled for attendance or behavior. The *only* counseling I'd *ever* received in nearly 12 years had been at least five years earlier, when I accidentally priced a 5lb bag of private label sugar ($4.99, I believe) at $0.99.

That was it.

And yet, as I'm sure you'll be surprised to hear, my termination was upheld, and thus I found myself shit out the corporate pipes.

Hello, midlife crisis!

So, how did I get to where I was in early 2019, four years after having my world rocked so hideously? How did I end up careening into such a hideous depression?

I gather you'll want to hear a bit about my life so far.

And if you really want to hear about it, the first thing you'll probably want to know is where I was born, what my lousy childhood was like, and how my parents were occupied and all before they had me, and all that Holden Caulfield kind of crap, but I don't feel like going into it, if you want to know the truth (to paraphrase J. D. Salinger).

Oh shit, who am I kidding? Of course I feel like going into it!

I was born in Brunswick, Maine, on September 12, 1972, in Regional Memorial Hospital. My mom said I was a good baby, but that it took me forever to grow hair. And now, after my hirsute high school days, it seems I've come full circle!

The fog of time and the fact of events unfolding before an undeveloped mind have obscured most of the picture of my earliest years, but the pertinent details of my earliest memory remain. First core memory: at age four or five, I got lost in Grand City Department Store, Brunswick, Maine. I was old enough to know that something was wrong, but young enough to not know what to do. I was found on the sidewalk in front of the store with a Wonder Woman coloring book in my hand (red was my favorite color, and I loved coloring in Wonder Woman's red earring)—so basically, I'd become a runaway and a thief in one day. This is my earliest memory. (My next earliest memory is of making Jiffy Pop before Super Bowl XIV— Steelers/Rams—in January 1980 and being in awe of quarterback Terry Bradshaw and terrified of linebacker Jack Lambert and his toothless scowl—but that's another story.) It must have been winter because I remember my dad hugging me tight to his quilted navy-blue nylon coat. I don't remember if this was inside or out. I don't remember being yelled at. I guess they were just thankful to have me back safely.

The safety of my insular world was shaken a bit that day. I'm now in my mid-forties, and looking at this event across the lens of those 40 years, I still remember the dark shades of feeling that came over me—and it is this very unease that has informed my life more than I've realized.

Other than getting lost and shoplifting, my early childhood was a mundane, happy one: solidly middle-class; no entitlements or luxuries, but also never wanting for anything. Growing up on such an even keel made me appreciate what I have and not lust after what I don't. This balance has served me well.

My dad was a travel agent for Stowe (yes, named after *Uncle Tom's Cabin* author Harriet Beecher, who also hailed from Brunswick) Travel, and my mom occasionally sold Avon. Her parents lived on the family farm in Whitefield, Maine, and my dad's mom kept her apartment in Bay Ridge, Brooklyn, until I was eight, after which she moved in with us. I never knew my paternal grandfather. We lived in a red ranch house on Thomas Point Road (after we'd moved out of an apartment on Pleasant Street, but I don't remember my time there), and my immediate family was made up of my older brother (Eric), my parents, an assortment of cats, and our beagle, Ginger. Ginger was a fat little thing, and I loved her. There was a little stream in the woods behind the house, and I remember my mom flinging Ginger's messes into the stream. Don't tell the EPA.

So, all in all, my younger years was pretty smooth sailing... but I see now that my early years in Brunswick were colored with many tiny niggling fears.

An example: just across from the school playground was a street with a few low-slung brick buildings and an overpass. We walked under the overpass to get to the corner variety store for Reggie Bars and candy cigarettes all the time. The buildings were nondescript and could have been either residential or commercial at one point. Regardless, now, they were abandoned, with the windows on the upper floors boarded up. I was convinced that this was a hideout for robbers and that there was a hostage inside trussed up on a meat hook. I was also convinced that if the robbers ever walked out of one of the buildings while I was passing, I would also be grabbed and trussed up, never to see my mom and dad again.

It was certainly a frightening way to get a Slush Puppie.

On my road, I had to watch out for the hippies. (I have no recollection of who called them "the hippies" or why, nor how many there were, but I knew that they had to be dangerous. Why else would they have such a reputation pervading them?) I only ran afoul of them once, but it was terrifying. There were two of them on one motorcycle, and they rode after me for a little bit. (Probably just revved their engines a little, really, but that was enough.) I remember hearing the engine gunning, seeing red and black plaid flannel and long hair, and hearing a laugh which, over the years, has turned into a maniacal cackle. I remember screaming and running like hell for the house, and the sickening feeling that I *might... not... make... it...*

My mom was probably home, and she probably hugged it all better. And I don't remember ever seeing the hippies again. But they have remained in my brain ever since.

Similarly, one time, we returned from a vacation at Disney World (more on that later) to discover that our lock had been picked. Nothing was missing from the house, and no arrests were ever made. Who knows what that was about? Not me—and yet I still remember the sense of violation that rooted me to the ground at the thought of a robber (one from the building with the meat hooks, perhaps?) being in the house and the visceral fear that they could come back. That they *would* come back, while we were home, and my dad would have to fight them all off...

And the intrusive thoughts that characterized my childhood didn't end there.

Example 2: on the bus to Jordan Acers, we drove by the end of the runway of the Brunswick Naval Air Station. At the time, BNAS was home to several squadrons of sub hunters, who flew P-3 Orions over the North Atlantic searching for enemy submarines. We lived about two miles away from the base, and so the sound of the propellers and the sight of the planes flying low and turning in graceful arcs toward or away from the runway was a perpetual background loop. On the bus, as we passed the runway or parked at the Dairy Joy or Fat Boy Drive-In, I often had an image in my head of a P-3 careening nose-first into the ground and exploding into a fireball. I could see the pilot frantically pulling the stick back through the cockpit window as the plane plummeted—to no avail.

It never happened, but the image was a frequent visitor in this brain of mine, and *extremely* vivid.

Fire was a common motif in these horrific imaginings. I saw the *Little House on the Prairie* episode where Albert accidentally burns down the School for the Blind by leaving a lit pipe in the basement at too young of an age, and the trauma settled in instantly: every clap of thunder, I was sure, brought with it the bolt of lightning that would hit the house and destroy my teddy bear and burn our cats alive. I remember my dad counting the seconds between thunderclaps to prove that a storm was moving away and reassuring me in general when a storm was on the approach, but the fear persisted.

I also remember walking through the woods one winter afternoon and seeing our neighbors' (the Thompsons') house burn to the ground. I don't remember the Thompsons, but I'll never forget the sight and sounds, and especially the *feel*, of seeing their house burning down, and the charred, smoldering wreckage after the fact. I remember this was the first time I ever heard of anyone having a "saltbox" house—we had a ranch, and most of my friends had ranches, split-levels, or trailers—and so to this day, whenever I drive by or see or hear mention of a saltbox, I immediately see the Thompsons' saltbox house fully engulfed in the cold winter woods of my youth. *It happened to the Thompsons*, I remember thinking, *so it's going to happen to us, too!*

In retrospect, I can see that this is where one of the narrative threads of my life started to come into play. This wasn't just the slightly overactive imagination of a kid who may have watched a bit too much TV; this was where my clinical anxiety and OCD really started to present itself. The obsession, the rumination, the spirals... it all makes total sense to me now. I don't recall any rituals or number obsessions or any other coping mechanisms I may have used back then, but I still find it very comforting somehow that my anxiety and OCD clearly go back this far. It explains a lot, and it makes me feel a lot (okay, maybe only a little) more normal. One of the most dominant traits of my internal wiring was right there all along, screaming for attention and being unintentionally ignored.

It's crazy the shit our brains tell us.

Nevertheless, I got my moments of respite in the form of family time—and, specifically, our regular trips to Disney World, Orlando. These trips were absolutely responsible for sparking my later travel bug. Dad was a travel agent, and we made the pilgrimage to Disney at least once a year (or, I guess, whenever he got comps for hotels, flights, etc.). Little did he know that these trips marked the start of my lifelong love for travel, adventure, and going *Someplace Else* and *coming home*.

Our trips began at PWM, Portland International Jetport. I feel like the name "International Jetport" conjures images of Jetsons-esque space flight (or at least early sixties postmodern optimism) around the world, like the swoops of latitude on the old Pan Am logo, but actually, "International" in this case meant "maybe one flight per day to Montreal", and the air—excuse me, *Jet*port—was, until very recently, an extremely small, extremely dated relic. Sit in the Staples parking lot next door for five minutes, and you may see takeoffs from JetBlue and DHL and a Cessna taking a father-and-son hobbyist team to the north Maine woods for a camping trip.

Still, it was, and still is, my home point of departure, and I'd always rather be at PWM than Hopkins in Cleveland.

The ticket counters were always a haze of impending adventure and cigarette smoke. I'd hand over my bag to a skycap in a blazing red blazer, and we'd hit the escalator. There was a restaurant at the top level called Jonah's Place (the J was a fishhook. Clever), and on the other side, there was a news stand and then the terminal, with endless rows of vinyl seats embroidered with the Delta logo.

We were on our way.

It was mostly 727s back then. I liked the planes with the symmetrical Delta logo on the tailfin, the navy-and-red widget forming a perfect triangle, but I *really* liked the ones with the more angular widget; with the bottom apex of the blue about three-fourths of the way over to the back of the fin. This logo was much sleeker, and suggested that our plane may very well get us there much faster.

Regardless of the logo angle or plane speed, the cabin décor was seemingly always straight out of a 1970s Good Housekeeping home remodeling book, the seats a slightly garish gold and red—a scheme I would imagine Marco Polo would have approved. I always got a Coke, a set of pilots' wings, and a pencil, and I would then amuse myself for hours reading the safety placards and vomit bag.

We almost always had a layover at Hartsfield in Atlanta, and in addition to all the wares featuring the logo of the Atlanta Braves and this newfangled (Ted) Turner Broadcasting System, there was a guy in the terminal selling a Styrofoam plane called the Super Looper. He would throw the plane while giving a spiel reminiscent of Vince from "ShamWow", and the plane would then do a loop and return to him. It was equal parts boomerang, model plane, and infomercial, and it was magic.

Eventually, we'd get to Disney, and those trips were always great, but (as you can probably tell) I remember the journey there more than being there. I was fortunate enough to have these trips during my formative years, when lifelong loves and habits and associations are born, and to any kid, an airport means the beginning of an adventure, a plane means escapism, and a logo means a brand you trust (even in the face of drastic changes to the company and the industry). I may never have a free lunch on a plane again, but to me, Delta still means flying to Disney, getting free pilots' wings, and going to that magical, mystical *Somewhere Else*.

That kind of love is for keeps, and even today, I'd rather be at an airport than anywhere else in the world. I *love* flight and the—yes—*romance* it entails. Don't get me wrong, I don't love being 45 minutes into a six-hour cross-country hump in a steerage seat without a USB port to charge my phone/entertainment center, but I love every other aspect of flight, especially the experience of being at an airport: I love parking in the garage and moving my car keys to the front of my backpack or roller bag (won't be needing those for a while), and I love printing my boarding pass. My boarding pass always becomes a bookmark for whatever I'm reading on the flight—meaning whenever I revisit many cherished books in my library, a boarding pass falls out. This is always a sudden reminder of place of page and a great journey undertaken, and I love this.

I also love people-watching: I love walking the terminal and speculating about all my fellow travelers. Where are they going? What do they have planned? What are they looking forward to most? I love passing international departure gates and speculating about what adventures await those fortunate souls waiting to board.

I especially love watching events at the terminal or on the plane as we wait to push back from the gate. I honestly believe that an airport provides the greatest coordinated daily ballet one could ever observe. You check your bag with a gate agent, and 90 minutes later, the same gate agent has crawled upstairs and is now doing your boarding call. Suddenly, you're handing off your bag, and the baggage crew gets to work, loading your bags on your flight (possibly after unloading luggage from your first flight, but that comes later). People serve you large coffees at Starbucks and double whiskeys at the bar; people sell you newspapers and issues of *Esquire*; people take your order at Chili's To Go and Wolfgang Puck's and Chick-fil-A.

And then, there is that magical moment when your boarding group is called.

I always tap the side of the plane as I'm boarding. Superstition. And then you watch out the window: the baggage crews are driving around in a coordinated dance around the shuttle buses; the ground crew pulls your plane back and hands it off to the pilot; the tower guides your flight from the gate to the taxiway and runway; you gaze back to the gate you just left and to the skyline on the other side. Conditions are extreme: either blazing heat and a brilliant orange summer sunset with potential thunderheads, or the lights of the city shimmering gauzily behind pitch-black darkness and snow.

You're tenth in line for takeoff, and you watch traffic on the adjacent highway, speculating, *Is that Ford Ranger heading home to supper after a long shift fixing the plane I'm currently sitting in? Is that Hyundai Santa Fe heading toward an evening shift at Best Buy... or a first date?*

Your taxi provides singular joys: the *FLY DELTA JETS* neon sign on the hanger at Hartsfield; the Empire State Building looming over Newark; the breathtaking view of Mount Rainier at Sea-Tac.

And, finally, takeoff.

You gaze back at the gate you just left, where they're getting ready for the next arrival. Meanwhile, a new group of departing aviators await their gate call while you hurtle down a runway at a speed that presses you back into your seat.

Then, you're airborne.

The tower hands you off to TRACON (Terminal Radar Approach Control facilities), who picks your flight up at about 10,000 feet (or 30-50 miles from the airport). The world you just left glimmers below, traffic and house lights and skyscrapers suddenly obscured by wisps of clouds and mist.

Mere hours ago, you were at the office or at home doing laundry, blandly going through day-to-day ritual and minutia. But now you're free. You're off. To *Someplace Else. The Big Adventure.*

It never gets old, and I cherish the experience every time.

And yes, I still look for the Super Looper guy every time I'm running for my connection at Hartsfield.

DAY ONE

MAY 8, 2019

I CAN'T HONESTLY SAY I'D waited my whole life up until that point for this day, but I *had* waited for four (long) months, and it was a delicious culmination: the thrill—the absolute *thrill*—of going *Someplace Else*, the thrill of *going to drive Route 66—The Big Adventure*—almost made me sick with excitement. It had been a while since I'd experienced that thrill, and I was all about inhaling it and letting it spread.

But first, a detour to explain the genesis of, and the rough plan for, this trip.

Like I said, I hadn't been waiting my whole life for this trip. It occurred to me early on that this trip—this Route 66 odyssey—didn't really make a lot of sense, not just in the sense of the magnitude and the timing and the other fundamental stuff, but also in the sense that it wasn't a lifelong obsession or anything. Honestly, for most of my life, Route 66 hadn't been on my radar at all; I hadn't even known it still existed until fairly recently. So, why was I embarking on Route 66: The Life-Altering Journey? Route 66: The Cure for Depression? Route 66: The Drive That Will Help Me Rediscover Myself and My Purpose? Why was the focus of my life now Route 66: The Great American Midlife Crisis Takes the Great American Road Trip?

Good question, isn't it?

Of course, I'd heard the old Bobby Troup song *Route 66*, rendered so memorably by Nat "King" Cole, many times growing up, and I was aware that there was a TV show called Route 66 in the sixties, but that all seemed like bygone stuff, dusty memories from an America I never knew and never would.

So, what brought it to my attention in any meaningful way?

To give some relevant historical context: the route designation "66" was decertified in 1985, when I was twelve. I had no idea what happened to a road after its route number was retired, so for all I knew at the time, Route 66 had been chopped up into powder and spread to the winds. And this attitude seemed to have also been held by many others: at the time of decertification, there wasn't the groundswell of nostalgia for Route 66 that has since emerged; rather, the route number was retired, and everybody yawned and got on the Interstate.

Big whoop.

Route 66 was gone with nothing but a spectral legacy, and not many people seemed to care.

But, of course, there's always nostalgia.

I wasn't really aware of the newfound appreciation for Route 66 when it began, but it didn't take long to sense it. I was aware of Michael Wallis' book *Route 66: The Mother Road* when it came out in the early nineties, but never picked it up. I then saw a few more new Route 66 books emerge over the years, and then an article about a Road 66 Warrior would pop up in my news feed... that kind of thing. It seemed like Route 66 was re-entering the public consciousness, and I found myself thinking of the road more and more frequently and wondering if anything was left of it. Peripheral thoughts, sure, but my interest started deepening, nonetheless.

I can pinpoint the culmination of my own Route 66 obsession to the random purchase of two coffee table books in May 2012: *Fill 'er Up! The Great American Gas Station* by Tim Russell and *Route 66 Lost & Found: Ruins and Relics Revisited* by Russell A. Olsen. The former is a treasure trove of gas station ephemera that traces the evolutionary story of the American gas station both in text and the form of hundreds of photos, old print advertisements, and yes, signs.

My six-year-old self would have lost his little mind over this gem!

The latter book, however, was the one that truly hit home. *Route 66 Lost & Found: Ruins and Relics Revisited* goes state-by-state across Route 66 with historic postcards placed next to present-day photographs of the same locations—and as a lover of history and Americana, I was captivated: I found myself starting at the Illinois chapter and slowly devouring the images and text, my curiosity piqued about American icons I was previously unaware of, such as the Dixie Travel Plaza in McLean and the Cozy Dog Drive In, where the corn dog was invented, in Springfield.

Then, I saw Ariston Café, Litchfield, IL, on page 26 and 27.

The 1935 postcard captures Ariston standing alone on the plains, a massive-looking art-deco barn with two gas pumps out front, *ARISTON* in block letters on the terracotta façade and a small *ARISTON CAFÉ* neon sign above an accompanying Budweiser neon sign. The 2003 photograph meanwhile documents just how little Ariston has changed since 1935: sure, there was now a billboard in the background, a tree in front of the building, an awning on the front of the building, some other additions besides, and removed gas pumps, yet the terracotta façade, block letters, and neon signs were *all* the same.

History preserved!

I found myself staring at those images, utterly sucked in, and thinking, *I'd love to eat at Ariston Café one day.*

From there, I continued through the book at the same deliberate pace, inhaling the images and places: Rolla and Devil's Elbow, Missouri; the Munger-Moss Sandwich Shop and the Devil's Elbow Bridge over the Big Piney River in the Ozarks; Galena, Kansas, and Eisler Bros' Old Riverton Store in Riverton, Kansas; Lucille's Gas Station in Hydro, Oklahoma; the U-Drop Inn service station in Shamrock, Texas; Tucumcari, New Mexico; Clines Corner, New Mexico; Painted Desert Trading Post, Navajo, Arizona; Amboy, California and Roy's Motel. For each page and each spot, my thoughts were exactly the same: *I'd* love *to see that one day.*

Naturally, this being 2012, I supplemented my reading with online research, and I discovered, much to my surprise, that a) Route 66 (the road itself) did, indeed, still exist, and b) that Route 66 (the road *and* the immortalized notion of it) was still beloved and well-visited.

Thus, my own obsession was born. My random purchase of *Route 66 Lost & Found: Ruins and Relics Revisited* changed everything; it reminded me that I *am* a traveler with images in my head that I want to be in.

Yes. Game on.

My gut was telling me *Route 66*, and sometimes in life, you just have to shut up and follow your gut, and whatever happens, happens. Sometimes, you just need a learning experience—and a solo road trip on Route 66 would probably tell me a hell of a lot about myself and my America.

Westbye, Commander of the Corps of (Re)Discovery, reporting for duty!

Now, theoretically, this should have been an easy trip to

plan. Why? Because I wasn't an obsessive or a classicist: unlike Clark Griswold, I'm fine if I don't drive 1,000 miles out of the way to see the House of Mud. I also was *not* about to bust my ass detouring 40 miles to see a two-by-five-foot slab of original Route 66 concrete accessible only by walking 20 yards over barbed-wire fences into a cow pasture, and I was *not* about to hit every single lovingly restored gas station on the route or gorge at every fried chicken and corn dog shack, nor visit the site where Mickey Mantle had his first lay, nor where Will Rogers once took a dump, nor where whatever other bit of arcane Americana happened. Hell, I wasn't even going to be *driving* on Route 66 (or what was left of it) for most of the trip.

Basically, I was seeking *experience*, not cult-like authenticity. I'm a practical sentimentalist. I don't give in to *nostalgie de la boue* (French for "longing for the dirt"), a sentiment that permeates far too many of our longings. For example, my fatherland, New York City: yes, I long for the New York that was affordable and reeked of excitement and danger before the Great Koch/Giuliani Sanitizing Project—a New York that I never lived through but knew well as a visitor and always wanted to experience first-hand—but I do *not* long for the muggings; the reek of bankruptcy; the arson; the piss-and-shit-befouled subways and the crunch of crack vials under one's feet that made such affordability possible. I *did* love the old Boston Garden, home of the Bruins since 1928 and the Celtics since 1946. It was cramped and cozy and wonderful, and stuff happened there: Bobby Orr and Larry Bird (among more of my heroes) owned the joint—but then again, who wants to spend three hours sitting in what was essentially a wood-slat kindergarten desk chair watching a game from directly behind a support pole and taking a leak in a horse trough (literally)?

Clearly, nostalgia only gets you so far.

Basically, I had no desire to drive a jalopy with no air conditioning, seatbelts, or navigation with a canteen of water, a blanket (so I could sleep in a field along the side of the road), and a preserved hog to trade for gasoline, just because that would be an "authentic" experience known by the first travelers along Route 66. *Nostalgie de la boue*? Nope. The facts were, Route 66 was, for all I knew, mostly gone, and the superhighway had won out fair and square. I don't long for the days when it took three hours on 66 to go 100 miles when it now takes half that time on the highway. I *wanted* to travel as much of the original 66 as was practical, but if I was on more of I-55 than 66 in Illinois or more of I-40 than 66 in Texas, so be it. Because Route 66 was so much more than the actual road; it was about the *experience*. And the experience was precisely what I was after.

Basically, I wanted to see my country as it really is and experience an authentic American adventure. I wanted to drive; I wanted to eat (copiously and often), see, and talk local; to get a feel for how the other guy lived; to see what else was out there and how I could incorporate these new findings into my everyday life. That's what almost everybody who's ever started out on the Mother Road has been seeking, and whether it's on the original macadam or the mega-artery that replaced it, it's all the same result—and pretty much the same exact scenery—in the end.

Notably, I wasn't creating any Spotify playlists for the drive. I loosely planned to do so after the fact (though it was more than likely that I'd just write and record the soundtrack myself), but at least for now, I wanted all local radio and television. I'm an NPR junkie, and I love hearing *Morning Edition* and *All Things Considered* framed by newsbreaks from a foreign American market, and I love seeing foreign American weather maps on the local six o' clock news. I wanted to hear how I'm going to Hell on Jesus Radio throughout Oklahoma; I wanted college radio throughout (that's where you always find the best stuff; kids playing what they like with no corporate playlists); I wanted western swing and Tejano across the Panhandle and southwestern folk in Albuquerque. And I didn't care if I got that on 66 or I-40, so long as I got it.

While the theme of this trip seemed to be "fly by the seat of your pants", I also knew that there were also some things I absolutely *had* to do, so I created a list of places and eateries by state and priority level that I wanted to visit. (I would highly recommend that you visit the Appendix for this, at least before the start of the Route 66 dispatches; it will help you make sense of our upcoming journey and give you some context for the places we'll be visiting. Or go ahead and visit the Appendix now! I'll wait.)

When it came to accommodation, the original plan was for me to book rooms for the sake of practicality and expedience in Chicago, St. Louis, and LA, but otherwise, I planned on winging it. Note I am but a humble traveler; I'm a Motel 6 guy, and I wouldn't know what to do with myself in a suite. Luxury, to me, is a scalding shower with good water pressure, a decent (not obscene, but decent) thread count, and walls thick enough that I can't hear the couple next door screwing. I've never raided a minibar, and I don't need a robe and slippers. I don't travel to stay at hotels ("Honey, let's go to the Marriot this year!"): I stay at hotels to travel. Hence, I had no doubt I'd be able to find plenty of budget chains along the way, and I didn't need anything else. And, naturally, I was planning to stay away from social media when making all my hotel choices. TripAdvisor, *et al.* are pretty worthless to me: most of the negative reviews come from Obviously Very Important People who are outraged at not having satin sheets, breakfast in bed, and a hand job for $50 a night at Motel 6. "This place is a sty! There was only *one* hand towel that probably came from *Kohl's!*" "The TV was *tiny!*" Well, life is full of disappointments, Chatsworth. Shut your entitled yap and try the Omni next time. Don't get me wrong, I pay some attention to legit criticisms ("Man, they *really* worked to crop the bloodstains out of those room pics!" "I woke up in the middle of the night to a caravan of rats crawling over the bed, and the front desk clerk just shrugged!"), but again, my baseline is pretty low.

Anyhow: in April (less than a month before my departure), I ended up booking rooms at all stops instead. I'd fully intended on winging it, but there's something to be said for having everything confirmed, especially on a trip where I was going to be doing a lot of it on the fly—and there was also something to be said for booking at places close to other stuff you want to do. Hence, along with The Inn of Chicago, City Place St. Louis, The Big Texan Steak Ranch Amarillo, and the Super 8 LAX, I booked The Campbell Hotel in Tulsa, the El Rancho in Gallup, and El Trovatore in Kingman. To elaborate on why...

- The Campbell. I had another booking in Tulsa, but canceled it when I read of this boutique gem in *Route Magazine*. Built in 1927 as a hotel, Safeway, drugstore, and barbershop at the end of the trolley line, The Campbell was once so derelict that the roof was exposed in places. Now completely restored and on the National Register of Historic Places, The Campbell looked to be an utter gem: a luxury hotel with great rates that welcomed its Route 66 import. There's a spa on the premises, and the cocktail lounge was open until 2AM. And it was a mile away from Ike's Chili and Centennial Park and the art-deco wonderland that apparently was downtown Tulsa. Could. Not. Wait for this one.

- And there's also something to be said for staying at places where stuff happened! El Rancho. Oh, the awesome. I'm not a huge connoisseur of Westerns, but I love Hollywood and Americana, and Bogart, Bacall, and the Duke stayed here. Errol Flynn rode his horse up to the 49er Bar here. A who's-who of signed eight-by-tens line the magnificent southwestern lobby. Spectral ghosts lingering in the night. History. The stuff of legends. Plus, the menu looked amazing, *and* the original staff were trained by the Fred Harvey company, famed for the legendary Harvey House restaurants and hotels that popped up next to depots along the old Atchison, Topeka, and Santa Fe railroad, thus setting up the literal and figurative roadmap for what would become Route 66. Hell yeah! 'Murica!
- Finally, El Trovatore. Marilyn and James Dean stayed here. One of the last pre-WWII motor courts left standing along the way. Magnificent neon in the heart of the desert. It looked like it had seen better days, but again, I didn't travel to stay at hotels; I traveled to have memorable American experiences, and El Trovatore looked to be exactly that. And you can't put a price on maybe staying in the same room Marilyn slept in. (Well, you can for $76 a night at El Trovatore, but...)

So, hotels were set. Now, I was back to waiting.

Until, that is, May 8, 2019.

PWM: GATE 12
5:01AM EST
Wednesday
05/08/19

I have on my person: the clothes on my back
(G.W. Bass cap, Harrington coat, G.W. Bass
flannel, Crow Bookshop Burlington, VT tee,
Levi's 511 33-32, Clark's desert boots), five
tees, three short-sleeve button-downs, a pair
of chinos, a pair of Vans, travel size
toothbrush and toothpaste, stick of Every
Man Jack Cedarwood deodorant, razor, ear
and nose hair trimmer (ah, vanity),
Propranolol (for familial tremor),
Amlodipine (sliiightly elevated blood
pressure), Atorvastatin (sliiightly elevated
bad cholesterol), Zoloft (depression) and
Omeprazole (my esophagus is shit),
Moleskine, pen & pencil, portfolio with all
directions, confirmations, tickets, iPhone
XR, MacBook Air, chargers, GoPro Hero 7
and car mount, the Penguin 50th
Anniversary edition of Travels With Charley
(for reading) and the copy of Travels With
Charley I had when I was 22 (for nostalgia
and because it travels with me). This
inventory represents the extent of my

worldly possessions. Why? Because I AM OFF TO DRIVE ROUTE 66, MOTHERFUCKERS. There is a chickadee flitting around the terminal, a fitting Maine goodbye. I'm expecting a very full flight to New York's JFK airport this morning (said in my best gate agent voice): joy. Short flight, at least. Unless the chickadee attacks...

More to come from Idlewild (sorry, I'm a traditionalist).

Thus began Day One of my Big Adventure.

Andrea dropped me off at PWM at around 4:30AM, and, just like that, I was on my own for the next eight days on my journey to (re)discovering America and myself. No pressure!

Now, as mentioned earlier, Portland International Jetport was, until very recently, an extremely small, extremely dated relic—and while it was still quite small, a massive renovation had changed everything, and the terminal (or at least the upper level leading to security) now felt like a Maine hunting lodge: pine paneling and joists; vintage prop planes hanging from the ceiling... magnificent, and perfectly of its place.

It was the perfect way to leave Maine, especially with a chickadee, the Maine state bird, flitting around!

There was no problem with security, and I got my fuel from Starbucks. I *love* airport Starbucks because they always play great jazz—in this case, Joe Henderson's version of the Kenny Dorham standard *Blue Bossa* from *Page One*, Blue Note Records, 1963, with Joe Henderson on tenor sax, Kenny Dorham on trumpet, McCoy Tyner on piano, Butch Warren on bass, and Pete La Roca on drums.

Yes. Another reminder of old passions and new passions reborn.

Gate 12 (my gate) lies within the new addition, but the gates from the old terminal, where I took off for Disney as a kid, remain operational, and whenever I find myself here, I always take a quick stroll through, checking in on my younger self. Sometimes, however, this is ever so slightly eerie and unnerving, since the old security checkpoint that Mohammed Atta passed through on the early morning of September 11, 2001, is still there (though not in use). Whenever I pass this, it hits me: *it all started here.*

But not today. Today, I focused on the old terminal and envisioned myself at age six waiting to board a flight to *Somewhere Else*, and reminded myself that I was now forty-six and was also about to board a flight to *Somewhere Else*. Namely, Route 66.

A 20-minute delay out of Portland ensued due to a "maintenance issue", which, I believe, turned out to be a dent or ding.

Okay, then.

This was followed by a short, uneventful flight featuring breathtaking views of Jones Beach and the

Verrazzano and lines of tankers heading out to sea on our landing—and then, before I knew it, we'd arrived at Kennedy. We deplaned at B43, and my departure gate was B42.

Awesome! No marathon hump across the terminal for this out-of-shape houseboy!

Hence, I set up with a smoked bloody at Urban Crave and whipped out the MacBook, taking my time and absorbing it all. The forecast for Chicago had improved from pissing monsoons with gusts up to 25 and highs in the 50s, to spotty showers with gusts up to 17 and 61 degrees. Nice! Might not get rained out at Wrigley after all! And, although conditions wouldn't be ideal, I also wouldn't be drenched like a sewer rat on my perambulations around the Windy City. Good to have optimism!

My second flight was also short and uneventful, and my MacBook was at the ready to chronicle this time:

Delta 3378, Seat 12D

9:57AM

Wednesday

05/08/19

34,000' over... somewhere in the east, a few minutes after takeoff from JFK. The thing about a journey is that it takes very little time until you are utterly catapulted into it. And I am completely catapulted into this journey now. A mere five hours ago I was house-boy, domestic, bank worker. Now I'm pounding out a dispatch for my book at 34,000' and heading for a week on the road solo. Strange. Not bad, but strange... like, great to get out of my comfort zone and revisit my own identity for a change strange. That's kind of awesome, actually. I can't believe I have an exit row to myself. Life is awesome. Oh, and much as I enjoy my day job, I'M NOT AT IT NOW. Nope, this week is all mine. I haven't had this luxury in years, and now it's time.

We landed at O'Hare before 11AM, I grabbed my bag right away, and then I smoothly got on the Blue Line to Grand.

I was instantly loving being back on the El through the northern 'burbs: Rosemont, Cumberland, Harlem, Jefferson Park, Montrose, Irving Park, the train paralleling I-90 into the city; the magnificent station announcements ("*This* is Rosemont"—solemn church bell—"*Doors* on the *right* at Rosemont"); three-flats with Cubs flags on balconies and the skyline getting closer. I took a video on my phone as we approached Addison, the Wrigley Field stop, so I could have the station announcement preserved (and, indeed, I found myself listening to it frequently later on).

And suddenly, I was steeped in the feel of Chicago; the feel of The Big Adventure. It really hit me on the train, and it kept building, and, truth be told, it hasn't really stopped yet.

I got off at Grand and hoofed it over to the Inn of Chicago Magnificent Mile, 162 E. Ohio St., in the Near North neighborhood, just off Michigan Ave. There, I was advised that my room wasn't ready, but I could leave my bag so I could head out again.

And just like that, glorious Chicago was all mine!

Electrified with my newfound freedom, I headed over to Michigan and turned south, over the Chicago River, heading for W. Adams Street and The Berghoff. I bypassed The Berghoff by two blocks, however: I had a pre-lunch mission to fulfil. Because on W. Adams St., between S. Clark St. and S. LaSalle St., is the official beginning of the Mother Road, signposted by the sign.

Source:
www.istockphoto.com

This was what I came here for. This was it.

I stood on the sidewalk, staring at the sign, lost in the magnitude of the moment. *I'm* here. *I'm* actually here.

Goosebumps.

No words.

I spent a good few minutes in the cool city afternoon trying to come to terms with the gravity of what I was experiencing—but I couldn't concentrate too hard because my stomach was growling too loud in the process of devouring itself. Time for lunch!

I backtracked two blocks and walked into The Berghoff, and this was like walking into a time capsule. This restaurant has had the same dining room since 1898, and has probably remained unchanged since 1898: checkerboard floors; paneling; elegant sconces giving off a soft, dim light. Old World Chicago. It was absolutely magnificent. I felt like an old-time Chicago politician; an Alderman with a cigar and a sack full of bribe money. City of Chicago Liquor License No. 1—the first one issued after Prohibition—hung on the wall, and I felt a big, dumbass grin spread on my face.

A spring in my step, I got my table, ordered a liter stein of Helles Lager, and settled in.

Soon enough, my waitress delivered an order of rye bread, and I proceeded to peruse the menu, though I already knew I was going with the chicken schnitzel with creamed spinach and whipped potatoes. (Normally, I hate whipped potatoes—it's a texture thing—but when you're in a dining establishment that has been serving whipped potatoes for 121 years, you get the goddamn whipped potatoes. And creamed spinach is classic chop-house fare, so I knew that would be perfect.)

I sat there staring out the window at W. Adams, basking in the joy of a) not being at my job, b) not being home, and c) being at the start of the greatest adventure of my life.

One does not get opportunities like this very often. Life falls out of the sky and into our laps. Take advantage of it.

The schnitzel was gargantuan and glorious: perfectly breaded, not too heavy, and ridiculously good—and, of course, the creamed spinach was fantastic. I even loved the whipped potatoes, texture and all.

After I'd demolished my plate, I sat for a few minutes absorbing (and digesting), overtipped ridiculously, and headed out for the rest of the Chicago afternoon. I didn't really have a plan, so I just kind of wandered over to Millennium Park and found a bench.

Millennium Park is a masterpiece: a 24.5-acre urban oasis of gardens, winding trails, and art installations on top of what were formerly parking lots and the Illinois Central Railroad Yards, all connecting seamlessly to the majestic 1901-christened Grant Park, home of Buckingham Fountain (the one in the intro to *Married: With Children*). Millennium Park is serene and centering, and a great place to while away some time while wondering what to do with the rest of the day.

But first, naturally, some mental drifting.

I thought of Old Chicago, the Chicago of Upton Sinclair and Carl Sandburg, who pretty much perfectly encapsulated the city in his iconic 1914 poem, aptly named *Chicago*:

> *Hog Butcher for the World,*
> *Tool Maker, Stacker of Wheat,*
> *Player with Railroads and the Nation's*
> *Freight Handler;*
> *Stormy, husky, brawling,*
> *City of the Big Shoulders:*
>
> *They tell me you are wicked and I believe*
> *them, for I have seen your painted women*
> *under the gas lamps luring the farm boys.*
> *And they tell me you are crooked and I*
> *answer: Yes, it is true I have seen the gunman*
> *kill and go free to kill again. And they tell me*
> *you are brutal and my reply is: On the faces of*
> *women and children I have seen the marks of*
> *wanton hunger.*
> *And having answered so I turn once more to*
> *those who sneer at this my city, and I give*
> *them back the sneer and say to them: Come*
> *and show me another city with lifted head*
> *singing so proud to be alive and coarse and*

strong and cunning.
Flinging magnetic curses amid the toil of piling job on job, here is a tall bold slugger set vivid against the little soft cities;
Fierce as a dog with tongue lapping for action, cunning as a savage pitted against the wilderness,
Bareheaded,
Shoveling,
Wrecking,
Planning,
Building, breaking, rebuilding,
Under the smoke, dust all over his mouth, laughing with white teeth,
Under the terrible burden of destiny laughing as a young man laughs,
Laughing even as an ignorant fighter laughs who has never lost a battle,
Bragging and laughing that under his wrist is the pulse, and under his ribs the heart of the people,
Laughing!
Laughing the stormy, husky, brawling laughter of Youth, half-naked, sweating, proud to be Hog Butcher, Tool Maker, Stacker of Wheat, Player with Railroads and Freight Handler to the Nation.

I know of few better depictions of place and time than this.

I also thought of Chicago literary icons Studs Terkel and Mike Royko. Stud's greatest works appeared before my time, but his appearances in Ken Burn's *Baseball*, which premiered in 1994 (when I was twenty-two) made me a convert. His 1974 tome *Working: People Talk About What They Do All Day and How They Feel About What They Do* introduced me to the joy of oral history and individual narrative, an artform ultimately mastered later on in a slightly different form by one of my all-time idols, Anthony Bourdain.

Royko, on the other hand, was a contemporary idol for me.

Mike Royko, the Dean of Chicago newspaper columnists, wrote five columns a week nearly every single week from 1963 until his death in March 1997, at the age of sixty-four. I repeat: *five columns a week nearly every single week from 1963 until his death in March 1997, at the age of sixty-four.* Over 7,500 columns over 30 years for the *Chicago Daily News*, *Chicago Sun-Times*, and *Chicago Tribune*. Mind. Blowing. And I was a contemporary fan because his columns were syndicated in the *Kennebec Journal*, and I'd devour them every time I visited my grandparents at the Homestead. (More on that later.)

By the time I started reading Royko in the early 1990s, he was largely focusing on national issues and had become fairly conservative, but he was still delightfully crusty, and reading those columns encouraged me to dig further back—and, sure enough, the earlier Royko swiftly became a hero to me. For the first two decades of his career, his main beat was Chicago, and his column was all about standing up for the little guy and taking on the power structure. Accordingly, Royko was a master of hanging crooked Chicago politicians on their own petard of hypocrisy with their own words. He championed MLK and put a spotlight on police brutality at the 1968 Chicago Democratic Convention, he savaged wealthy Chicago suburbanites who shunned African Americans who wished to move into their neighborhoods, and he tried to get answers when the city of Chicago inadvertently razed a man's apartment—an apartment that was clearly newly renovated and *not* slated for demolition.

What I'm trying to say is, it was sure nice to be in the spectral presence of literary gods.

This being Millennium Park, the bench I was currently sitting on was on the former Illinois Central Railroad depot, and so I also thought of a photograph taken by Jack Delano in April 1943 titled "Illinois Central R.R., freight cars in South Water Street freight terminal, Chicago, Ill". The photo is in the invaluable Library of Congress collection, and shows a freight train at night passing through this spot, illuminated by a giant Pabst Blue Ribbon neon sign with a clock. The clock appears to be set at about 12:05, and the lights of chic Michigan Ave. glimmer in the background. This shows two disparate sides of the city in one frame—industrial Chicago churning on below glamorous Chicago—a very long time ago.

Jack Delano notably worked for the Farm Security Administration and took many Kodachromes of the Illinois Central depot at all times of day and during all seasons, and they're truly magnificent snapshots of a lost industrial past: the bustle of commerce; the people working on the lines. Hard men and lean faces without an ounce of fat. Hard times. That one 1943 shot is the one that gets me every time, though: it's a snapshot of a world that no longer exists; a bustling world of industry and hope in the middle of the war effort, when Americans all came together and sacrificed for a common cause: the belief in our country and our shared stake in it.

And here I was, sitting at that very same place, wondering what to do with my day of leisure.

The nice thing about not having a plan is that... well, you don't have a plan. So, you're free to freelance. Hence, I got back on Michigan and started back north, past the *Chicago Tribune* building, the Wrigley building (1924, one of my favorite buildings in the world), and back to the hotel. There, I checked in, crashed for a little bit, and then set back out—again, without a plan.

I ended up having a single malt at Michael Jordan's on Michigan, just to say I'd been there, and then got on the Red Line headed for Addison.

1060 W. Addison. Wrigley Field.

A day game at Wrigley is always preferable: it was the last park to have lights installed (in 1988), and so night games are still something of a novelty, yet Wrigley is Wrigley, and Wrigley is a magical experience. It opened in 1914 as Weeghman Park, and the original tenants were the Chicago Whales of the Federal League. The Federal League folded after two seasons, however, and so the Cubs moved in for the 1916 season. The park has been modernized since then, of course, but peel your eyes away from all the digital glitz, and you can still put yourself right back in time: the original manually operated wood scoreboard still remains above the bleachers; the National League team flags still fly above the scoreboard in order of the standings (first place team highest, second place team just below, etc.); and after every game, a white flag with a blue "W" or a blue flag with a white "L" is still raised announcing the final result: a win or loss for the home team.

Tradition. Hardball purity.

I love this feeling of history and connection, and I feel it every time I'm at Wrigley. There, one surreal thought echoes through your mind: *somebody sat in this very spot and watched Ernie Banks and Ron Santo. Somebody sat in this very spot and watched the Cubs win their first World Series since 1908.* Yes, I'm a nostalgist, and I love being in the presence of ghosts—and that's one reason why I love baseball: it allows me to feel that connection, and I cherish it.

Tonight, however, as I would soon find out, the wind was whipping in off the lake, and it was absolutely miserable. Regardless, I passed through the turnstiles, walked up the ramp, bought a Chicago dog, and got to my seat... and it was at around this point that I was reminded that Wrigley Field Chicago hot dogs suck: the bun nearly disintegrates, and the tomatoes, relish, and mustard (never ketchup on a hot dog—*never*) splat all over your lap like a surrealist Jackson Pollock. So, I changed tact and got a small Giordano's cheese pie. This was a good enough pizza, but it didn't feel nearly deep enough to be a true Chicago deep dish. I'm used to Uno's, and I've never been to Giordano's, so I could be selling Giordano's short, but it just didn't feel right.

Meh. Can't win 'em all.

I was loving being back at Wrigley, but also not really, what with the wind and chill. I felt like I was on Hoth, the Ice Planet. Plus, I had an early start in the morning, so I left after one inning.

Hey, I've been there before. I'll be back.

From there, I had an Old Style at The Cubby Bear (just to say I'd been there), and a guy in the band that was setting up looked almost exactly like Deep Purple drummer Ian Paice, circa the *Fireball* album. I resisted the urge to scream out a request for *Child in Time*, but the thought was there. With that, I got back on the El and headed back to the hotel, where I set up in the lounge and ended up bullshitting with Juan, the bartender, for a good stretch of time.

Hell of a nice guy.

I also ended up bullshitting with a guy named

Gregory—a writer of crime novels, as it turns out. Thus, I was up way later than I should have been, but I wouldn't change this for the world, since the conversation was great, spanning from my trip to the writing craft to prog rock to jazz to Chicago politics to Mike Royko and beyond.

What a great experience, and one I so rarely have. Yes, I'll always gladly trade a bit of sleep for such a gift at the start of a trip!

As I drifted to sleep, I couldn't help but ponder how much I love this town (easy for me to say as a white male, age thirty-four to fifty-two, and a non-resident who doesn't see the other side of the city daily, and that bothers me—but nevertheless). It was so great to be back, and though I didn't get to do nearly enough while there, this trip was all about getting tastes of what I knew and tastes of what I didn't know and wanted to find out more about. So, so far, so good.

CHAPTER 2

MAINE, I MISS YOU

TRAVEL (WELL, LONG-DISTANCE TRAVEL, that is) was not the only thing to have made a huge, lasting impact on me and my worldview during my childhood: it occurs to me now just how much my passions in life were also informed by shapes and colors—specifically, advertising signs, preferably neon (foreshadowing of my destiny, if you will, to travel Route 66, perhaps?).

Growing up in Brunswick, Maine, in the seventies and eighties, I was treated daily to great living examples of American advertising. Exhibit A: on Rt. 1, there was a gigantic vertical sign for Maclean's Restaurant formatted in vertical block letters:

M
A
C
L
E
A
N
'S

I loved how the apostrophe kicked the *S* over to the side a bit. This sign was also near a similar Texaco sign. Both together offered twice the visual joy.

Meanwhile, in town, on Main St., there was (and still is) J&J Cleaners, with its canopy and butterfly sign with "J&J" in classic script. I seem to remember the "J&J" having flashing bulbs, but I could be imagining that.

And out by the Naval Air Station is Fat Boy Drive-In. In 2006, they replaced the classic neon and bulb sign with a hideously bland LED sign, and I still haven't gotten over this spiritual gutting.

You may think this obsession unusual, but you have to remember that I entered my formative years at the end of a great era in gas station signage in terms of design, shapes, and especially the use of neon. This was the time of the old neon splendor of an angled Sunoco sign next to an oval Amoco sign with a torch flame on top (I drew one once and my teacher told my mom that she "couldn't get over it". I thought she meant she couldn't jump over the paper, or something, not possibly that she couldn't get over my nascent talent), and, in truth, the Texaco star still inspires me. Those classics are unmatched in today's era of generic LED signage. And in those waning days of great gas station signage, I often visited my grandmother in Brooklyn, which gave me the opportunity to see the greatest gas station sign ever, no arguments: Gaseteria.

Gaseteria stations were all over the Big Apple back then, and I fell in love with that American hamburger on the sign immediately. It was like a cross between an Amoco sign and a Burger King sign, and when I saw it, I knew I was home and in one of my favorite places in the world: New York City. This was the beauty of the era: mass chain homogenization didn't yet exist on the scale it does today, so I *couldn't* see a Gaseteria sign anywhere but in New York. And seeing that crazy sign made our trips much more special for me.

Sadly, most of these great signs of my youth are now gone, and I give in to nostalgia and lament the change. Of course, people my age no doubt called the old J&J sign vulgar and an eyesore when it was first installed and probably longed for the days of tin signs on storefronts, and that's fair enough, but I was shaped into that landscape of vulgar neon dreams. I am of that great American cloth, and those old signs inspired in me a love of Americana, history, and pop culture... and it is that very love that ultimately guided me on my trip on Route 66.

Besides my (perhaps unusual) enthusiasm over signage, I was also briefly interested in soccer—"briefly" being the key word: I got hit in the nuts with soccer balls a lot as a kid. I don't know if that's a *skill*, exactly, but if it is, I had some serious game. Because of this (and my generally subpar skills), my soccer career only lasted for one season of Brunswick rec league, but it was enough to do some physical and psychological damage: I suffered the pain of not winning a single game, not scoring a single goal or steal, and still not escaping from this stint without a few good whacks to the manhood. Also, wearing shin guards seems to have killed off all my follicles. My legs below my knees would not be miscast in a Nair commercial. I remember pulling sweat-soaked shin guards out of my socks after every game, and now, I've got bald legs. This may be a spurious connection, but I can't find a better one.

I also played one year of tee-ball on a team that, too, went completely defeated. I played right field very badly, and I had a penchant for swinging and missing spectacularly.

Swinging and missing a ball on a tee: yet another skill I had.

I love watching sports, but I learned pretty quickly that I wasn't going to be the Maine boy that beat the odds and started playing for the Sox at Fenway. Not a chance. Take enough soccer balls to the junk, and you just know whether that's gonna happen or not. So, instead, I'd spend hours in my room spinning the dial and watching the vinyl spin, and, slowly but surely, my life developed in the spaces between those stations and grooves.

Something was always playing in the house or in the car; on the radio or on the turntable. My parents' record collection was vast and varied: Sinatra; Torme; Judy Collins; Simon & Garfunkel; The Beach Boys; Bach; Barry Manilow; The Carpenters; Elvis; The Monkees. It seemed they were always listening to a record, and nearly every childhood memory I have comes with a sonic association. I soon set up my own record player in my room, and with that, I became the proprietor of my own neighborhood bar. I made a neon sign by shining a flashlight through a straw, and the house special was water in Dixie cups. My parents were regulars, and they were treated to regular doses of Bill Haley & His Comets on vinyl.

The oldies obsession stuck because I was a regular listener of WJTO Brunswick. I used to call my favorite DJ, Candy, and ask her to play Mark Dinning's 1959 hit *Teen Angel*. I love the fact that at five and six years old, I was obsessed with a song about a girl being hit by a train. I started traumatizing myself early!

But more (a *lot* more) on music (and trauma) later.

During my younger years, sports was my main salve, and my winter nights in Brunswick were always warm, cozy, and full of hockey. By birth and geography, I was a Boston Bruins fan, but I loved the game thanks to the sheer brilliance of the era. I missed the Big Bad Bruins of the early seventies with Bobby Orr, forward Phil Esposito, and goalie Gerry "Cheesy" Cheevers, with his scars-and-stitches mask, but I fell in love with the Lunch Pail Bruins of the late seventies, hard-edged guys who played hard for 60 minutes like Cheevers, the ferocious enforcers Wayne Cashman and Terry "Taz" O'Reilly, and the brilliant goal scorer Rick Middleton. This was hockey at its finest, and I caught the bug at an age when these things mean everything.

My dad was born in Bay Ridge, Brooklyn, in 1940, and in addition to the Brooklyn Dodgers, he remains a passionate fan of the New York Mets and Rangers. Hence, by virtue of my environment, the Rangers became my second on-ice love, and I came to know them intimately through radio and Dad's 1976-1977 yearbook. That team included Esposito (traded by Boston in a move that crushed all New England, except my dad), the stately forward Rod Gilbert, defenseman Ron Greschner, goalie (and future beloved TV fixture) John "J.D." Davidson, and New York City's own Nick Fotiu.

Dad had a silver GE transistor, with the band and dials on the front and an army-fatigue green grill on top,

Boston Garden, home of the Bruins since 1928. They called it the Old Barn on Causeway Street, and it looked as cozy and homey as Grandma's farmhouse. I only caught one game at the old Garden before it closed in 1995, but it was as cozy and homey (and cramped and uncomfortable) as it looked on the tube.

These were the days before advertising permeated

every available inch of surface, so the lines were clean, and the pure white ice and boards really popped on our TV. These were also the days before helmets became mandatory, so you could really *see* the players in all their 1970s hockey-mullet-and-walrus-mustache glory. It was truly a magnificent time for the game, and for me to discover it.

Although I never learned to play (or skate, for that matter), my passion for hockey was born here. Things changed in the nineties, when the commissioner made a ridiculous push to bring the Canadian game to the Sun Belt (the Minnesota North Stars became the Dallas Stars; the Quebec Nordiques became the Colorado Avalanche; the Hartford Whalers became the Carolina Hurricane; the Winnipeg Jets became the Phoenix Coyotes), and after this point, more teams were born in markets with no hockey passion (Atlanta, Nashville, Columbus), and with the game diluted and spread so thin, my interest waned—but even still, I (clearly!) hold these memories dear.

At this time, school life came with few trials and tribulations. I attended the elementary school across from First Parish Church, next to the Bowdoin College campus, and I remember I had a black, white, and purple blanket for naptime. Then, first grade through to third grade, I went to Jordan Acres Elementary. The principal was Ms. Kurz and the music teacher was Ms. Elser. I didn't know this at the time, but Ms. Kurz and Ms. Elser were a couple. My teacher, meanwhile, was Mr. Barrett, and he could be a mean bastard, but I suffered no trauma (again, at the time).

I had friends, and on the long scenic bus ride (from the trailer park to the tidal basins of the Sheepscott River), we spent the time rocking out to Huey Louis, Greg Khin, and Christopher Cross [sic] on the bus radio and dreaming of playing at Fenway for the Sox. And when we were out of school, Eric and I played Nerf football in the yard and basketball in the paneled hall leading to the bedrooms. We played KISS, the Bee Gees, and the *Star Wars* and *Saturday Night Fever* soundtrack records on our turntable.

I once backed into a wall-mount space heater in the bathroom, and I had griddle marks on my ass for a long time afterwards. We went to Thomas Point Beach and viewed all the artefacts from Admiral Peary's exhibition to the North Pole at the Bowdoin College Museum. We visited my grandparents at the farm, and we visited my grandmother in Brooklyn. We saw *Star Wars* and *Poltergeist* and *Raiders of the Lost Ark* in the theater, and we played Atari at home. We played on the rocks at Bailey Island, and we bought Smurf figures and other toys at the Maine Mall. We went roller-skating at the Brunswick rec center and we watched the Blue Angels from our driveway when the air show came to the Brunswick Naval Air Station. We ate out at Pizza Hut and enjoyed home cooking at home.

Basically, we were a happy American family unit in the

seventies and eighties. It was middle-of-the-road America, and it was all I knew and all I knew to want—and this is further illustrated by our trips to my grandmother's in New York. I say that our trips to Disney likely sparked my love for travel, but really, these regular drives were equally formative.

We had the Plymouth then, and it was full of AM magic as we set out on golden cold Thanksgiving mornings for my paternal grandmother's apartment in Bay Ridge, Brooklyn. The Beatles' *The Long and Winding Road*, Carly Simon's *Nobody Does It Better* (a song I always associate, for some reason, with the NFL and Alcoa "We Can't Wait Until Tomorrow!" commercials), Nicolette Larson's *Lotta Love*, Peaches & Herb's *Reunited*, and, as we got closer to New York, the perfect disco funk of Herb Alpert's *Rise:* the sonic cloth of memory, always associated with Thanksgiving and drives to visit my grandmother in Brooklyn.

Eric and I were good travelers, content to listen to the radio, color, and sightsee. Nothing was ever more thrilling than the little things: the Portland skyline that looked just slightly like New York; the pilgrim-hat-with-arrow logo on the Massachusetts Turnpike signs; the grids on the turnpike toll tickets; a water tower; a factory smokestack... all captivating. I was always fascinated by the minutiae of travel. The McDonald's signs in Massachusetts were different from the ones in Maine, and there were no billboards in Maine, so I had plenty of reading material starting in New Hampshire. Plus, the style of road signs and streetlamps were different from state to state: the traffic lights in New York City were yellow, unlike in Maine, for example.

I am still enthralled by these regional differences, and this all started on the road to my grandmother's apartment.

Mom and Dad always had a red and black plaid thermos full of steaming coffee, and they always had a Wash 'n Dri towelette ready. They appeased us with Happy Meals, and the miles passed by uneventfully: I-95 through Maine and New Hampshire; I-495 to the Mass Pike; I-84 to Hartford. Then, finally, one of the highlights of the trip: the West Rock Tunnel, just outside of New Haven. The sign instructed motorists to remove their sunglasses for the tunnel, so my mom always did, even though she was always a passenger, and then we'd be in the tube—and it felt like it lasted for hours. The tunnel itself was and is beautiful: the granite wall and arches; the soft red glow from taillights and the streetlamps on the ceiling. And the tunnel meant *almost there*; almost New York.

And then, finally, we'd arrive. My grandmother lived in a building called The Bay Shore at 275 Bay Ridge Parkway in Bay Ridge (Tony Manero's 'hood! Yes, *Saturday Night Fever* was filmed in this very same neighborhood). I'll never be able to articulate the smell in the lobby of that building—some kind of mélange of garbage, cooking, coffee, and natural gas—but whatever it was, it smelled like home. The tile in the lobby was black-and-white octagon, and it was *always* dark, and Grandmother's apartment had huge French doors, glass doorknobs, pre-war wooden frame windows with yellowed shades and cloth pulls, and threadbare runners over hardwood floors.

I remember waiting for the tubes in her TV set, which sat on a gold stand that seemed too rickety for its weight, to warm up blue and orange—like the Mets uniforms—through the vents in the back of the set. I remember vintage radios and her paintings, many of which hang in our house to this day. I remember Grandmother's diploma and class photo from nursing school and the pole in the closet. I remember a musty (but pleasantly so) smell in the bedroom that mingled with the fresh smell of the Narrows. Somehow, a box of Ivory laundry detergent also plays into the scene, as well as a copy of the *NY Times* with a photo of Richard Todd (the man who replaced my idol Joe Namath at quarterback for my Jets) celebrating a touchdown throw. I remember Grandmother's etched-gold Manhattan glass. I remember planes in the night heading to or from Kennedy, or maybe LaGuardia, and the static they produced as they passed over the antenna. I remember all the lights of the city seeming green and safe. From our bedroom window, we could see laundry hanging on clotheslines with pulleys, and the apartments across the courtyard had keystone arches—and hovering above it all from the living room, close enough to touch, was the Verrazzano. I knew the bridge from *Saturday*

Night Fever, but I really knew it from watching the lights dance across the real thing, right before my very eyes.

Among my earliest Brooklyn memories is one that involves me returning from somewhere—probably the Museum of Natural History or the Central Park Zoo. I remember driving by the old Brooklyn Gas tanks off the Kosciuszko Bridge on the Brooklyn Queens Expressway and seeing the red-and-white checkerboard pattern at the top of the tanks, and I know I drew them and colored in the squares (my red crayon at work again!). Most distinctly, however, I remember there being talk of a gas tank fire (possibly my dad telling of the time he and my mom were stuck on the Jersey Turnpike due to said fire), and I remember feeling very, very scared: I don't like fire (that fucking episode of *Little House* where Albert burns the School for the Blind down again!), and, driving into the city in the late seventies and early eighties (the height and decline of the fiscal crisis in New York), I see burnt-out buildings everywhere and can still hear my dad explaining that landlords sometimes burn their own buildings down to get money from insurance companies. (*It's going to happen to us, too!*) I, recalling all of this in the present day, feel unsettled all over again, seeing the scorched shells of buildings and the gentle smell of smoke in the background of these 40-year-old memories.

How much of these scenes is true memory, and how much is co-opted from multiple experiences, overheard anecdotes, and misinterpretations? How much have I imagined? How much have I invented and reassigned after the fact?

How strange memory is, and how it presents itself, demanding I revisit and backfill the story.

Basically, I don't remember the actual Thanksgiving dinners we drove down for; instead, I remember the etched-gold of Grandmother's Manhattan glass, and little else. I remember the drives; the sounds; the feelings. I remember the air smelling different to Maine's, full of more and different kinds of foods, car exhaust, piles of garbage, smoke (from buildings abandoned to arson), and the tides of the Narrows. And I remember being thankful, even then, for the sensory snapshots that have since proven to last a lifetime.

But let's get out of the city and see how the other half lived. Let me take you to the family farm in Whitefield, Maine—a.k.a., the Homestead.

I was afraid to leave my mom for overnight visits for a long time, but by the time I was six, I couldn't get enough of the Homestead. We visited during all seasons, of course, but the fall and winter especially stand out in my mind.

My grandparents would arrive at our house in Brunswick to pick us up, and as the baby-blue Oldsmobile pulled into the driveway, my mom always said, "Look who's here!"—and Eric and I would go nuts. Grandpa was always clad in forest green Dickies, and Grandma always had a mod seventies sleeveless polyester shirt and, in the coldest weather, a knit sweater.

We would load into the Olds, bathing in the magnificent cigar smoke wafting through the interior, and we were off.

I always loved the sound of the turn signal, though it seemed sharper when it was cold out. The sound was a comforting *click-clock*, like a large interior clock. But (as I would learn after the fact by analyzing the memories) the rhythm was eight notes, so the *click* had a bit more urgency: *CLICK-clock-CLICK-clock* rather than *CLICK*-pause-*clock*-pause-*CLICK*-pause-*clock*-pause.

My sense of rhythm and tone may well have developed here, within these memories.

My grandfather's wood pile towered in the yard by the henhouse, always big enough for us to climb all the way to the top and observe our kingdom. We would play Nerf football on the leaf-strewn great lawn, puffs of woodsmoke from the stove hanging low, or play on the tractor in the toolshed, the smell of sawdust, kerosene, and WD40 folding itself in the crisp air.

Before my time, my grandparents also had cows—but by the time I came along, this farmyard population was diminished to just sheep and hens. The sheep pasture spread for hundreds of acres, from the barn to the woods, and it was a minefield of fresh and calcified crap. Of course, my grandmother named all the sheep. The one I most remember now is Red Spots (I remember him being all white, but whatever), who had a mean streak. He was fond of charging, thus making feeding time an... adventure. But I loved having them, and I loved hearing their *baah*ing in the night. Gentle. Pastoral. Perfect.

On St. Patrick's Day, 1989, a sickly lamb was born. My grandmother named him Patrick (of course), and he slept in a box behind the woodstove and was hand-fed by my grandmother with a bottle. Hearing a little baby lamb bleating in the house was a joy. Another symbol of youth and innocence, I suppose.

The main event of the day came when the light left the sky in the afternoon, however: the sunsets at the Homestead during the cold months to this day grip my heartstrings and leave me speechless. I love the absence of light from November onwards: the sun leaves the sky by 4PM—the precursor to those amazing sunsets on the farm—and to me, there is nothing cozier than returning home and settling into the night immediately. During this time of year, the backroads are covered in a fog of woodsmoke—the most intoxicating smell in the world—and these are the days of stews and pies and baked bean suppers and finding comfort and warmth wherever we can.

I love winter and I embrace it, thanks to these Homestead memories. I love all the outdoor fun that comes from a good, deep blanket of New England snow and the sharp cold: tobogganing, ice fishing, pond hockey, you name it. And as a Maine man, I also love the romance of winter and the pride that comes with merely surviving day-to-day in extreme conditions. It takes a special character to survive and thrive in a Maine winter, and we pride ourselves on having this fortitude of spirit. Besides, there's something wonderful about loved ones arriving home during the cold months: the door opens and a blast of fresh chill follows, infused with the smell of cold, leaves, and Earth. My grandfather also always carried the scent of the barn, hay, his work clothes, kitchen matches, woodsmoke, and cigar smoke after he returned from feeding the sheep, and this remains a magical olfactory concoction in my mind.

After dark, with a fire roaring in the wood stove, we would gather in the living room, and my grandfather would smoke his cigars, my grandmother would make Jiffy Pop, and we would watch the classics of the seventies and eighties: *Vegas*, *Quincy*, *Dallas*, *Hill Street Blues*, *Love Boat*, *Fantasy Island*, *The Rockford Files*, *Alice*, *One Day at a Time*. We weren't studying for the bar, but we were together and warm and happy.

As the days got colder, the pile of blankets and afghans on the beds upstairs got thicker. My grandmother would kiss us to sleep, and from then, we were off to dream of breaking through coverage for touchdowns, playing a Les Paul through a wall of Marshall Stacks at a sold-out Madison Square Garden, and skiing or tobogganing from the edge of the woods to the house.

I was never in my life warmer than I was during those short, cold days, and this all comes back to me every time I return to visit my parents in the old house on the farm.

*

The 11-mile stretch between my grandparents' farm and the town of Gardiner, Maine, bore several farms. There was the Maple Tree Farm (which had a plank sign above the barn doors) and the Chip Off the Block barn (a red barn with its name and an Amish seeing-eye design painted on), to name a couple, but my favorite was the "LENTY TO DO FARM". I never thought about what it meant to have "LENTY TO DO" or what it took to accomplish "LENTY", and it certainly never occurred to me that perhaps a *P* had fallen off somewhere. It was the "LENTY TO DO FARM", and that was that. No questions. Nothing to see here.

As my grandpa whipped us past these farms in the Oldsmobile, I always wished we had a finger bar mower, just like the one on the tractor, attached to the passenger side. Grandpa would attach the mower to the tractor, lower it so its gruesome, pulsing teeth spread out six feet from the tractor and six inches above the ground, and drive out into the fields to mow the hay. I always pictured the mower on the car destroying everything in its path—mailboxes, telephone poles—all the detritus of the sidewalk decapitated and lying in a swath of rural destruction at the hands of the Rocket Delta 88.

A trip to Gardiner always meant a haircut for Grandpa and shopping for toys at Wilson's Department Store for Eric, Grandmother, and me. We'd park next to the Kennebec River and walk up the stairs of the arcade to

Water St. The arcade was narrow and rickety, and always smelled of musty river water, greasy paper plates with pizza slices from Gerard's in some form of forgotten decomposition, and, occasionally (if we were lucky), urine. The toy section was upstairs at Wilson's, and it was a magical world of Hot Wheels cars, car and airplane model kits, *Diff'rent Strokes* and *Dukes of Hazzard* coloring books, and, my favorite, Topps Baseball sticker albums with shiny stickers.

After we had done our trading (as Grandma would call it), Grandpa would get behind the wheel of the Oldsmobile and floor it home.

Some grandfathers sit on the porch and tell grandiose fishing stories; some grandfathers play bingo at the VA and volunteer for bean suppers. *My* grandfather drove like a fucking maniac, yelling at everything and nothing, dropping cigar ashes, and eating (driving never deterred him from any of the above). Why? His temperament combined with lax traffic enforcement, I guess. Why the hurry? Probably to make it home in time for the start of his favorite soap, *Another World*. (We always seemed to make it just in time.) Meanwhile, I, unfazed, would be sitting in the back of the Delta 88, driving my new Hot Wheels across the bench seat, breathing in that wonderful cigar smoke and plotting the destruction of rural Maine by hay mower as we pushed 60 in a 35. Anything that existed within six feet of the road was a goner. I probably would've spared the "LENTY TO DO FARM", though. Whatever

"LENTY" was, I was pretty sure I didn't want to have it to do.

As you can probably tell, my grandfather wasn't exactly the squishy type. Sure, he drove a baby-blue Oldsmobile Delta 88 (1979, used) with a baby-blue slipcover for the bench seat and finished his farm work every day at 2PM so he could watch *Another World*, but other than that, his default mode seemed to be "exacting bastard", and he seldom spoke an encouraging word. Don't get me wrong, I know he loved us (and we'll get to that), but it was tough never feeling like anything we did around the farm was good enough. My grandmother always consoled Eric and I after one of my grandfather's biting critiques, saying, "Don't mind him; his bark is worse than his bite," but it was still hard to take. If you were to do a mashup of sound bites from people who played football for Vince Lombardi in Green Bay or Bear Bryant at Alabama, the running narrative would be, "We hated the son-of-a-bitch's guts, but he made us winners," and while I never felt all fired up to beat the hell out of the Bears or Auburn, I do know that feeling. I wanted to impress Grandpa with everything I did—and my memories of him are mostly happy ones. Visits to the Homestead meant a wonderful haze of smoke from his Wm. Penn filter-tip cigars, and *Hee Haw*, *Lawrence Welk*, *Dallas*, and *The Rockford Files* were all interrupted upon Grandpa's return from the kitchen with a big Pyrex mixing bowl full of Jiffy Pop and the *thwack* of peanut butter cups tossed in our laps. On snowy winter days, he'd sit at the kitchen table next to the woodstove playing solitaire, and while we bundled up to go tobogganing, he always offered the admonition, "Watch out for automobiles." Always "automobiles"; never "cars" or "vehicles".

As we were saying our goodbyes at the Portland Jetport after our Christmas vacation in 1982, Grandpa leaned down and gave me a kiss on the forehead. You could tell he'd sincerely wanted to give me that kiss, but you could also tell he was kicking his own ass internally for doing so. Even still, it was... nice. An all-too-rare and unexpected moment of unspoken mutual love.

The biggest crack in the armor, however, came during his last summer, when I was twelve. It was July 13, 1985—the day of Live Aid. I woke up on that blistering morning, turned on the Zenith, and was blown away at the sight of Ozzy reunited with Black Sabbath. Awesome! What a great day! Grandpa was off in the fields mowing the hay, and so Eric and I spent the day rocking out.

By the evening, everything would be different.

Grandpa invited me along to the general store to pick up some smokes. I was feeling rather adult that day, for whatever reason—perhaps just because he invited me—so I bought a Perrier. It was when we were on the way back that Grandpa, the tough-as-shit bastard, said out of nowhere, "I guess I'm not much of a grandfather."

Heavy thing for a twelve-year-old kid, already fragile in the presence of the speaker in question, to hear.

I felt myself desperately trying to be an adult and comfort him on his level, saying, "No, you're doing a hell of a job!"

I don't remember the rest of that five-minute drive or dialog or anything else ever being said about it, and I certainly don't remember the rest of Live Aid—but I do remember feeling much softer toward him from then on, and I like to think that during his remaining eight months, he felt a little softer toward us, too.

So, was my grandmother the yin to his yang; the cute, domestic, baking-and-cooking-with-love, pearl-donning grandma? Well, put it this way: one Thanksgiving Day, unbeknownst to all of us at the Homestead, one of the cats pissed on the stove. Sometimes, a smell indelibly sears itself into your memory bank, and that incident, fairly and unfairly, confirmed the fact that my grandmother was a disaster in the kitchen. It's not like she put the cat on the burner herself, but her cooking was atrocious, and the cat burner fiasco definitely formed a Pavlovian connection in us between Grandmother and bad food. Her specialty, as it were, was pork chops and biscuits—specifically, Shake 'N Bake pork chops. She always managed to find these tough little chops that were mostly bone, and the Shake 'N Bake coating always slid off in one greasy sheet. The biscuits were made from scratch, possibly out of rocks. Nary a hint of flake in those things.

Many nights, my brother and friends and I would

make a show of eating and then bring our dinner outside for games of Pork Chop Toss and Biscuit Shooting. The house down the hill was maybe 300 yards away, and with a good flick of the wrist and crust on the snow, a pork chop could make it a long way in the direction of the property line, and a biscuit could take two BBs at close range and barely even flinch.

Indeed, when it came to my grandmother's culinary efforts, all was almost lost—but not quite: she made the most amazing donuts from scratch. On frigid winter mornings, we'd come downstairs and find her covered in flour, stirring a fresh batch in boiling Crisco on the woodstove. And they were *spectacular*—unless and until you bit into a "prize" donut and found yourself choking on a nice big clump of gray hair. *Those* donut mornings were then swiftly turned to heaping-bowls-of-Boo-Berries-or-Fruity-Pebbles mornings, the remaining donuts instead saved for the birds—and target practice.

She tried, and I loved her for the effort. And we certainly didn't go without. But the woman was an absolute nightmare around the stove, with or without the noxious fumes of burning cat urine.

All that said, she was a kindly, loving soul, with a perpetual sense of mirth and play. Grandma was born in 1897 and taught in a one-room schoolhouse. She lived to be 95, and until a few years before her death, she was out in the fields in 90-degree heat lifting 100lb bales of hay onto the tractor trailer and feeding the sheep and hens. Even into her nineties, she was sharp and observant: her diaries are treasures of observation and documentation. As we will see, I subliminally took her example to heart. She was a devotee of *The Old Farmer's Almanac*, but she was even more accurate. Grandma could always predict how severe a winter would be just from observing nature: the thickness of a bird's nest; the thickness of a deer's coat. She had some arcane set of mathematical calculations she used to predict how many storms would hit, and her diaries are snapshots of a Maine Winter foretold: *February 22nd, heavy snow today, seven storms left.* And she was always right.

Moreover, she was always kind and nurturing, and I always felt loved in her presence.

So, the above was about as complicated as my childhood got. Until, that is, at some point in the summer of 1982, before I turned ten, when it was announced that my dad had got a job at a travel agency in Jacksonville, Florida.

As you know, we'd visited Orlando and Disney World plenty of times, thanks to his work, but now, we were *moving* to Jacksonville, a mere two-hour drive away from Orlando.

Okay, then.

I don't recall being particularly upset or excited about this, and I don't really remember any of the dirty business of moving, saying goodbye to friends, or any of the rest. I vaguely remember a Paul Arpin moving truck and boxes, but that's about it. What I *do* remember is that my dad picked up my mother, Eric, and myself at Jacksonville International, from whence we drove to our apartment complex in our silver-and-rust-with-black-vinyl-interior 1979 Ford Fairmont station wagon—and before I knew it, we'd stepped into our new home, which was already furnished with two metal wire chairs—the same kind of chairs, it would turn out, as the ones at the Regency Square Mall Food Court in Jacksonville, where I would soon discover the joy of Chick-fil-A waffle fries.

My dad, the bachelor.

We had Apartment 5G of The Gloucester Apartments at 4915 Baymeadows Road. The complex has since been converted into condos, and apparently, one of its previous management companies is wanted in Florida, Ohio, New York, and Nevada for fraud, embezzlement, absconding of funds, and breach of contract. Fun and games! But, of course, that was long after my time.

The buildings of The Gloucester were a strange mix of Tudor and southern Colonial: Olde English font on the sign at the front of the complex, more pine trees than palm trees, gabled roofs with dormer windows, brick, and shutters, and coach lanterns. The effect was a bewildering middle finger to the endless waves of palm tree-shrouded Spanish plaster and stucco that adorned the rest of the neighborhood.

I remember walking into the bare living room and saying, "Well, there's not much to it," and with that anticlimax, we were home.

My favorite parts of my new home presented themselves immediately: the pool was great—right next to the tennis court—and in the dark, Astroturf-carpeted hallway between the pool and the rental office was a vending machine with Mr. Pibb, which didn't exist in Maine. It was love at first taste. It was like Dr. Pepper on crack. And, perhaps best of all, we had TBS, which brought us Atlanta Braves baseball *every night*. As soon as the daily thunderstorms cleared out, it was Joe Torre's Braves with Dale Murphy and Claudell Washington in the outfield, Bob Horner and Chris Chambliss at the corners, Phil Niekro, Al Hrabosky (the Mad Hungarian), and Steve Bedrosian on the hill, and Bruce Benedict and the immortal Biff Pocoroba behind the plate. Skip Caray and Pete Van Wieren meanwhile provided the play-by-play.

I was a diehard Red Sox fan from New England, but the 1982 National League West-winning Braves became my second team.

The humidity was heavy, and the neighborhood reeked of sulfuric water from sprinklers on every lawn— but by the close of summer 1982, I was settling into my new home, happy to have Chick-fil-A, Mr. Pibb, a pool and tennis court, and a ballgame on the tube every night.

It was an easy transition.

And then, school started.

My first day in fourth grade at Beauclerc Elementary, Jacksonville, FL, instilled in me a sense of terror and dread that I still carry to this day. I was the "new kid", a strange outlander from *Maine*, of all places. ("Do y'all have snow up there all the time?" "Do y'all live in igloos?") It was difficult being so recently removed from all my friends and all that was familiar in my life in Brunswick.

Even still, I eventually found a few friends. Yet I will never fully recover from the horror that was Ms. Jelks.

Ms. Jelks was morbidly obese, with shimmering curls hanging into her eyes. I can see her now, sitting on her desk, cross-legged and leaning slightly to the right, as if she was so exhausted that she wanted to lie on the desk, but was too tired to get her legs up all the way. The following year, when *The Empire Strikes Back* came out, I saw Jabba the Hut on-screen and immediately thought of her. And her personality wasn't much better.

She didn't waste any time establishing the lay of the land: not long after the bell rang during my first morning in my new school in my new home, Ms. Jelks informed her class, "Now, class, you done heard that Headmaster Blah-Blah's paddlin' arm done been broke, but I'm here to tell you that his arm done been healed over the summer, an' that paddlin' arm is *ready to go!*" She paused for a second, and then repeated, "*Ready to go!*" as if any of us really needed emphasis.

I, a ten-year-old from a progressive Yankee enclave, had never heard of anything as draconian as corporal punishment in school, and the mere idea of a fully healed and "ready to go!" paddlin' arm was enough to make my butt cheeks clench.

And then, class began.

Memory lies and moves the goalposts around, so I'm not sure if this incident was on my first day or later, but it definitely feels as though it was the first day. It was at least my first week. At any rate, the equation on the board was "9 x 8". I was called forth to solve it, and... well, I stood before the board in terror.

I stood there in mortified silence, hearing the snickers of the class growing louder and louder. I trembled, trying desperately not to cry, feeling the raging disapproval in Ms. Jelk's icy gaze boring into my skull. I wasn't a dumb kid, but I was perhaps a bit slow with math (a safe bet, since I ended up failing pre-algebra twice in high school), and I just couldn't *get* 9 x 8 on a dime.

The seconds seemed like years in my head, and the snickers grew into a full-on William Tell overture of laughs, catcalls, and withering scorn.

Eventually (not soon enough), Ms. Jelks put me out of my misery. Did she kindly help me out? Did she offer a hint? Pat me on the shoulder? Applaud me for trying? Nah: "It's 72! Now *sit*! *Down*!"

I slinked back to my seat, feeling Ms. Jelks' palpable disgust and the tears at last welling up in earnest. I don't know if I actually let loose with a gusher, but it felt like I did.

Needless to say, I *can* answer 9 x 8 on a dime now (with a shudder), even if I may not be sure *why* one gets 72 from it. But why bother with piddly details such as process and meaning?

Basically, during that first day and week, Ms. Jelks broke my confidence and left me a shellshocked wreck, paranoid of getting paddled for my next incorrect answer and even more paranoid that my next public humiliation was impending.

And this served as a pretty accurate indicator of what the next few years were going to be like—and, in truth, it was the times I spent *outside* of Florida that I look back on with the most fondness. That is, the times we (that is, me, Eric, and Mom) briefly returned to Maine every summer from 1983 to 1986 after moving to Florida to spend time at the Homestead, where, across the dirt driveway lay the great lawn, the lawn chairs, picnic table, kettle grill, cold bottles of Pepsi and Shur Fine grape and strawberry soda, potato chips, games of wiffleball and Nerf football, and the general joy of summer in Maine, thousands of miles from our new Florida "home".

DAY TWO

MAY 9, 2019

Chicago, IL, to St. Louis. MO: 296 miles.
Time Out: About 6:30AM CST.
Time In: Checked into City Place, St. Louis, at about 5PM CST.

Highway 66 is the main migrant road. 66—
the long concrete path across the country,
waving gently up and down on the map,
from Mississippi to Bakersfield—over the
red lands and the grey lands, twisting up into
the mountains, crossing the Divide and
down into the bright and terrible desert, and
across the desert to the mountains again,
and into the rich California valleys.

66 is the path of a people in flight,

refugees from dust and shrinking land, from the thunder of tractors and shrinking ownership, from the desert's slow northward invasion, from the twisting winds that howl up out of Texas, from the floods that bring no richness to the land and steal what little richness is there. From all of these the people are in flight, and they come into 66 from the tributary side roads, from the wagon tracks and the rutted country roads. 66 is the mother road, the road of flight.

—John Steinbeck, *The Grapes of Wrath*

ND SO, IT BEGINS.

On Day Two, I awoke early with the above passage in my head, wondering where the hell Steinbeck got Mississippi and Bakersfield from: Route 66 doesn't come within *miles* of either location. I know Steinbeck was a novelist, but really? Just...

Regardless: I was in a bit of a haze after the previous night. I'd been hungover before (obviously), but never as wonderfully as this—and not in terms of the magnitude of the hangover, but in terms of the *experience* leading to it. Because what a fantastic first day! Glorious Chicago all to my own; an amazing lunch; Wrigley Field; great, deep conversation. No terms and conditions. No strings attached. Just the experience of a lifetime, worth the trip by itself. And now I was embarking on Day Two—and Day One of actually being on the road.

I commenced this day with an Uber ride over to National on LaSalle in a soft spring rain, and then signed out my car from a guy in a Notre Dame cap named Darius. (I hate Notre Dame, but he was a nice guy, so I didn't hold it against him.) Andrea had suggested naming my rental "Rose" in homage to Rocinante, the camper truck Steinbeck drives across the country in *Travels With Charley.*

She's a wise chick.

Rose was a silver 2019 Nissan Altima with 2,832 miles on the odometer. Practically brand-goddamn-new, and my new best friend for the next eight days!

I spent about ten minutes in the garage trying to figure out the oddities of the car. Back home, in my "real" life (ha!), I drove a 2004 Hyundai Elantra and a 2011 Hyundai Sonata, so this 2019 Altima was a bit of a mindfuck: a key fob with no keys? A push-button ignition? A navigation screen? Say wha...?

I also spent a few minutes trying to make the $30 suction cup I bought for my new GoPro stick to the dash. No soap: it works fine on flat surfaces, but dashboards, apparently, are not flat surfaces. Who knew? Shit! But okay, if this is the worst that happens, well...

I eventually gave up and drove over to Lou Mitchell's for the Traditional Route 66 Starting Point Breakfast.

Some Lou Mitchell's trivia for you: the restaurant has

been in business since 1923, and has remained in the same location (well, across the street from the original location) since 1949. It started when William Mitchell opened a small diner on Jackson and named it "Mitchell's" before he then changed the name to—you guessed it—"Lou Mitchell's" in honor of his son. Before long, lines formed out the door for the breakfast rush, and the rest is history.

Even better: Chicago-based Leaf Candy was renowned for its Slo Poke Bites and suckers, and, while making the latter, the caramel would drip, and they didn't know what to do with these leftover "duds". The owner of Leaf, who was a Lou Mitchell's regular and a pal of Lou's, got the idea to coat the duds in chocolate, and wanted a market to test-drive the new product. So, in 1958, "Uncle" Lou Mitchell, a Greek known for his hospitality, started handing out donut holes and boxes of Milk Duds to all waiting women and children—and thus, a tradition was born.

God, I love this stuff: beloved local institutions with singular traditions. Nothing I can access regularly at home, but something I can subsume myself in for half an hour and take the experience of home with me!

And yes, I did order the Lou Mitchell mouse pancakes from the kids' menu! It's one regular pancake, two small cakes for ears, whipped cream for a smile, and some Milk Duds for the eyes and nose. And yes, it made me very happy. Fuck all y'all haters. Mouse pancakes are for kids young *and* old!

On another note: Lou Mitchell's proclaims to have the

"World's Finest Coffee" on the neon sign out front and on the menu... and to this I can only say that I was slightly less than whelmed, *especially* since they proclaim this in *neon* and on the *menu*, fachrissakes! Don't get me wrong, not the world's *worst* coffee by any stretch, but certainly not menu-proclamation-worthy, much less *neon*-worthy. In my humble, worthless opinion, of course.

Naturally, I still got one for the drive.

After this brief respite, I got back to the car, which was parked a block away on Jackson, so it was easy in, easy out: I plugged my first coordinates into my phone, and I was off! Finally, off on The Trip of an American Lifetime!

Now, one thing I'd noticed at this point: I repeatedly caught myself wearing this big, dumbass grin—a rarity in my day-to-day life. I first noticed this when staring at the "Begin Route 66" sign the day before, and then I noticed it spreading many times again after that, including when crossing the river on Michigan Ave. and seeing the *Tribune* and Wrigley buildings. Not that I don't have lots to grin about in my day-to-day life, nor that I don't appreciate all that I have—but let me drive home that this was the grin of renewed wonder and pure, unbridled excitement; the grin of feeling like a kid again.

Of course, I was kind of loving this grin. I decided it was a good look for me.

With that revelation, I managed to wedge my GoPro into the window, and it stayed... mostly. It was good enough, anyway. So, I commanded the GoPro to start a timelapse, turned on to Adams, and navigated toward I-94 W. and I-55 S. toward St. Louis. Gray with spits of rain, but the traffic wasn't bad at all, and I had WBEZ Chicago on the dial for my NPR fix.

As I pulled off onto the Mother Road for the first time in Joliet, I was listening to a story about Chicago's recycling program and loving life. My knowledge of Joliet started and ended with *The Blues Brothers*, but the research I'd conducted prior to going on this trip made me appreciate Joliet as one of the spiritual starts of Route 66. Founded in 1673, Joliet also lays claim to the 1926 Rialto Theater, one of the ten most beautiful theaters in the country, as well as the first Dairy Queen—and the latter alone is certainly good enough for me! I also wanted to hit up the old Joliet Prison, where Jake Blues memorably served his term, but, unfortunately, there was not enough time on this trip. Even still, it was good enough just knowing I was in Joliet and on Route 66. An *amazing*, surreal realization.

66 through Joliet was largely two-lane and hectic, suburban Chicago. McDonald's, school buses, Route 66 Raceway, shopping nodes... all great, but no real feel of Route 66 yet. Even still, I *was* on Route 66, and this made me feel on top of the world—or, more fittingly, on top of the Good ol' U.S. of A.

I made my first unscheduled detour (I'm going to call these "ADD Stops" from now on, since that was precisely what they were) at the Route 66 Food N Fuel in Joliet, where I found an exact replica of the Bluesmobile on a pole with a plaque featuring Elwood's immortal line, "It's got a cop motor, a four-hundred-and-forty-cubic-inch plant. It's got cop tires, cop suspension, cop shocks. It's a model made before catalytic converters, so it'll run good on regular gas."

Yes. Yes, yes, yes.

After that, I stayed on 66, cruising through the southern 'burbs, through Elwood to Wilmington, just loving the knowledge that *I was on Route 66*. And now that we were most definitely in the thick of 66, it was time for Mission I: The Launching Pad in Wilmington, IL, 60-odd miles south of Chicago and home of the Gemini Giant, one of several Muffler Man statues known to still exist along Route 66.

What the hell is a Muffler Man statue, you ask? That's a very good—and a very timely—question! Allow me to divulge: in the early 1960s, the Prewett Fiberglass Company of Venice, CA, started building 18- to 25-foot-tall statues for advertising. The statues were all men (sexist, I know) holding the desired advertised product—anything from hotdogs to mufflers—hence the colloquial name. The first was a Paul Bunyan holding an ax, which was built for the Paul Bunyon [sic] Cafe in Flagstaff, AZ. That one is still standing, as is the Gemini Giant.

And who is the Gemini Giant, you ask? The Gemini Giant is a spaceman with a silver helmet and green spacesuit holding a rocket. (Obviously.) It was installed at the Dairy Delite at the height of the space age in the early sixties, thus inspiring the drive-in to rechristen itself "The Launching Pad".

The Launching Pad was a beloved local institution, but when the Eisenhower Interstate Highway System was completed, I-55 diverted traffic away from Route 66 and, as often happens, the original owners sold, new owners couldn't keep the magic, the restaurant closed, and the Gemini Giant fell into disrepair.

Enter Holly Barker and Tully Garrett. (My Twitter bud, Brittni—a Route 66 veteran from *Australia*, believe it or not—recommended I stop in and chat with Holly and Tully, and I took her advice to heart.) Holly and Tully bought The Launching Pad in 2017 and set to work restoring it for relaunch, and this was no minor undertaking: years of neglect had resulted in significant damage, and one hell of a renovation was needed. Yet the community of Wilmington was ecstatic to have The Launching Pad reborn (witness all the local contractors who donated their time and equipment and efforts to the cause!), and so Holly and Tully pressed on and kept the dream alive.

Tully was taking care of odds and ends when I walked in, but Holly was working the counter. I bought an issue of *Route 66 Magazine* with the cover story about The Launching Pad and a bottle of Route 66 Black Cherry, and from there, Holly talked me up, asking about my stopping in, where I was from, etc. I mentioned my book, and she beamed and half-demanded that I connect with their

Facebook page because my story was "what they lived for".

I immediately felt so at home with Holly's warm, welcoming glow, and I instantly felt like I'd found friends for life. What a joyful experience on my first (official) day on the road!

I didn't know their story at the time, but I cherish them both all the more now that I know it: Holly and Tully met via Holly's Facebook page, Grief Anonymous, after they had both lost life partners to cancer, and as of May 2019, they're together, happily engaged, and (re)launching this amazing institution.

My kind of people; my kind of story!

But back onto the Mother Road: I stayed south on 66 (now known as IL 53), through Braidwood, Gardner, and Odell, to hit up Mission II: Pontiac, IL, 45-odd miles beyond Wilmington. I spent this time nursing my sluggishness and looking forward to putting myself in my images of Pontiac.

Pontiac, IL, was established in 1837, before the railroad and automobile age. As a result, the town was centralized and grew out of a town square—a concept that died off after the rails became prominent and towns became more spread out. This lives on in Pontiac, however, in the form of Main St., Mill St., and Livingston County Court House—all characteristic of quintessential, smalltown-America. While here, I knew I had to check out the Walldog Murals, painted by "Walldog" artists on multiple downtown buildings, and walk at least one of the three swinging bridges over the Vermillion River. So, I found a spot near the magnificent City Hall and walked downtown, checking out the murals. What I hadn't known before setting off was that music is pumped across the town square from speakers atop multiple buildings—Top 40 hits from today and yesterday—and I gotta admit, it was more than a bit unnerving hearing Vincent Price's manic cackle from Michael Jackson's *Thriller* reverberate through the streets while walking the square of Pontiac, IL! And my mood remained unimproved once that segued into Kenny Loggin's *Footloose*, and much less so after hearing Ringo caterwauling *With A Little Help From My Friends* (I love Ringo dearly, and think he was the most essential Beatle, but really, there's a reason he only had one vocal bone tossed to him each album). I don't know, Pontiac, maybe tap the brakes on your soundtrack?

Unexpected and subpar street-wide playlist aside, I eventually found one of the bridges and walked halfway out, and it was lovely: I could feel the ghosts of shoe workers crossing it to go to their mill jobs, with no conception that one day, a swell like myself would be walking their route and marveling at the "quaintness" of their hometown. Standing on that bridge, my nonlinear-ADD brain kicked in, and I thought of my office at work, which was just across a similar railroad bridge, and thought of how far I'd come in the last few months, from desperate unemployment to working an amazing job in an amazing historic mill—the same mill where uniforms were once made for the Union forces in the Civil War and where the great Ray Lamontange once worked making shoes and, upon hearing Stephen Stills on the PA, decided he wanted to play guitar and sing.

Goddamn, I'd arrived in a great place, despite my many hideous experiences. And if that wasn't endlessly hope-inducing and inspiring, I didn't know what was.

I loved Pontiac, and I was psyched that I'd actually made it after dreaming of it for all the months of planning before the trip. It proved the epitome of smalltown America, and I spent maybe 45 minutes just walking around, skipping the museum in the process, before heading back out.

Next, a quick ADD Stop at Dixie Travel Plaza in McLean, IL.

The Dixie Travel Plaza, originally known as the Dixie Truckers Home, was established in 1928 by J.P. Walters and John Geske. Originally, it was a sandwich shop inside a garage, but business soon boomed, and so they started operating as a full-service restaurant in 1930.

The Dixie is arguably the first truck stop in America. The original building burned down in 1965, but this iteration has been here since 1967.

Upon arrival, I got a lousy iced coffee and then got back on the road, The Scorpions on the juke. Yes!

On to Atlanta, IL.

I had to hit up the Hot Dog Muffler Man in Atlanta as a quick ADD Stop. The Hot Dog Muffler Man had stood serenely in Cicero, IL, for generations before being moved, and, after a quick ten-minute diversion, there I found him. Two of the known Muffler Man statues in one fell swoop!

A quick pic, and back to it.

I knew I'd be blasting through Springfield—this time, at least—and I was fine with that: I got right back onto I-55 and balled that jack, as Kerouac would say.

Here's an observation I never would've imagined I'd make: downstate Illinois reminded me a lot of the drive from Burlington, VT, to Montreal, Quebec, via I-89: the way the fields stretch out forever with the farms on the far distant horizon; the endless highway; the granaries and power lines cutting through... I never would've thought Illinois would remind me of Quebec, but there it is.

And so with these musings flitting around my mind, I kept on, treated to heavy doses of Wings, Rush, and Heart all the while and digging it immensely.

It's about 65 miles and theoretically about an hour's drive between Atlanta, IL, and Auburn, IL, but it took a *smidge* longer than that. I tried detouring off I-55 to get back on 66 a couple times, and both times I got lost and ended up backtracking. Plus, the drive was a bit of a drag due to my still being a bit hungover.

But Wings, Rush, and Heart...

So, now we were on to Mission II: The Brick 66 in Auburn, IL. Ten-mile detour, but totally worth it: the Brick 66 in Auburn is a perfectly preserved stretch of the Mother Road on its original 1926 alignment with original brick paving. I drove it ever so slowly, sucking it all in and stopping at several points for pics in a gentle spring rain. Original Route 66, original brick, verdant green farmland, barns, and silos. Goddamn, what an experience. This is what the original 66 pioneers knew. This is living breathing history. No other cars, no other souls. It could've been 1926, for all I knew.

I didn't want to leave it. But I *did* want to get on to lunch...

It was about another hour between Auburn and Litchfield, and I started to feel a bit of a second wind during this time. Not much, but a bit. I found myself thinking of the symmetry of driving between Auburn and Litchfield: I drive between Auburn and Litchfield, Maine, every time I visit the Homestead, and here, I was making the same drive in Illinois... which looked like Quebec.

All of my worlds, coalescing again.

Now, let's segue into Mission III: Ariston Café in Litchfield, IL. I found this gem in the early afternoon, and within, I also found memories that will surely last a lifetime. By this point, it had been years since I'd initially spotted the pictures in *Route 66 Lost & Found: Ruins and Relics Revisited*, and I *knew* it was going to be as great as I imagined.

First impressions when walking in: Astroturf carpet, rickety tables (told ya!), "soft" rock on the juke—Brandy, Seals & Croft, etc. Yes... perfect.

I was seated in a booth and handed a menu by a sweet

grandmotherly type named Tina. I ordered the chicken sandwich, and Tina was kind enough to inform me that this was a bone-in situation, so I changed my mind and ordered a cheeseburger, and she talked me up, asking about my stopping in, etc. In return, I told her about my trip, and I could see her visibly fretting at the enormity of my undertaking.

Yeah, a familiar theme.

The cheeseburger was fantastic, and Tina wondered if I'd like dessert—and now I felt like if I *didn't* order dessert, I'd break her heart forever... so, naturally, I asked for the menu. She replied by walking over to the front of house, bringing back the entire *tray* of desserts available, and giving me a dissertation on all.

I went with the blueberry cheesecake, and it was beyond amazing. And after shuffling off again, she came back and said, "I got you a magnet and a postcard."

Yeah, I'll display both forevermore. *And* she fixed me up another Dr. Pepper for the road, on the house.

And just like that, I'd visited a spot I'd dreamed of visiting for years: I'd put myself in a picture I'd had in my head for years, and it had been just as I'd imagined it.

I did it.

I pulled out of the Ariston feeling very *verklempt.* Route 66 had treated me very well so far: my very first day had bestowed upon me memories and connections that I would carry with me for the rest of my days.

At this point, I was almost crying, so moved by the

enormity of this trip; by both gratitude and fear—fear over the perceived impossibility of traversing this monster America by myself. What had I gotten myself into? Thoughts of canceling all my reservations and changing my flight plans danced through my head. Plus, I was feeling like pounded shit from my Ariston gorging...

It's about another 57 miles from Litchfield, IL, to St. Louis, MO, on I-55, and before I could second guess myself further, I found myself barreling across the Heartland on my way to the Gateway City. Gray, lowering clouds and lush green scenery—and then eventually, the land opened up on the left and I got my first look ever at the St. Louis skyline and the Gateway Arch.

My first view of the Arch felt like my first view of America. There it was, looming over the grasslands, beckoning me. I felt an incredible sense of pride and joy at this sight: I was *finally* seeing such an American landmark with my own eyes! I felt incredibly excited knowing that this was my destination.

And so this brings us to the Gateway Arch—the Gateway to the West.

In 1935, President Franklin Delano Roosevelt started plans to build what was known as the "Jefferson National Expansion Memorial", but is now known as Gateway Arch National Park. Land was found along the river in front of the Old Courthouse and cleared for construction, and in 1948, a national competition was held to choose the design for a memorial. The winner? A relatively unknown Finnish architect named Eero Saarinen. Saarinen wanted "...to create a monument which would have lasting significance and would be a landmark of our time... Neither an obelisk nor a rectangular box nor a dome seemed right on this site or for this purpose. But here, at the edge of the Mississippi River, a great arch did seem right." And mission accomplished, I'd say! Construction began in 1963, and the Gateway Arch was completed in 1965 (sadly after Saarinen's death, brought about by a brain tumor, in 1961). The Gateway Arch is Eero Saarinin's masterpiece, though he also designed the terminal at Dulles International Airport and the breathtaking TWA Terminal at JFK.

Once the Arch was completed, Gateway Arch National Park naturally grew around it, and the park is now a delightful urban oasis of lush gardens and trails. Or so I'd read.

But anyhow, to bring us back to our narrative: there I was, watching the Gateway Arch looming in the distance, calling me home to St. Louis. Almost there. But first, Mission IV: the Chain of Rocks Bridge over the Mississippi.

This was the spot where the GPS (inevitably) fucked me over: I remember *seeing* the original Chain of Rocks bridge while crossing the new Chain of Rocks bridge and, at that very moment, hearing my electronic overlord saying, "You have arrived." ...but I hadn't. Nevertheless, it looked like an amazing walk. I pulled into an Aldi parking lot and allowed the GPS to guide me through an industrial stretch off Lewis & Clark Blvd. and past the Kraft-Heinz plant. (I can now say I've seen where my ketchup and mac and cheese come from. So, there's that.) My mood was saved when I realized that I was cruising a part of the country that produced two major sonic influences of mine: Miles Davis and Jeff Tweedy.

Miles. What can I say? I started listening to Miles during his be-bop years when I was in high school, and started studying the *Kind of Blue* album in college. Miles grew up affluent, the son of a doctor, in East St. Louis, IL, and he kicked heroin on his father's farm there. Seeing where Miles came from informed and expanded upon my mental images of young Miles making his way in the clubs on 52nd Street in Manhattan with Charlie Parker and Dizzy Gillespie. So, seeing this land—the place from whence he came—was a revelatory moment; a fresh bit of context for a favorite artist.

And the same was the case for Jeff Tweedy. His first band with high school pal (though soon-*not*-to-be-pal) Jay Farrar, Uncle Tupelo, blasted out of Belleville, IL, in '87, and set the template for alt-country, sporting equal doses of Ramones and Gram Parsons influences. Uncle Tupelo blazed and imploded in '94, from whence Jeff Tweedy took most of the band and rechristened it Wilco. Being in this area allowed me to actually get a lot more context for Jay Farrar's output: he was the working-class middle-America guy, with songs like *Graveyard Shift* and *Still Be Around*; a twenty-something kid with the voice of a guy who'd spent decades running a machine in a mill and lamenting his declining fortunes on a barstool.

I love Farrar and Tweedy equally, and it was *very* cool to become immersed in their world for a spell.

After taking this moment of appreciation, I eventually crossed over the Mighty Mississippi and checked into City Place, St. Louis—though not before catching the wheel of my roller in a drainage gate and nearly pulling off a Mary Lou Retton move, naturally. I then got upgraded to a suite with an amazing view of the Gateway Arch... and from then, it truly felt as though I'd arrived in St. Louis.

Duty first, though: I called my mom to wish her a happy eighty-fourth birthday, and set out on foot for Busch Stadium. This walk took me past the Old Courthouse and the Dred and Harriet Scott statue.

Dred Scott v. Sandford, 1857.

As some background: the Dred Scott decision voided the Missouri Compromise, thus making African Americans not entitled to citizenship. Under the three-fifths compromise (ratified at the Constitutional Convention of 1787), it was determined that three-fifths of each state's slave population would count toward the state's total population for the purpose of determining the number of seats in the House of Representation.

Yes, you read that right: a slave—an African American *person*—was considered three-fifths of an American citizen.

Accordingly, these slaves were not entitled to

citizenship and had no voting rights—not to mention the fact that their "owners" (and the south in general) now boasted outsized power in the legislative process.

In 1820, northern states wanted to stop the expansion of slavery, while southern states wanted to continue with such expansion: Maine and Missouri both petitioned for statehood, but northern lawmakers attached amendments restricting slavery to Missouri's petition. Southern lawmakers balked, claiming slavery was a states rights issue, and thus, the Missouri Compromise was struck: Missouri was admitted as a slave state and Maine was admitted as a free state, and as a compromise to Missouri's statehood, slavery was prohibited in the rest of the lands acquired in the Louisiana Purchase, including the Michigan Territory (Michigan and Wisconsin), the Missouri Territory (Montana; the Dakotas) and the Oregon Territory (Washington; Oregon; Idaho).

Dred Scott was one such person born into slavery— "property" of the Blow family of Virginia. The Blows moved to St. Louis in 1830, but sold Scott to Dr. John Emerson due to financial hardship. Emerson, an army officer, served in Illinois and the Wisconsin Territory, where slavery was prohibited by the Missouri Compromise, in 1836, but eventually Emerson, Dred, his wife (Harriet), and their surviving children (Eliza and Lizzie) returned to St. Louis in 1840. In 1843, Dr. Emerson died, and for the next three years, his widow, Irene, continued to "lease" the Scotts out.

Hired slaves.

Scott, heartbreakingly, offered Irene Emerson $300 for their freedom, and the offer was refused. Thus, the Scotts filed "freedom suits" in the Missouri Circuit Court, which were tried in the Old Courthouse.

The first court upheld the "once free, always free" doctrine, which held that slaves who resided in a free territory for two years were considered emancipated and would retain their freedom if they returned to a slave state. In *Scott v. Emerson*, in 1847 (also tried in the Old Courthouse), the Emersons' "ownership" of the Scotts was established, and it was also established that, because of their residence in a free territory, the Scotts were, indeed, emancipated.

Irene Emerson appealed, and in 1852, the Missouri Supreme Court overturned the verdict on the theory that Missouri didn't have to abide by the laws of free states.

By 1853, Irene Emerson had moved to Massachusetts, but not before transferring "ownership" of the Scotts to her brother, John F. A. Sanford, a citizen of New York. This was an interesting rub, since the Scotts would be citizens of Missouri if granted their freedom, and Sanford wouldn't be subjected to suit in Missouri due to his state of residence. So, in *Dred Scott v. Sandford* (the defendant in the case name is "Sandford" rather than "Sanford" due to a clerical error), Dred and Harriet took their fight for freedom to the U.S. Supreme Court.

Chief Justice Roger B. Taney wasn't having it. His opinion in the seven-two majority twisted history and his own logic into a fetid, rotting pretzel. While Taney admitted that African Americans were citizens of certain states and could vote in certain states, ultimately, state citizenship had no relation to national citizenship, and therefore, African Americans could not sue for freedom in federal court because they could not be citizens of the United States. Never mind that the Constitution requires that if one state considers a person a citizen, all states and the federal government must accord that person "all Privileges and Immunities of Citizens in the several States" (Article IV, Section 2), and never mind that Article III (which established jurisdiction of federal courts) says nothing about national citizenship and states that judicial power shall extend "to Controversies... between Citizens of different States".

But Taney wasn't done yet: he determined that Congress had exceeded its authority by enacting the Missouri Compromise, arguing that the Scotts had never been free and so could not contest their freedom because, once they returned to Missouri (against their will, by the way), their status depended on local (slave) law.

Basically, the U.S. Supreme Court found that no persons of African descent could claim citizenship in the United States, and that the Scotts' time spent in Wisconsin and Illinois did not grant emancipation under the Missouri Compromise. Why? Because their emancipation was unconstitutional because it would "improperly deprive [the] Scotts' owner of his legal property".

Happily, the Scotts finally earned their freedom when the Blow family "repurchased" the Scotts and granted them enfranchisement in 1857. From then, Dred worked as a porter in a hotel... and the kicker is, he died of tuberculosis just over a year later.

Not a part of our history to be proud of, but one that should absolutely still be told and reflected on, nonetheless.

I got choked up at this point while soaking up all the history. How could we have *done* this to our own *people*? How could we have possibly considered *any* human being to be three-fifths of a person? The stain of America's dark past really hit me there. I definitely had a lot of mental fuel to ponder.

And all this on the way to see a ballgame!

I hadn't been to Camden Yards in Baltimore—the ballpark that started the whole *nouveau* r*etro* stadium craze—before, but I loved her offspring, including Busch Stadium III. The Cards originally played in Sportsman's Park (renamed Busch Stadium by Anheuser Busch scion Augustus "Gussie" Busch in 1953; he wanted to name the park Budweiser Stadium, but Commissioner Ford Frick was aghast at such brazen commercialism—*pah!*—and turned him down. Gussie, not being one to sleep on an opportunity, asked if he could rename Sportsman's Park Busch Stadium, ostensibly after himself, instead, which Frick was fine with. Not long after, Busch Beer was launched...). Busch Stadium, *née* Sportsman's Park, was razed in 1966. Busch II, a prototypical multipurpose "cookie cutter" stadium where the baseball and football Cardinals (before they moved to Arizona in '88) played on Astroturf, stood from 1966 to 2005, until Busch III opened in 2006.

I was quite impressed by Busch III: classic brick-and-steel exterior; statues of the greats (Musial, Bob Gibson, Ozzie Smith, *et al.*) out front; nice wide-open concourses; tons of grub options inside and out. It smelled like barbecue and turkey legs, had great sightlines, and the upper deck didn't feel so steep that you felt as though you were about to roll to a grisly death behind home plate (I'm looking at you, old Shea Stadium!). Plus, the view of the Arch and the Old Courthouse were stunning—though that view was somewhat swallowed up by the new skyscrapers. Even still, the views were fantastic, and I was digging it.

I found myself staring over at the AT&T logo on a gorgeous art-deco tower (turned out to be 1010 Pine St., the original Southwestern Bell Building), and from there, my mind (as it often does, clearly!) wandered across the ages. I imagined Chryslers and Buicks, men with fedoras and women with pearls around 1010 Pine, a Benny Goodman soundtrack playing in the background... and then drifted back even further, hearing in my head the prose style of the days of Lewis & Clark. "A dispatch arrived from Saint Louis..." "We arrived on horseback, at Saint Louis, and set camp for the upcoming winter..."

Magnificent. And now, I have yet another favorite art-deco tower in the world.

It was cold as hell in the upper deck, and I was feeling a bit pukeish from my cheeseburger and cheesecake at the Ariston, so in the end, I only lasted a few innings. But hey, I got a taste, which is what this trip is about! Once I'd had enough, I hoofed back to the room, flipped on the telly to watch the game I'd just left, crashed for a bit... and then I realized I hadn't gotten to the Gateway Arch or the museum. Major bummer, but my fault: I hadn't thought ahead enough to buy my tickets well in advance, and the only times left on the tram to the top of the Arch were too late in the morning. Next time, for sure—and yes, there *will* be a next time! To compromise in the meantime, I left my bedroom, went to the living room, and stared at the Arch for a while, which... kind of counts, right? (Yeah, I know...)

I didn't know it at the time, but the view from my living room counted even less, because the Arch lighting system was turned off due to bird migration season. Yeah, I love preservation, but *fuuuuuuuuck*! Okay, I'm coming back to St. Louis.

I also realized at this moment that I hadn't eaten since Ariston. It was too late (and I was feeling too bloated) for St. Louis ribs, so I decided to walk over to Gringo on Washington & 7th, and had queso and Mexican rice. Good. Nothing spectacular, but good. I then left Gringo and wandered aimlessly for a while in the frigid dark—and this was when an interesting observation hit me: there wasn't much foot traffic in St. Louis. I'd kind of noticed this on my walk over to Bush: there was the usual gameday foot traffic, but beyond that, not much. And now, wandering around 11th and Pine and Olive, I barely noticed any people at all—and it also seemed like all the stores and restaurants were closed. Strange. This was a major metropolitan city, right? So, where the hell *was* everybody?

Simmering on this, I walked back to the room alongside a horse-drawn carriage with bells and shakers that made a perfect, rhythmic beat to its clop. I'm not a fan of horses, but that sound was *magnificent*, and with this cadence, I once again conjured up the St. Louis of Lewis & Clark for a few blocks, imagining the sound of hoofs without engines and sirens and satellite linkups. The Gateway to the West.

Goodnight, St. Louis.

CHAPTER 3
GOODBYE, DIXIE

THERE WAS RARELY ANY RESPITE from the torment that was now my Florida upbringing; from the spiritual de-pantsing that was about to continue with great speed over the next four years.

Not that it was *all* doom and gloom: it was while living in Jacksonville that I got my first "big boy" bike—a Huffy with a banana seat, which, believe it or not, I actually *wanted* at the time because the banana seat said *HUFFY* under my butt, and I thought that was pretty "rad". It didn't take long for me to realize that I was a lost bit of chum in the shark pool of kid-dom, however: I was vaguely aware of BMX in Brunswick, but Florida was an entirely different world. As I casually rode my Huffy around my new neighborhood, all the other kids were riding track-approved bikes from GT and Mongoose. It was 1982, after all: biker and gear impresario Bob Haro was a featured stunt-rider on the big screen in *E.T.*, *BMX Plus!* was on every newsstand, and my new home pulsed with the culture of bicycle motocross. My Huffy and I were surrounded by surf-and-skate rats on tricked-out bikes, like a slightly younger Daniel LaRusso surrounded by the Kobra Kai.

Clearly, things had to change.

Right away, I *needed* a new bike—preferably a GT. But I'd also need to trick out the bike with Haro rims, a number plate, an Oakley handlebar, frame pads, and those bitchin' Oakley handlebar grips. Oh, and of *course* I'd need a GT helmet and jersey and pants. Not unreasonable demands from a ten-year-old.

Ultimately, I "settled" on a Mongoose with the grips and pads but without the rims—an entirely acceptable compromise—and, with my new bike in tow, I spent hours shredding the trails in the woods, practicing new jumps, and loving the feeling of fitting in (or at least fitting in outside of school). On my bike and with my friends, I was free—free to catch air; free from the bullying and awkwardness that resided in the classrooms and halls; free to be me; free from having a Huffy banana seat.

It was also shortly after that that I got my first guitar. I don't remember exactly where I got my first real six-string (sorry, Bryan Adams); just that it was some music store in Jacksonville. It was November 1983, I was eleven, and it was a $30 student acoustic bought with the money I'd saved up.

It came in a cardboard box and smelled like wood polish, and it was everything to me. I also got a Hal Leonard book and started taking lessons at the same store. The first song I ever learned was Pink Floyd's *Wish You Were Here*. I quickly learned that the whole song was basically a G chord and that I could do different things with that G chord. Lightbulbs started going off, and 40 years later, they still are.

The first record I bought for myself with my own money (at the long-lost DeOrsey's Records in Brunswick) was AC/DC's *For Those About to Rock (We Salute You)*. It was 1982, and this record nicely supplemented the 45s I was obsessively collecting: Anita Ward's *Ring My Bell*, Paul Davis' *'65 Love Affair*, and Greg Khin's *The Breakup Song*. My father was kind of pissed at me for blowing my money on such "trash", but that shimmering copper cover held sway, and my AC/DC obsession was born.

Next stop: Ozzy.

The early eighties were a wash of sonic inspiration born from big, creamy guitars. This was when I first started really noticing guitar players and what they were playing. Elliot Easton's massive-sounding solo on The Cars' *Since You're Gone* and the emotive melody of Steve Clark's solo on Def Leppard's *Bringin' On the Heartbreak* just hooked me in with the tone; the feel.

This was also when I started noticing the emotive power of music. Certain songs would just make me cry for no reason. Great example: both the Bee Gees' and Tavares' versions of *More Than a Woman* from the *Saturday Night Fever* soundtrack—specifically the pre-chorus ("Oh, say you'll always be my baby, we can make it shine") and chorus. I now realize that this is because of the way the chord progressions set up the melodies, but back then, all I knew was that I got weepy over certain songs for no reason.

Basically, music was fast becoming an obsession.

I started reading about and dreaming of playing Gibson Les Pauls through a wall of Marshall amps. And then, I started doing.

I have made many suspect life choices, but never a bad sonic choice. I had a good, solid aural foundation, and from that, I became an obsessed listener, a deconstructionist, constantly tearing down songs to hear how and why they worked—the composition, the instrumentation, the mix— and a reconstructionist, constantly rebuilding songs into my own interpretations.

And I never left a song behind. The common logic goes that when one "grows up" and discovers classical, jazz, talk radio, whatever, the music that one enjoyed as a child becomes a quaint anachronism; an adorable reminder of immaturity. To that I say: well, we may have aged, but the music has remained exactly as it was, so why ditch it? I'm now forty-six, but the Dead Kennedys record I was listening to at age thirteen hasn't changed a bit, and listening to it just reminds me of being thirteen again. What's wrong with that? Why should I ditch a lifetime of music in favor of a world-weary self-condescension? Why not just *add* to my repertoire, rather than trying to constantly tear it down and rebuild it?

I personally feel that my life has been greatly enriched by my keeping all my original musical loves close to my heart.

Music is passion. And it all started in those magical childhood spaces between the stations and the grooves.

Upon returning to Florida for sixth grade after one of these summer trips to Maine, I embarked on my second new start in two years—another uprooting that would this time come with sociopolitical underpinnings. 1984 was the subject year of George Orwell's novel, Reagan's trouncing of Mondale, the Ethiopian famine, Maine Girl Joan Benoit ruling the LA Olympics, Bhopal, Bernie Goetz, the launch of the CD player, *Ghostbusters*, *Beverly Hills Cop*, *The Karate Kid*, Van Halen's *1984* (the last album with Diamond David Lee Roth before Sammy Hagar took over and ruined the band, though *1984* was really the first "Van Hagar" album—spiritually, at least), and the rise of Mötley Crüe, and hints and intimations from major underground bands such as The Dead Kennedys, Hüsker Dü, and R.E.M.

It was also (in my case) the year of sixth grade, which, as we're about to see, didn't go too well for me.

After two years at Beauclerc Elementary (which was in my neighborhood), I was now, as a new sixth-grader, bussed across the whole of Jacksonville (the largest city in the country in terms of square mileage) to R.V. Daniels, a predominantly black school in a predominantly black neighborhood.

Now, I walked into this situation knowing nothing of prejudice. It wasn't in my heart then or now, and if I bandy about words that are racially charged today, that's because it was just what we knew in 1984. But goddamn, it was a weird situation. I mean, bussing happened in Boston in the *seventies*, right? Weren't we over that shit by 1984?

In truth, I'm not sure why I was bussed. Maybe some pencil-pusher in the Duval County School District dropped a cigarette ash on a demographic report and missed a figure, or maybe they just threw a dart, or played eenie-meenie. Who knows how bureaucracy really works? Regardless, it was determined that I would be bussed 45 minutes each way for sixth grade. In this, I was joined by a few friends from Beauclerc, so I had some solidarity, and the bus ride, while long, was pleasurable: the driver always played the radio loud, so my commute was filled with Chaka Khan's *I Feel for You*, Diana Ross' *I'm Missing You*, Don Henley's *Sunset Grill*, and UTFO's *The Real Roxanne* (yes, it was played on commercial radio). Plus, crossing the Mathews Bridge and taking the Arlington Expressway meant plenty of bumps, so I always sat in the back hoping to hit the ceiling. I think it actually happened once, although I don't quite remember. (There may be a correlation here...)

Basically, there were many great moments from this

time, and the school itself had its happy spots: I remember getting together an air-band performance of Def Leppard's *Rock of Ages* for a talent show, I had warning track power at recess, and I pulled off a few nifty doubles.

But then again, there was always "my man" Cedric and "my friend" Chad to cloak a storm cloud around my sunshine.

I often "loaned" Cedric my lunch money, and once "loaned" him my new Casio computer watch. I ended up getting that one back in pieces and—shocker—I never got my lunch loans back. But Cedric had a way of smoothing things over. "We tight!" he'd say—and I'd believe it. "You my man!" he'd tell me—and I'd buy it. I heard him call me a "dumbass honky motherfucker" behind my back a few times, but no matter, because we tight! Right?

Chad was meanwhile a pure St. John's River redneck, well-versed in Hank Jr. and Charlie Daniels' lyrics and the content of *Guns & Ammo* and *Field & Stream*. We were never all that "tight", and even less so after the day he produced a pair of handcuffs on the bus, hooked my right arm up to a seat, and punched me until my arm was completely numb and lifeless. Why did he do that? Who the hell knows? The bus driver saw this attack himself and told Chad to get off the bus early—somewhere in ghetto downtown Jacksonville. I have no idea what happened to him from there, but with the way my arm was feeling, I must admit I didn't care too much.

At least I still had my music.

Sometime in 1985, I got my first electric guitar: a red Aria Pro II. I don't remember how much it cost, but it was comfortable to play, and I had no problems with it at all. I got this guitar at LV Music, which was in a strip mall less than a mile from our apartment. The proprietor was one Vance Val (apparently, he was the "V" half of LV Music; I never knew who the "L" half was), and he was a seriously cool guy: perpetual Marlboro, long black hair, Star of David tattoo on his picking hand between his index finger and thumb, and player of a Stratocaster painted with the Union Jack. He inspired me to *shred*—though apparently, he also had sticky fingers and fast feet (or cashflow issues), since one day, Vance Val and LV Music were both suddenly gone.

My dad always referred to him as a druggy, but I didn't care. I still carry his influence to this day.

I also got a little five-watt practice amp with a distortion channel so I could finally seriously rock out. Coping strategies for the win!

My parents knew I was having problems at school, so they decided to try sending me to private school. This was a good, well-intentioned idea on paper; in practice, not so much. Regardless, my third new start in three years came in the form of Hendrick's Methodist School.

I was not Methodist, nor anything else: my family went to church as often as we flew first class—which is to say, never. I also wasn't in the same tax bracket as most of my new chums—a point which was never more painfully obvious than when I stepped out of our silver-and-rust Fairmont station wagon past classmates stepping out of Porsches and Mercedes'.

Once again, I was the new kid, but now, I was also the new *poor* kid. Fun! By which I mean, traumatic!

I was a weird kid. I began noticing this after my arrival in Florida, but this was the time it *really* started to become obvious. Like, I'd throw out a line I'd heard on a TV show in class, taking for granted that everyone else had seen the show and knew what I was talking about. Of course, *nobody* knew what I was talking about, and the awkward silences and titters that inevitably followed exacted a toll on a fragile soul desperate to fit in; to belong. Now, I laugh and say that my brain is a garbage dump—and throw out another obscure *The Simpsons* reference for good measure—but at the time, I felt as though I was from another planet... and in so many ways, I was.

Besides this, I don't remember much about Hendrick's other than the teasing. I also remember getting the wind knocked out of me playing basketball in gym and feeling like a John Hughes outcast.

Oh, and I got a Swatch watch that year.

That's about it.

Basically, I may have left Maine physically, but I never left it spiritually.

Of the four years we lived in Jacksonville, the only year we didn't return to Maine for Christmas vacation was 1985. That year, I transferred my homesickness to a familiar stand-in: living my dreams of a white Maine Christmas through Frogtown Hollow, home of Emmet Otter.

Christmas in Florida (even northern Florida) was depressing for a Maine boy: it was chilly—maybe in the 40s or, at most, 30s—but nothing like the pure Maine winter cold I wanted. And there was certainly no snow. My only lasting impression of Jacksonville Christmas cheer is an aluminum tree with the most garish lights imaginable on the roof of Jax Liquors.

Bing Crosby clearly hadn't visited my neck of the woods.

But we *did* have HBO, and with that came salvation. *Emmet Otter's Jug Band Christmas* had been a favorite of mine since it premiered in 1977, and the Jim Henson special, adapted from the 1971 Russell and Lillian Hoban book, came along at exactly the right time during Christmas 1985. The Frogtown Hollow inhabited by Emmet and Ma Otter served as a virtual Maine Christmas at my grandparents' farm as I sat in my Florida apartment: the fire-red sunset as Emmet and Ma row home from running errands made me dream of the sunsets I knew from the living room window at the Homestead; the sound of the snowmobiles driven by Chuck and the River Bottom Boys echoed the sound of snowmobiles heading up our path and into our woods; the brilliant full moon that shone over Ma, Emmet, and his jug band as they walked home in defeat from the Waterville Talent Contest was the same moon that shone over Eric and I as we played football or went tobogganing by the barn light in the crystalline snow.

I suppose I've always had this ability to adapt to circumstances and to try to improve my lot, and this certainly served me well over that Christmas vacation in 1985.

Christmas Day wasn't all bad that year, despite it being spent in a small Florida apartment rather than a snowbound Maine farm. We got our first VCR that day (the remote control was attached to the console by a wire), as well as our first VHS movie: *Gung Ho* with Robert Mitchum. I also got my first blank VHS tape, with which I taped Celtics/Knicks at Madison Square Garden and, later that day, *Emmet Otter's Jug Band Christmas*. Even still, I was pining for Maine and all the quirks that came with its lifestyle, including one of the most critical aspects of surviving a Maine winter: dressing for the occasion, a.k.a., *layering*. From November through April, my standard wardrobe is a T-shirt and a flannel, and often, I also go for a T-shirt, long-sleeve Henley, and a flannel, frequently adding a pair of Long Johns for extra warmth below the equator.

Layering is a time-honored Maine winter tradition, but ironically, the lesson was driven home in Florida, on a day of national tragedy. January 28, 1986.

Eight days earlier, my science class, led by Ms. Harm, had taken a field trip to Kennedy Space Center in anticipation of the launch of the Space Shuttle *Challenger* and the first teacher in space, New Hampshire's own Christa McAuliffe. It was a brilliant cold day, and I had Led Zeppelin's *IV* and Mötley Crüe's *Too Fast for Love* for my Walkman. We devoured all the exhibits and went crazy in the gift shop, and as we were herded back to the bus, there it was: the great ship on the giant transport tractor, making the slow journey to the launchpad. *Challenger* and her booster rockets practically glowed against the brown and orange of the fuel tank. It was a magnificent sight, and we all felt a sense of pride in the upcoming mission.

Eight days later, as *Challenger* launched on her doomed flight, one of my chums spilled a full carton of chocolate milk all over my lap. The humiliation of my entire table laughing at me as my crotch and legs were doused was bad enough, but there was also a practical problem: my jeans were soaked, and it was literally freezing out. What the hell was I going to do to stay warm?

I must have thought of my days tobogganing at the farm and my trusty Long Johns, because I went to my locker, grabbed my gym sweats, and put them on before pulling my jeans back on. I reeked like stale chocolate milk and humiliation, but I was warm.

I remember sitting in Ms. Harm's science class, warm with my sweats on under my jeans, when she said, "The *Challenger* has exploded, and there were no survivors."

My class gasped and cried, and we all went outside—and 160 miles to the south, we saw the smoke in the sky:

the unmistakable Y-shaped cloud of death with the huge ball of fire in the middle where the shuttle had blown up and the rockets separated.

I stood there in the cold, stinking like sour chocolate milk but layered in warmth, gazing at the smoke in the sky and realizing that the world had just changed forever.

Later, at home, I watched President Reagan's "Touch the Face of God" speech in a fresh pair of pants. I remember the sky outside the Oval Office and how much it reminded me of the winter sunsets in Maine.

Despite the horrors of the day, I remember dreaming of being back at the farm; back home in Maine. I dreamed of those 4PM sunsets and cozy early evenings; the woodsmoke and sitting by the woodstove safe and warm; playing in the snow in the glorious winter cold. And I remember thinking that when we moved back home, whenever that would be, I'd spend the rest of my winters layered and happy.

By the time I hit eighth grade, not much was working, so I returned to public school: Duval. My fourth new start in four years. I only ended up attending Duval for a few weeks (more on why below), so I really don't have any impressions of that time. The preceding years were enough for me!

Several weeks after I started eighth grade, it was announced that my dad had accepted a job in Brunswick, Maine. Thus, on September 12, 1986, I got the greatest fourteenth birthday present ever: we loaded up the silver-and-rust Fairmont, got the fuck out of Jacksonville, and began our three-day journey back home to Maine.

This time, I welcomed the change. *I was going home.* Even in the back seat, squished against the passenger side door by Eric and two giant ATA-approved cat carriers (which housed our slightly incontinent cats Snowflake and Tiger), it was the greatest day and car ride of my life. I remember I had an issue of *Circus* with an article on Ronnie James Dio, and I think I was listening to Dio's album *Holy Diver* on my Walkman.

We stopped at South of the Border and loaded up on fireworks and cheap Americana. We spent the first night in North Carolina, and I had the worst meal I've ever had in my life. I don't remember where it was, or even *what* it was, but it was *bad*. Then, on the second night, we settled somewhere in New Jersey. I remember a guy who looked like a serial killer smiling at us at dinner and a live-action *Chipmunks* variety show special on the TV.

The next morning, I was home again, driving I-95 through New York City. The Giants were rolling toward the Super Bowl, and it was great to be in Metro NYC again.

Later in the afternoon, we arrived at the Homestead. Home again!

I'd missed Maine like crazy, but I'd also gotten used to the life of a pre-teen Florida beach bum/skate rat. Every day in Jacksonville had been like a Cameron Crowe film, and I was straight out of central casting, bedecked with a devil-lock (nicely highlighted by 14 bottles of Sun-In), surf and skate tees, Jimmy'Z skate shorts, and violet Chuck Taylors. This meant that my new Maine chums were, to put it mildly, a little taken aback by me. Walking into Sugg Middle School, Lisbon Falls, Maine, circa 1986, was like walking onto the set of a documentary about the Nixon years. I'd decided to dress up in a Cosby sweater that first day—to find my classmates were all sporting bowl cuts and bangs and were bedecked in jean jackets. I was listening to The Dead Kennedys, Black Flag, The Ramones, and Agent Orange, and a skateboard was how I got around, while the preferred mode of transportation for the rest of the class revolved around the most extreme engines on two or four wheels. Plus, the Maine airwaves were filled with Grace Slick and John Kay and Steppenwolf on the dinosaur station, and there were only two feet (mine) clad in violet Chucks for many miles around.

I was fourteen and finally back home after four years of dreaming of exactly this—and I was about to become a middle school pariah; a purple-wearing faggot.

Right away, like some sort of sick joke, I was back home, but I didn't fit in.

So, immediately upon my arrival from Florida, I was marked as a weirdo; a perfect target. And the trauma began immediately. Once my new chums discovered that I was nervous and jumpy, the Hot Ass became a go-to trick. The Hot Ass was a pithy variation of the Hotfoot, wherein the perp holds a lighter under the victim's plastic chair until they jump out of said chair, shrieking in agony and, hopefully, tossing their books and pen around the room in the process. This was especially popular during tests, when my sudden screech and flame-induced dance would inevitably make me the focus of the otherwise-quiet room. Often, my perp—usually M-W—would say something snarky about me causing a disturbance as the eyes of the class bore into me and their howls of laughter carved into my soul.

In response to these taunts, I developed a rather nasty defense mechanism during this time—one that still haunts me. I had no self-esteem, and my sense of self-worth was such that I thought I could make myself feel better about myself by ripping others and getting laughs. Hence, I developed an acid snark and made fun of others in my class for their clothes, hairstyles... anything. I was desperate to get laughs—but, of course, the people I was trying to impress thought I was an asshole, and my self-worth tanked further as a result of my failed efforts.

I hurt people, and I will hurt over that for the rest of my days.

DAY THREE

MAY 10, 2019

St. Louis, MO, to Tulsa, OK: 394 miles.
Time Out: Checked out of City Place at about 6:30AM CST.
Time In: Checked into The Campbell Hotel at about 4PM CST.

I T OCCURS TO ME THAT we haven't gone over the history of Route 66, and since we're now heading to Tulsa (the spiritual epicenter of Route 66) and are on Day Two of being officially on the road, this feels like the perfect spot to do so.

So, how did Route 66 come to exist? Why was it so important after its initial establishment? And what led to its demise... and rebirth?

The story of Route 66 starts with the Santa Fe Trail, and it continues with the Atchison, Topeka, and Santa Fe railroad, Harvey Houses, and the Ozark Trail Highway. It was born with Cyrus Avery, and it ended with decertification. And then, it continued (and continues to this day) due to nostalgia.

But let's start with the Santa Fe Trail.

The Santa Fe Trail was the original Gateway to the West, a wagon trail running 900-odd miles from Franklin, Missouri—roughly halfway between St. Louis and Kansas City—through Kansas and Colorado, and onto Santa Fe, New Mexico, and, by extension, to Mexico City via El Camino Real (the Royal Road). Originally laid out in 1821, the trail became a critical link between the east and the west, and a major trade route with Mexico: it was the route the U.S. Army used to invade New Mexico during the Mexican-American War, and it also became a route used by the Pony Express.

William Becknell, a Missouri trader, headed for Santa Fe in 1821 to drum up trading opportunities (and to avoid prison for his debts), and in the process, he blazed the now-famous trail there—and, at this time, French colonists, now freed from Spanish rule under the Louisiana Purchase, established trade with Santa Fe, and were happy to deal. Thus, the Santa Fe Trail saw a major influx of traffic from the east, and the route thrived until 1880.

So, what happened in 1880?

The railroad.

The Atchison and Topeka railroad was chartered in 1859, and ran from Atchison and Topeka, Kansas, to the

Colorado border. Rechristened the Atchison, Topeka and Santa Fe in 1870 (obviously they named the railroad with an eye on posterity!), it *finally* reached its namesake terminus (Santa Fe, New Mexico) ten years later, in 1880, thus ensuring the demise of the Santa Fe Trail and the birth of the iron horse era.

Atchison, Topeka and Santa Fe founder Cyrus K. Holiday wanted to build a rail line that paralleled the New Mexico stretch of the old Santa Fe Trail—and by 1887, the tracks ran from Chicago to Los Angeles, with stops including Oklahoma City, Amarillo, Santa Fe, and Barstow.

Sound familiar?

And if you're going to be humping the rails for days on end, you're going to want a place to crash and get a good home-cooked meal, right?

Enter Fred Harvey.

Born in Liverpool in 1835, Fred Harvey arrived in New York in 1850 and dove into restaurant life immediately— and, after his St. Louis restaurant bombed, he hit the rails traveling the Great Plains... and soon noticed that dining options along the rail routes in the southwest, well, sucked. So, in 1876, Fred Harvey signed on with the Atchison, Topeka and Santa Fe, and took over concessions for the trains and dining operations at the Topeka depot, which led to rapid expansion of his hospitality empire along the rail line: Harvey House restaurants soon appeared adjacent to stations all along the Atchison,

Topeka and Santa Fe, soon followed by Harvey Hotels.

Harvey House became the first American restaurant chain, and the concept was the same throughout: locations convenient to the rail depot and quality food with quality presentation, cleanliness, and efficiency.

Shortly thereafter, Harvey Girls appeared in 1883 in their trademark black-and-white skirts, and Fred Harvey's staff was, unfortunately reflecting the times, all female and all white. The girls were expected to have impeccable manners in exchange for a generous salary and room and board, and their 10PM curfew was strictly enforced by the elder Harvey Girls, who took on the role of house mother. The Harvey chain, amazingly, lasted into the 1970s.

So, we now have a railroad stretching from Chicago to Los Angeles, through Santa Fe, with pre-existing infrastructure including built-in restaurants and hotels.

But wait a second, you may be thinking, *Route 66 goes through Albuquerque! Why are we blathering on about Santa Fe?* Well, hold on there, partner: we haven't gotten to the Ozark Trail Highway yet.

The Ozark Trail Highway was laid out in 1913 by William "Coin" Harvey. Harvey predicted that auto travel was coming, and so formed the Ozark Trail Highway Association to establish a road connecting St. Louis to Las Vegas, New Mexico, with the road running through Missouri, Kansas, Oklahoma, and Texas. Cyrus Avery established the Oklahoma branch of the Ozark Trail Association in 1914, and the trail eventually ran from St.

Louis south to El Paso, with a western spur stretching from Lawton, OK, to Santa Rosa, NM. The original 1926-1937 alignment of Route 66 continued along this path and featured the "Santa Fe Loop", which ran from Santa Rosa to Santa Fe and then south to Albuquerque. After 1937, the route was shortened, bypassing Santa Fe and running straight from Santa Rosa to Albuquerque. And *that's* why we're blathering on about Santa Fe: it was on the path of the *original* Route 66.

But let's get back to 1913. Again, we have a railroad stretching from Chicago to Los Angeles, through Santa Fe, with pre-existing infrastructure including built-in restaurants and hotels. Might be a good path to follow for a road, right?

Enter Cyrus Avery.

Born in Pennsylvania in 1871, Cyrus Avery eventually made it to Tulsa, OK, establishing the Avery Oil & Gas Company along the way. With the advent of the Ford Model T in 1908, Avery, like William "Coin" Harvey, soon sussed out that auto travel would be huge and that, consequently, there might be a bit of demand for his petroleum products. By all accounts, Avery was a good, civic-minded guy and a shrewd businessman... and he also knew that a major road running through Tulsa would be good for his adopted town. So, Avery started pushing for road improvement across Oklahoma and joined the Oklahoma Good Roads Association (in addition to the Ozark Trail Association) and, by 1923, the Oklahoma State

Highway Commission. There, he implemented a gas tax to fund the department before he eventually moved on to the federal Joint Board of Interstate Highways.

Meanwhile, Congress was pushing for a cross-country road running from Virginia Beach, VA, to Los Angeles, CA, passing through Springfield and Joplin, MO, Kansas, Colorado, Utah, and Las Vegas (Nevada, this time), and on to LA. Hearing this, Cyrus Avery thought it would be cost-prohibitive to run a road through the Rocky Mountains, and instead suggested a route starting in Chicago and running through St. Louis and on through Tulsa and OK City before crossing the Texas Panhandle, New Mexico, Arizona, and California.

Again: sound familiar?

So, Avery's plan was approved.

Now what? Well, the road needed a number!

Under the conventions of the time, north-south routes had two-digit odd numbers and east-west routes had two-digit even numbers. Cyrus Avery was pushing for this new route from Chicago to Los Angeles to be certified as Route 60, but Kentucky balked, since that would leave Kentucky as the only state without a "0" highway designation. Kentucky pushed for Route 60 from Virginia Beach to Los Angeles, with the Springfield to Chicago stretch called 60 North. Avery thought 60 South would be good for the Virginia Beach to Springfield stretch, but Kentucky threatened to take a walk. Eventually, however, Kentucky offered a compromise: the highway from

Virginia Beach to Springfield (originally designated as Route 62) could be called Route 60, with the Chicago-to-Los Angeles stretch designated as Route 62. Avery responded that he didn't like 62 and proposed that the entire Chicago-to-Los Angeles route be called Route 66 instead.

Sold.

From there, Avery became Vice President of the U.S. Highway 66 Association, and pushed tirelessly to have the entire route paved. Which, eventually, it was. But this compromise also guaranteed pop-culture immortality for his new highway.

So, we now know how Route 66 came to exist and that within a few years, it was paved for the entire 2,278 miles. But how did it become so iconic?

Enter John Steinbeck, Bobby Troup, Nat "King" Cole, and Jack Kerouac.

Steinbeck coined the phrase "the Mother Road" in his 1939 classic *The Grapes of Wrath* and wrote eloquently about the plight of the Okies fleeing the Dust Bowl in Oklahoma and traveling 66 to California and the "promised land".

Bobby Troup wrote *Route 66*, and Nat "King" Cole recorded it in 1946. And really, what could Bobby Troup have done with "Route 62"? Think about that. The fact that "kicks" and "66" rhymed so perfectly really was a godsend. "Visit a drive-thru... on Route 62"? Well, okay, I *guess*, but *this* is much better:

If you ever plan to motor west
Travel my way, take the highway that's the
best
Get your kicks on Route 66

It winds from Chicago to L.A.
More than two thousand miles all the way
Get your kicks on Route 66

Now it goes through Saint Looey
Joplin, Missouri
Oklahoma City looks mighty pretty
You'll see Amarillo
Gallup, New Mexico
Flagstaff, Arizona
Don't forget Winona
Kingman, Barstow, San Bernardino

Won't you get hip to this timely tip
When you make, when you make, make that
Cal-I-fornia trip?
Get your kicks on Route 66
Get your kicks on Route 66
Get your kicks on Route 66

Three verses, one middle eight. And in this compact
format, Troup managed to reference major cities in seven

of the eight states along the route (no Kansas, but again, only 13 miles of Route 66 in Kansas) *in geographic order from Chicago to Los Angeles*. And the iconic rhyming chorus. *And* in those verses, he perfectly encapsulated the thrill of the joyride: getting your kicks; a 2,000-plus mile odyssey; heading to California, *the promised land*. The Big Adventure. Catchy as hell, and inspiring as hell. Songwriting 101 right here!

And Bobby Troup was lucky enough to have Nat "King" Cole record his song, and it became a major hit and an iconic touchstone of time and place.

And Jack Kerouac celebrated his journeys across 66 in the infamous *On The Road*, and that book has resonated for generations.

That's it, really.

Okay, so there's more to it than that: Route 66 was the original American superhighway. It was heavily traveled from 1926, and many iconic businesses opened up along the way and thrived as a result of their location. A short, extremely incomplete list of treasured Route 66 businesses that opened after the certification of Route 66 in 1926 includes (and this only includes establishments still operating as of 2019):

Illinois
- Del Rhea's Chicken Basket, Willowbrok (opened 1946).
- The Launching Pad, Wilmington (opened early 1960s).
- Dixie Travel Plaza, McLean (opened 1928).

- Cozy Dog Drive-In, Springfield (opened 1949).
- Ariston Café, Litchfield (opened 1935).

Missouri
- Ted Drewe's Frozen Custard, St. Louis (opened 1941).
- Meramec Caverns, Stanton (opened 1947).
- Wagon Wheel Motel (opened 1934).
- Munger-Moss Motel, Lebanon (opened 1946).

Oklahoma
- Waylan's Ku-Ku Burger, Miami (opened 1965).
- Rock Cafe, Stroud (opened 1939).

Texas
- U-Drop Inn, Shamrock (opened 1936).
- The Big Texan Steak Ranch, Amarillo (opened 1960).

New Mexico
- Blue Swallow Motel, Tucumcari (opened 1936).
- El Rancho Hotel, Gallup (opened 1937).
- Clines Corner, Clines Corner (opened 1934).

Arizona
- Wigwam Motel, Holbrook (opened 1950).
- Jack Rabbit Trading Post, Jack Rabbit (opened 1949).
- Delgadillo's Snow Cap, Seligman (opened 1953).
- El Trovatore Motel, Kingman (opened 1937).

California

- Roy's Motel & Café, Amboy (opened 1938).

Again, to reiterate, that is a short, *extremely* incomplete list of treasured Route 66 businesses—and seriously, look at that list! Unbelievable! And what's more, *all* of these locations are going strong as of 2019, so they must be rather beloved. And what's the connective tissue between them all? Yep, Route 66.

So, Route 66 is long and has many well-loved institutions—so surely that'd be enough to preserve it? Well, it appears not; so why exactly *did* Route 66 fall into decline? I'll tell you: an American war hero did it! Well, not intentionally, but still.

In 1956, the Dwight D. Eisenhower Interstate Highway System was initiated. Ike, of course, was a five-star General of the Army, oversaw the invasions of North Africa and Normandy during World War II, and became the 34th President of the United States in 1953. He was inspired by the efficiency of the Autobahn, and wanted to bring a similar four-lane system back home. And so the Federal Aid Highway Act passed in 1956, and the wheels started turning for a plan involving massive four-lane highways spanning across the United States. Construction began in 1956 in, depending on who you ask, Missouri (I-44), Kansas (I-70), or Pennsylvania (the Pennsylvania Turnpike). By the early sixties, I-55 in Illinois, I-44 in Missouri, Kansas, and Oklahoma, and I-40 in Oklahoma, Texas, New Mexico,

Arizona, and California, were all open. The new highways mostly bypassed Route 66, and as such began to draw traffic away from the Mother Road—and, as a result, many businesses along 66 suffered.

Many didn't make it.

But what officially "killed" Route 66?

On June 27, 1985, the American Association of State Highway and Transportation Officials officially decertified the route number "66" and voted to remove all Route 66 signs along the entire route. The road remained, of course, but it was renumbered and reassigned by the state.

So, that was it. The end of the line for Route 66.

But.

Route 66: The Mother Road by Michael Wallis was published in 1990, *On The Road* and *The Grapes of Wrath were* still widely read, the Route 66 Corridor Preservation Society was launched in 1999, and the U.S. 66 Highway Association was launched in 2015.

All of these efforts helped to preserve the physical Route 66, and also helped to keep the dream of Route 66 alive in the public consciousness.

So, with these small movements, Route 66 started to matter again... and, most importantly, people were actually fighting to save it. And this proved a relatively straightforward feat thanks to the fact that all of the above-cited, beloved businesses were still there—and, with the advent of the Internet, they started getting noticed.

Frank Zappa once theorized that the world would end

by one of two causes: death by paperwork, or death by nostalgia. His reasoning for the latter was that the cycle between "the event" and the nostalgia for "the event" was growing shorter and shorter as time went on—and I personally think this is the case with Route 66... and I am ecstatic over this: nostalgia can be dangerous, sure, but sometimes, it reminds us of what's important and what's worth holding onto, fighting for, saving, and preserving.

And now, thanks to that very phenomenon, here we are.

Okay, so now that we're all enlightened, back to Day Three.

This proved a memorable day from the get-go: I started by rousting the front desk manager from a dead sleep, making him drop his iPhone in the process. I then continued blasting 75 along I-44... before noticing that my hood was fluttering and threatening to blow wide open.

Shit! Fuck! Motherfucker!

Well, I needed gas, anyway...

I pulled off, found a Circle K, took care of the hood, filled up, and sat for a minute composing myself.

Okay, I'm good...

There are 400-odd miles between St. Louis and Tulsa, and I spent most of it on I-44 out of expediency. I knew I'd be blowing through a lot of the Show-Me State by doing this, but I was only okay with this because I knew I'd be coming back. Again, I just wanted a taste of what I didn't know, not the whole buffet. So, I started on I-44, passing by barns with advertisements for Meramec Caverns in Stanton all the while. It was very cool seeing these, as I knew they were original.

In case you were wondering, Meramec Caverns (along the Meramec River) is a series of underground caverns that were once used as a hideout by Frank and Jesse James. In 1947, it became (arguably) America's first theme park, and so hand-painted advertisements started appearing on barns in many states—sort of a precursor to the South of the Border billboards which today run from southern Florida to New Jersey.

The Meramec Caverns didn't make my to-do list (for this trip, at least), but it was awesome seeing those bits of bygone Americana still standing.

Anyhow: I was making good time on I-44, but I did want to experience *some* Heartland Missouri Route 66—and I did.

I pulled off I-44 onto 66 somewhere around St. Clair or Stanton, and cruised for a good stretch through Cuba and Rolla (a town supposedly phonetically named by a North Carolinian who wanted to call the town "Raleigh"). Bright sun, small towns, train tracks, quarries, and rolling hills. *America.*

I flipped on St. Louis Public Radio and listened to Sada Jackson's heart-wrenching story of losing her mom to breast cancer and subsequently becoming a mom herself on StoryCorps while wending my way through smalltown

Missouri on Route 66, very much aware that, rather than being in the throes of my daily life, I was *instead wending my way through smalltown Missouri on Route 66.* Hello again, dumbass grin! I missed you!

I paused to grab a very large Dr. Pepper at a Kum & Go (for sure the most unfortunately named convenience store chain in the world), pulled back onto I-44, and sucked it down while listening to David Greene's interview with Paul Stanley on the final KISS shows on *Morning Edition*, loving life and the beautiful state of Missouri all the while. Though I was surprised to see so many dead armadillos on the side of the road. I hadn't thought they were indigenous to Missouri, but clearly, I was wrong. I'd been expecting plenty in Texas, but Missouri? Crazy. Made me very sad, as I hate roadkill: I once accidentally ran over a squirrel on the way to work, and (as Andrea can attest) I was bawling, inconsolable for a good 30 minutes, thinking of the squirrel; hoping it hadn't suffered; thinking of the little squirrel family left behind. Sad. So, yeah, it was kind of sad and surprising to see all these dead armadillos all over Missouri. But that's life: a fresh surprise around every corner—some nicer than others!

I was also surprised at how much Missouri reminded me of Maine, Connecticut, and The Berkshires. I was expecting endless farmland, and there was that, but there was also a *verdancy* about Missouri that I wasn't prepared for: deep green; lush; quite beautiful. The Ozarks, at last.

I crossed the Big Piney river and the Gasconade river...

and in the process realized that I'd forgotten all about Hooker Cut and Devil's Elbow. Oops! My first brain-fade on the road. Oh, well, I'll be back. And gladly: Missouri was a lovely surprise!

Another big dumbass grin moment was crossing into Kansas. I don't know why, as Kansas had honestly never been on my radar. It was just the knowledge that I was in Kansas, I guess; the surrealness of that.

I stopped in at Cars on the Route in Galena, snapped a few pics of the trucks that inspired *Cars*, bought a Route 66 road sign and postcard, and headed out, bound for Waylan's Ku-Ku Burger in Miami, OK. But first, a semi-planned ADD stop: the Eisler Brothers' Old Riverton Store in Riverton, KS—another site that entranced me in the *Route 66 Lost & Found: Ruins and Relics Revisited* book all those years ago. The 1930s postcard in that book depicts one child and four adults: a woman in what appears to be a nurse uniform, a grizzled gent in a fedora sitting in the back, a semi-sullen teenager in what appears to be medical scrubs (arms folded and behind the counter), and a man in a butcher's apron standing in front of the counter. The man in the apron has a half-smile/-smirk and a flop of hair over the right side of his forehead, like his Vitalis failed after half a morning of hard work refilling the stockroom. I stared at this man for a long time the first time I got the book because he looked like my grandfather might have looked when he was a younger man. Plus, old photos in general captivate me: who were these people? What were they thinking of and going through the moment the shutter was pulled? What can their lives tell us about our own?

I will admit that I almost forgot about the store, and I almost missed it, but I caught the sign and beautiful flowers out front out of the corner of my eye and pulled a U-turn (not difficult to do in Kansas). The store had been in business since 1925 (the year before Route 66 came to be), and then, in 2019, it was basically the same as it had been then: front porch with a tear in the screen on the slat door; pressed tin ceiling; a basin filled with sodas in what was once "ice" water; a deli counter in the back... wonderful. A time capsule on the prairie.

I got another bottle of Route 66 Black Cherry and headed out, glad for peripheral vision. And in the parking lot, in the cool Kansas sun, I saw another guy get out of his car and line up his shot on his iPhone.

I went over and said, "You too, huh?"

Yep; he was apparently from Michigan, and was going all the way—and turned out his wife grew up in Portland, ME. Amazing how small the world really is! Another big dumbass grin moment. And yet another big dumbass grin moment was realizing that in the past 24-odd hours, I'd visited two places I'd dreamed of visiting for many years: Ariston Café and the Eisler Bros' Old Riverton Store—and, in the process, I'd put myself in two images I'd co-opted from the *Route 66 Lost & Found: Ruins and Relics Revisited* coffee table book I'd randomly picked up seven years earlier and had wanted to visit ever since.

Not. Bad.

On to Picher, OK, and then Commerce, OK.

Picher both fascinated and haunted me. It was a spectral town twice destroyed, and there, I could feel the town's former vibrancy; feel the souls that had worked in the mines that destroyed the town. Lead and zinc mining contaminated the water supply and the soil, and in 1983, Picher was declared a superfund site. It was eventually cleaned up, but in 2008, a tornado took the rest. The EPA offered a buyout for residents to move, and most did, and now, there's not much left of Picher, Oklahoma, but ghosts. I felt them around the water tower; around the abandoned houses.

Onwards, though: I couldn't be in this part of the country without seeing where The Mick came from! I hate the Yankees as an organization, but I love the Yankees themselves, especially DiMaggio and Mickey Mantle. Mickey is a classic American archetype: the kid with the straw suitcase—half bumpkin, the other half yokel—who came out of the mines and made it big in the Big City, couldn't quite live up to his own superhuman gifts, and lived a complicated, often-tragic life. Mick briefly worked the same mines his father, Mutt (who named his boy after the great Philadelphia A's catcher Mickey Cochrane), worked in Commerce, OK—and, when seeing the town, the mines, and the yard where Mutt taught Mickey how to switch-hit (536 career homers: 372 left-handed, 164 right-handed), I got a real sense of context and connection; a sense of place and perspective.

Awesome.

And after that historical deep dive, time for lunch! Waylan's Ku-Ku Burger, Miami, Oklahoma.

Ku-Ku Burger was originally a chain dating from 1965, and the Miami location (which has been run by Eugene Waylan since 1973) is the last one standing. It is a beacon on Route 66, nestled in by a Pizza Hut, a Long John Silver's, and a Domino's. And it's the only place on that part of 66 you want to go to.

I saw the sign and felt that big dumbass grin spread across my face again. I was torn between a chicken sandwich or a pulled pork sandwich (an Oklahoma specialty)—so I split the difference and got a pork tender sandwich and some tots.

Great bun, good tots. And another check on my to-do and to-eat lists!

After that, I was keen to get on to Tulsa, so I got back on I-44, the Will Rogers Turnpike, and balled that jack. There are 90-plus miles between Miami and Tulsa through Afton, Venita, Claremore, and Catoosa, and the gorgeous afternoon sun was cool yet somehow bestowed a feeling of warmth. When approaching Catoosa, the drive on I-44 reminded me greatly of the drive from the southern office of my former grocery chain in Salisbury, NC, to Charlotte, and my flights home from CTW: I-85 through China Grove and Kannapolis, the metropolitan nodes becoming denser and closing in on the highway and the city skyline suddenly appearing. I thought of how far away those days seemed: another job; another time; another lifetime. Another world; another me. As much as I'd enjoyed those previous drives, I was *so* much better off now—and now, I was here in Tulsa.

Tulsa, OK, settled between 1828 and 1836 by the Lochapoka band of Creek Native Americans. Tulsa lies on land originally inhabited by the Kickapoo, Osage, Creek, and Caddo tribes, and is still part of the Muscogee Creek nation. The tribes established a settlement, and Chief Tukabahchi and other Trail of Tears survivors were reminded of their original home in Tallahassee, Alabama. Their name "Tallasi" (Creek for "old town") was later bastardized into "Tulsa", and the town was officially incorporated in 1898. A mere three years later, oil was discovered there, and the population skyrocketed: Tulsa was the "Oil Capital of the World", and the new inhabitants spearheaded a major construction boom—and, with it, a design ethos heavy on art-deco.

In 1921, Tulsa saw one of the worst race riots this country has ever known: the Tulsa Race Massacre leveled the Greenwood District, which was known as the "Black Wall Street". Over Memorial Day weekend, James Rowland, a nineteen-year-old African American shoeshine boy, was accused of assaulting seventeen-year-old Sarah White, an elevator operator. After Rowland's arrest, rumors circulated that he was to be lynched, and a group of African Americans descended upon the jail to protect

Rowland.

A shot went off, and chaos ensued.

White residents, armed and "deputized" by city officials, lay waste to the Greenwood District, and after two days, the "Black Wall Street" was a smoldering ruin, 10,000 African American residents having been made homeless and over $1.5 million in property damage losses having been incurred.

The riot was largely buried, yet it remains a stain on American history.

The starting point of the Tulsa Race Riot took place behind what is presently center field of the Tulsa Drillers' (the LA Dodgers AA team) ballpark.

Welcome to America, 2019.

I pulled off I-44 onto 11th Street (a.k.a., Route 66) and checked into The Campbell Hotel.

Damn, what a gem.

The Campbell (in the Campbell Building) was originally called the Casa Loma Hotel, and the building also featured a Safeway and a drugstore. It was right on the Double Six, but was also at the end of the trolley line—convenient for downtown workers and for pass-through travelers alike. Naturally, the building fell into disrepair when the Eisenhower Interstate Highway System diverted traffic away from Route 66 in the late fifties and early sixties (notice a theme developing here?), and the Casa Loma was once so derelict it was on the verge of condemnation. Today, however, is a very different story: The Campbell today is truly one of a kind; a boutique luxury hotel boasting 26 rooms and a spa. All the rooms have a unique theme championing the hotel's Tulsa, Oklahoma, and Route 66 import, and all have *crème de la crème* features and fixtures. And it's right on Route 66, *and* the rates are extremely reasonable.

A total no-brainer.

After check-in, I got back into Rose and headed for downtown, where I paid a buck an hour for on street parking. A *buck an hour*! In *Tulsa*! That'd pay for a tenth of a nanosecond in New York! Unreal.

Mindfuck recovered from, I hoofed up S. Boston and past the fountain (which was whipping water around in the breeze) and over to the Philcade Building and the Tulsa Art Deco Museum.

Okay, it's not a museum per se, but a collection of displays in the lobby. But it's a treasure, nonetheless—as is Tulsa.

The Philcade Building dates to 1931, and is art deco at its finest! It was, of course, the headquarters of Phillips 66, Standard Oil, and Amoco for many years. The building topped out at 13 floors so as to not overshadow the pyramidal-topped Philtower next door, and the facade is terracotta with elaborate engravings, Egyptian columns, and papyrus reeds. The lobby is meanwhile the shape of a *T* for "Tulsa", and has terrazzo floors and marble walls with mahogany and gold leaf. Side note: it was a shopping arcade in the Phillips 66 building, hence Philcade.

Let me rephrase this above paragraph: this building is in Tulsa, Oklahoma, and it is just as stunning as the Empire State Building. Tulsa was a beautiful town, an art-deco dreamscape on the open prairie, when I'd previously assumed Oklahoma would be nothing but shit-kickin' cowboys, oil tycoons, and brutalist 1960s urban renewal towers. What a great surprise to discover such a gorgeous, manageable, and, yes, though I hate the word, *hip*, town! I'd gone in with an open mind, and I had left delighted.

Now, time for some chili—of course at Ike's Chili, 11th Street, Tulsa, Oklahoma. Except Ike's Chili, 11th Street, Tulsa, Oklahoma, closes at 3PM... and I only discovered this when I got there at 5:30PM.

Y'know the moment in *National Lampoon's Vacation* when the Griswolds finally arrive at Wally World and the Marty Moose statue out front greets them with a, *Sorry, folks! We're closed for two weeks to clean and repair America's Favorite Family Fun Park!* message? Yeah, that was me: I kept waiting for someone to come out the kitchen and say, "Sorry, we close at three. The moose out front should have told you." I didn't punch in a window, but I did pout a bit (okay, a lot). But when a door closes, a window opens, and thus I headed across 11th to the Mother Road Market.

Honestly, this might just be my favorite food hall in the world now—and I say that having spent five years living with easy access to Quincy Market, Boston: it's a 1939 grocery building repurposed with exposed brick and joists and Tulsa-centric murals and 20 food stands offering everything from BBQ to rice bowls to crazy gourmet ice cream and cookies, and so on and so forth. A paradise for the senses.

I "settled" for a gargantuan slice and gelato samples from Andolini's, and promptly felt much better about the world. And I felt even better after seeing the Meadow Gold sign! This neon landmark was recently restored and relit, thanks to Tulsa's Route 66 Neon Sign Grant Program—one of the most awesome uses of civic funds I can imagine: the city matched, dollar-for-dollar, the restoration of the amazing neon beauties that line Route 66, and, as of 2019, $40,000 has been raised, with more to come.

The Meadow Gold sign reads:

> Meadow Gold
> Milk, Ice Cream
> Beatrice Foods Co.

The sign dates from the 1930s and was *this* close to being demolished by the new owner of the building it formerly sat atop. Now, however, it's safe.

Tulsa, you're all kinds of awesome.

I stood there staring at the sign for a few minutes, thinking of the J&J Cleaners sign and the original Fat Boy sign from the Brunswick, Maine, of my youth, and again felt that big, dumbass grin coming on. My worlds and my passions were coming together, renewed, and I was feeling pretty damn good by this point—even after my first-world crisis of chili deprivation. And, naturally, I felt even *more* spectacular after leaving the bar at The Campbell: not a soul in the joint when I walked in, save for Jennifer behind the bar, so I ordered a Laphroig neat, and we engaged in great conversation, deep and shallow, for the next two-plus hours. She made me the margaritas she learned how to make for Cinco de Mayo (and couldn't serve because she had no customers) and tried to teach me how to play gin rummy. And yet again, that big, dumbass grin stayed with me, and once again, I felt like I'd made friends—or at least memories—for life.

It was as I was walking back up to my room that night that it occurred to me: if this had happened even a few years before, I'd have been replaying the entire evening out in my mind for hours (okay, days) from that very moment, scanning the conversation, wondering if *x* came out too awkwardly and almost *looking* for things I could blame myself for. And yet I *didn't* do that tonight. I was fine: I'd left a good impression, and ya know what? Neither Jennifer nor anybody else on this trip was going to remember me the following week, let alone the following *month*, when I'd usually still have been flogging myself over my imagined *faux pas*.

That night, I let all that fear go. And I felt light as a feather for it. Getting out of my comfort zone, engaging in

169

small talk, not scanning the entire conversation in my head all night, and not kicking myself for saying something dumb I might (or might not) have said, was... well, nice.

Hmm... was I actually *evolving* on this trip?

CHAPTER 4

HELLO, *CARRIE*

NOTHING IN IN MY LIFE EVER filled me with terror more than gym class in my freshman and sophomore years at Lisbon High School.

Because my toes turn in ("Just like Jackie Robinson!" I'd say to the great amusement of my chums, who couldn't have given less of a shit about Jackie Robinson), gym class was utterly traumatic: my fear of running, making an idiot of myself, and being exposed, was all-consuming.

One was allowed to skip five gym classes per semester with impunity, and after that, it was laps in the gym after school... and I think I may have cashed in all five of my skips during just that first week. So, I'd skip class and run my penance laps after school, and then walk the four miles home. Which was easier. Much less humiliating.

I often walked home along the train tracks—the same

tracks Stephen King walked when he went to Lisbon. I think he may have gotten a story out of those walks... something about a dead body...

Remember the Cookie Monster anthem, "C is for 'cookie', that's good enough for me"? During this time, I was serenaded with my own personalized version: "W is for 'Westbye', that's weird enough for me!" But nothing would ever come close to the hell and agony of being known as "Twacker". In hindsight, I love the fact that this incident occurred in the very same gym that inspired *Carrie* (ahh, that was one of the Stephen King stories!), because at the time, it was my own version of that very same story.

Freshman year: I was standing at a urinal shaking off after using it for... its intended purpose, just before gym, when K-L came up behind me and jumped to the conclusion that would break me for the next two years: "*He's twacking off! He's twacking off!*"

I knew in those first few nanoseconds that this was going to be a game-changer for the worst, but I couldn't imagine how bad it would actually be.

Well, word spread like so many proverbial wildfires (or Hot Asses), and I became known as Twacker, thus indirectly preceding Pee-Wee Herman and Fred Willard on the path of self-gratification-in-public infamy.

It stuck.

In a quiet science class, my desk-mate, Katie, asked if anyone had any hand lotion, and M-W immediately piped up, "Why, is Westbye horny?" The memory of the entire class laughing and staring still burns under the scar tissue of time.

And so it went—and it didn't stop, or at least ease up, until midway through my sophomore year.

And why did it stop then?

Music.

(Are you seeing a running theme yet?)

My high school years may have been largely defined by trauma, but in retrospect, they were probably more defined by triumph. After a day of bullying, I would arrive home and reach for my guitar, and from then, I channeled the pain of not fitting in into the pleasure of my craft: learning favorite songs and writing my own versions.

During my sophomore year, I joined the Lisbon High School band and jazz band, where I remained until graduation. My band teacher, Mr. Judd (nicknamed "Bluto" for his resemblance to the *Popeye* character and, sadistically, "Hot Lips" due to the obvious prurient resemblance his large lips and curly goatee suggested), was a mentor, and he encouraged me to take chances and broaden my sonic horizons. Even then, I knew that life falls out of the sky and into our laps, and I took to all his suggestions: Gerry Mulligan, Miles Davis, Charlie Parker. Mr. Judd saw me, a sixteen-year-old heavy metal shredder, and encouraged me to go further—but he also encouraged me to develop who I was. He even brought me into the One Night Stand Rock & Roll Band, a pickup group of Lisbon High teachers, guidance counselors, and our principal, for the 1988-89 Winter Carnival Talent Show. Our repertoire included the Roy Orbison standard *Pretty Woman* and, of course, I Van Halen-ized the fuck out of it, throwing in crazy solos and flourishes fresh from the 1982 Van Halen cover version on *Diver Down* and throwing in a few screaming licks in between songs for good measure. The packed gym—the same gym where I ran my penance laps under the specter of Stephen King and *Carrie*—went ballistic, and I fed on it under the white-hot glare of the spot-lamp. And later that night, my band, Rampage, nailed covers of Metallica's *Creeping Death* and *Master of Puppets*, and the utter fucking rockstar adulation still rings in my ears.

And yet, after the show, my principal and guidance counselor excoriated me, ripping into me for "showboating" and stealing the thunder of the mighty One Night Stand Rock & Roll Band. I was absolutely humiliated, convinced that I was a horrible kid who'd never be able to recover; never be able to repent.

HSP rumination at work, and it was on overtime that night.

The next day, however, every single one of my classmates were in utter awe, and several teachers (all of whom were unaware of the tongue-lashing I'd received) expressed their admiration and wondered why I hadn't gotten more time to shine. Hence, my humiliation was quickly saved by affirmation. Even still, the tongue-lashing taught me a critical lesson: always be humble and never show up your creative partners, no matter the situation.

This lesson has served me well.

So, in this way, I became known as a great musician midway through my sophomore year, and this helped immensely with the bullying. But the trauma of the prior bullying held, and I never really got fully comfortable in newfound acceptance. Like, you're being nice to me now, but what are you *really* saying behind my back?

It took me years (and lots of therapy) to come to terms with the word "trauma" in this context: trauma was what one experienced after seeing their entire family bludgeoned before their eyes, or after escaping a fiery plane crash, not after getting picked on a little in school. Right? But the more time I spent on that couch analyzing myself, the more I realized that I was, in fact, traumatized. There's no other word to describe the toll that was exacted on my psyche during those years. I've since come to terms with all of this, and I'm becoming okay with it.

This has been helped by the fact that I've had many last laughs over the years: Lori, our prom queen, is one of my best friends now, and she didn't even remember the whole Twacker thing—and I doubt that M-W's band has sold out House of Blues Boston on a Tuesday night.

That said, trauma runs deep, and it will take many more years (or maybe forever) for me to undo that level of damage. But I realize now that I look back on those talent show triumphs and adulations more than I do the trauma of the bullying. And that's got to count for something.

Anyhow, to resume our narrative: our marching band played football games every Saturday, and we were *mortifyingly* bad. Combine the fact that nobody ever practiced to save their ass with a cheesy songbook featuring *Iron Man*, *Paranoid*, and *Smoke on the Water*, plus fire-engine-red polyester coats and hats with plumes, *and* the fact that I had a kid hauling my bass amp around in a wheelbarrow with a generator, and you sorta get the picture. The band missed nearly every touchdown because its members were off in the woods stealing a smoke, copping a feel, and doing basically anything but sitting ready on the risers. Mr. Judd tried his hardest, but it was hopeless.

Not to worry, though: on the weekends, I was playing in my heavy metal band, Rampage, so I was still keeping my musical ear largely intact. (Yes, I kinda nicked our logo from Metallica—also the band that formed half of our repertoire.) We played a few talent shows and keg parties, with absolutely glorious and hideously ignoble results. Yet by the time I entered my sophomore year (1988-89), I was burning out on metal, and my old Smiths, Smithereens, and R.E.M. influences were kicking in. But more than anything, thanks to our psychotic friend Dana, I was getting into Bix Beiderbecke and Glenn Miller.

Dana was a Korean War vet who lived in a cabin he'd built on a pond in the woods by my grandparents' farm. Many nights, we rode out on our four-wheeler to pay Dana a call, tapping into his bottomless well of cold Schaeffer beers while he held forth on the rot of modern culture, how everyone in the town was after him, and how we had to kill our neighbors (and how to do it). Dana Getchell had extremely high military clearance, and was also a soccer coach at Harvard... and he was also known as "30-Second Getch" because that was how long his Korean captives usually lasted before spilling their secrets.

In his cabin, lit low by a kerosene lantern and the glow of the woodstove, Dana, in a frothing cloud of rage and beer spit, taught us how to shank a man in the kidneys so that he'd become so incapacitated by pain he couldn't scream, instructed us on how to hang piano wire across a snowmobile trail so that our neighbors would face instant decapitation, and relayed every slight and grievance he'd suffered that would necessitate our committing these acts—all set to a soundtrack of hot swing on his transistor: Glen Miller's *In the Mood* ("This is good fucking music. You can really fuck a girl with this one") and Artie Shaw with George Wettling on drums ("Great drummer, not like these fucking glass breakers today! Now that piano wire, ya gotta fuckin' do it! That son of a bitch swindled me out of a quarter acre of that garden plot!").

If visits to the cabin left me a bit shellshocked, they also left a great sonic impression: thanks to Dana, I started listening religiously to Marian McPartland's *Piano Jazz* on NPR every Sunday night, and I heard a lot of greats on the show.

All these disparate influences started to coalesce

around 1989, and by the time I got to UMA in 1991, I was *so* ready.

Before we dive into that time, though, I realize that there is one notable story from my high school years missing from this repertoire, and that's the story of how I got my first ever girlfriend in my senior year of high school (1990-91), with the arrival of Anne the Psychotic from Akron just before the start of the school year.

Anne and I "went out" once and started horsing around on our second "date". Of course, now that a girl had (finally) shown some remote interest in me, I was convinced it was love. Finally! The One!

A few weeks later, she dumped me for the other guitarist in Rampage. Naturally, I kicked him out of the band ("creative differences": it was a "mutual decision"), and a few weeks later, Anne the Psychotic dumped him, and we were back together. Things then went swimmingly for a few weeks—that is, until she dumped me *again*, this time for the sax player in the marching and jazz band, who she'd apparently been pining for since she left Maine and moved to Akron after the third grade, or some shit like that. This one kind of didn't work out, since he was the only kid in our class with a Madonna T-shirt. (You can do the math on that one.)

After dumping Madonna, Anne the Psychotic and I picked up where we left off, although by this time, she was wearing the class ring of *yet another* classmate on a necklace. Yet (with apologies to The Hollies), by January, she was mine.

Over the next year and eight months, I was subjected to a laundry list of borderline-criminal behavior. These acts included, but were not limited to:

- Her breaking into my house, stealing my guitar, and holding it for ransom.
- Her stabbing me in the forearm with a steak knife.
- Her stalking me at work.
- Her stalking me on-campus.
- Her shaving my nuts and rubbing some kind of hellburn balm on them because she "may have seen what may have been a crab on one of her other boyfriends". (I felt this was quite a conscientious move, actually.)
- Her forcing me to watch *The Little Mermaid* and to listen to Andrew Lloyd Webber soundtracks *ad infinitum*.
- Her "almost" driving off the road with me in the car as a "suicide attempt".

And I took it. I had such horrible self-esteem at the time that I didn't think I could find anything else, and I didn't want to hurt her (sic). Then again, in retrospect, I also held my ground to a surprising degree. She once bought a pack of Marlboros, I guess expecting me to be appalled and throw them out the window, saving her from herself with my shining-armor chivalry, but instead, I bummed one and lit up. I also declined invitations (i.e., demands) to join her and her jarhead "friend" for an evening of bowling on many occasions, often flat-out lying that I was "spending the weekend with my ailing grandmother".

Basically, I took it until I couldn't take it anymore, and in September 1992, I broke up with Anne and never looked back. And as soon as she realized she'd lost her power over me, I never heard from her again.

In thinking of my high school years, I've noticed an interesting recurring characteristic—one that I've only faintly recognized before, but one that has guided my path more than I realize nonetheless: discipline, despite feeling lost. For example, I, of course, had terrible acne in high school, and somehow—and I have absolutely no idea how, considering how utterly fantastical the idea is—I came to the conclusion that "dark" soft drinks (i.e., Coca-Cola, Pepsi-Cola, Dr. Pepper) and chocolate were contributing factors. This brilliant theory failed to take into consideration the heat and humidity of my environment and the mounds of grease I was also mowing down in the form of pizza, potato chips, French fries, etc., but nevertheless, I held onto the theory and—here's the critical part—*abstained* from Coke and Twix bars *et al.* during the rest of my high school semesters (and then went crazy during the summers, when I didn't see many people and didn't care).

Convoluted brilliance! Discipline in the service of a (futile) cause!

I *wish* I had recognized this discipline in myself 30

years ago. It would've saved me a hell of a lot of trouble! Though I suppose discipline and self-preservation are sort of the same thing, and I've always been hyperaware of my self-preservation streak but not my discipline. Potato, potahto.

My point? Whatever feats of overindulgence I've allowed myself to sabotage myself with—whether it's eating an entire frozen pizza when I was in my twenties, downing a 12-pack, or not writing in my journal for two weeks—I always overcome: I always find my way back to salads, water, and a pen and a blank page.

Always.

Example: in 2011, I found myself in a position where my drinking was getting out of control, and I could see it getting worse. I didn't like the thought of the potential outcome, so, as a pre-emptive strike (as I see it now), I checked in for a night in detox and entered counseling, and ended up abstaining for eight full months. This proved to be extremely fortuitous, because it allowed me to hit the reset button and re-evaluate my relationship with drink. And that relationship has been much healthier ever since because I allowed myself to revisit my discipline.

Clearly, I've *always* had major discipline; I've just never allowed myself to realize it. Yet another trait to revisit and recultivate for the rest of my days!

DAY FOUR

MAY 11, 2019

Tulsa, OK, to Amarillo, TX: 365 miles.
Time Out: Checked out of The Campbell Hotel around 6:30AM CST.
Time in: Checked into The Big Texan around 3PM CST.

G RAY SKIES AND RAIN HEADING out of Tulsa, befitting my mood about leaving this fine town. But Texas was calling. I'd never been, and I'd always wanted to.

I knew that at some point along the way today, I'd be leaving the east behind, spiritually and physically, and setting into the west, and my mind buzzed at this realization, wondering where that change would occur.

Let's find out.

I got a delightful French press from 918 Coffee on 11th St., Route 66, got back on I-44 (now the Turner Turnpike), and headed toward OK City. Along the way, I got off somewhere and stopped at a general store type place for a water, where I found a table full of farmhands having a heated discussion about some local issues over truly monstrous breakfast sandwiches. Black Stetsons, Bolo ties, work shirts, vests, Wranglers, boots. Honest working folk. I felt that big, dumbass grin spreading again in that moment; don't ask me why.

Hydration at hand, it was time to embark on Mission I: Pops Soda Ranch in Arcadia, which was 90-odd miles from Tulsa.

I think it was somewhere around Bristow or Depew that I pulled back onto the Mother Road, and from there, I could feel things changing just a bit: lush, verdant farmland in the rain, though not the New England birches and sugar maples I was used to, but black elm and walnut trees instead. Just enough of a shift to be tangible, yet it did still feel very New England-esque; a dense, old-growth copse framing an overgrown meadow. Robert Frost by way of Will Rogers, without any mending walls.

66 was narrow and winding, and I imagined myself making the same journey in 1929 in a Model T with no air conditioning, seatbelt, or option to jump onto I-44 to save time and stop at a Love's station for a Coke and a donut. I thought of what a mindfuck it must have been for the earliest 66 pioneers: probably four, five, or six days out of Chicago, driving this forlorn stretch and pondering how much further California was.

Mulling these things over, I cruised past the famous Arcadia Round Barn and pulled into Pops, past that magnificent 66' neon soda bottle sign. And my God, what a caffeinated wonderland it was! Over 700 varieties of soda from all around the world beautifully lined up in marching formation against the angled glass windows and rain. Space-age fuel.

I got an orange Nehi (do they even make Nehi anymore?) and a tee—and yes, I even got gas, and could have gotten breakfast, if I'd wanted.

Now, I'd thought of taking a little time for Oklahoma City—at least the monument at the Murrah Federal Building, where Timothy McVeigh committed his notoriously hideous act of cold-blooded murder—but I decided it would be too emotionally heavy. Plus, rain. I saw some of the OK City skyline through the lowering fog and murk, listening to Cards' great Ozzie Smith guesting on *Wait, Wait... Don't Tell Me!* on NPR, then got another water, and "christened" the facilities at a 7-Eleven.

Just outside of OK City, I left I-44, picked up I-35 South, and navigated to I-40 West. I'd been on I-44 since St. Louis, and it was a little sad leaving it behind. I-44 had been very good to me, and I couldn't wait to get back on it one day.

As I continued, there was still the pervading question of, where would the west begin?

El Reno, Oklahoma, as it turns out. Or, at least, in my opinion.

Here, I pulled off into a Love's, got a Dr. Pepper with a shot of cherry, and took a few minutes by a buffalo statue with a painted headdress outside the Cherokee Trading Post to soak it all in. I observed that there was much more prairie land than trees here; the land felt much more open and spread out, and half the stations were in Spanish all of a sudden. It wasn't like a topographical light switch went off, but there was definitely a topographical dimmer being slowly pulled.

As I stood by this buffalo statue, I took in the rolling plains and watched the kids play around the statue—and that made me think of the Fisherman's Memorial Statue at Land's End, Bailey Island, Maine. We always climbed on and around this statue (which depicts a lobsterman kneeling and tending to a lobster) when we were kids. The original was created for the 1939 New York World's Fair, and bears the inscription, *To all Maine fisherman who have devoted their lives to the sea.*

Well, I knew nothing of the El Reno, Oklahoma, buffalo when I was six, and a six-year-old kid playing on the El Reno buffalo likely knows nothing of the Bailey Island, Maine, Fishermen's Memorial hard against the Atlantic Ocean—but you can bet that anywhere there is a public monument, kids will play around it, and therein lies American continuity: we all have so much more in common than not.

And with that thought, I was on the other side.

*

Mission II: The National Route 66 Museum in Elk City. Which, as it turns out (after driving 85 miles to get to it), was the "wrong" museum! I'd been thinking of the Oklahoma Route 66 Museum in Clinton, but Andrea sent me a link to the National, and I ended up there instead. Hey, just another reason to go back to Oklahoma! And, to be fair, the National Museum was fine. It felt like the kind of museum you love going to on school field trips as a kid: tons of classic rides (the '48 Indian Chief was especially choice) and a fun film (fun save for the *Kung-Fu Theater*-style synch-lag between film and dialog, that is). A pleasant diversion, and a lovely goodbye to a new favorite state.

In that moment, I honestly felt very proud to be in Oklahoma: it was a proud state of proud people; the Cherokee Nation; the nation of Cheyenne and Arapaho, Caddo, and Apache, and the Trail of Tears.

I hope my respect showed, and I hope I have represented the Sooner State well in these pages.

That's not to say that I wasn't insanely giddy when crossing the border into Texas, however. What's more, I landed on Moe Bandy's *I Cheated Me Right Out of You* on the dial just as I crossed over for the first time, which was *perfect*. Texas is many things, but it is made more proper with a little honky-tonk on the juke.

And there I was, on the Panhandle with endless scrub grass and, pleasantly enough, windmills. Yes to clean energy! I was glad to see the fossil oligarchs hadn't taken everything quite yet.

And with that, we were on to Mission III: The U-Drop Inn in Shamrock. Naturally, it was closed when I got there (obviously), but I made it, nonetheless.

Built in 1936, the U-Drop Inn was opened by J.M. Tindall. Architect J.C. Berry designed the structure based on a sketch drawn out in a patch of dirt in a parking lot, and an eight-year-old boy won the naming contest with the "U-Drop Inn", though the inn was only half the business: the U-Drop Inn was the café and Tower Station was the Conoco station. Both are a spectacular example of art deco, with glazed tile, geometric detailing, and neon galore. I snapped a few pics, sucked in the surprisingly cool air of the Lone Star State, and jammed back onto I-40.

And here I was, in Texas, driving through McLean, Alanreed, and Groom. Endless flatland and scrub brush, cattle grazing along the lonesome highway, the land spreading out impossibly far and flat with little signs of water and non-bovine life. The Texas Panhandle felt like one giant endless ranch—but occasionally, I did see wrought-iron fences with different ranch names, so it was really *many* giant endless ranches.

I thought of Southfork and watching *Dallas* at the Homestead as a kid, and how far away from Whitefield, Maine, I was. And again, I imagined it was 1929 and I was puttering along in my jalopy (probably with a rakish newsboy cap) with only a canteen of water, no conception of where the next filling station might be, and no hope of finding a Motel 6 to lay down for the evening.

I can't even imagine—yet this was reality for the early 66 pioneers. Braver souls than I'll ever be!

95 miles to Amarillo. Because of the weather and my fear of fatigue, and because I was meeting a friend in Albuquerque, I was back-and-forth on Palo Duro. I figured I'd just get to Amarillo and wing it from there, and if I made it, great, and if not, I wasn't going to kick myself. First time, a taste of what I don't know, blah, blah, blah.

Amarillo. Spanish for "yellow". The Yellow Rose of Texas. Founded in 1887, Amarillo grew out of a cattle shipping market founded at the intersection of the Atchison, Topeka and Santa Fe and Fort Worth and Denver City railway lines. The railroads provided a thriving business node, and commerce blew up when the Pecos Valley & Northeastern railroad connected Amarillo to Roswell, New Mexico, in 1898. Cattle shipping was king, and Amarillo was smack-dab in the middle.

But to go back to our story:

The Big Texan has been open since 1960, and has been in operation in its current location since 1971. It is gaudy and glorious: perfectly Texas; perfectly America.

I checked in in the early afternoon and realized that my laundry situation was a bit dire... and that I hadn't packed enough boxers. Back out we go to find a store... and it was here that I made the brilliant decision to get a burrito at Taco Villa.

Yes, I went to Taco Villa mere hours before gorging myself at The Big Texan Steakhouse. Not *quite* like going to McDonald's before eating at Momofuku, but almost. Plus, I got hot sauce all over my white tee. Brilliant! And yes, I got my pack of boxers.

I headed back to the hotel and got a Tide pod (which I did not eat, for the record) in the lobby. I then hit up the Big Texan coin-op before retiring to my room with an ice-cold six-pack of Lone Star.

Even in my room, you could *very* much tell I was in Texas: pine paneling, the Lone Star, steer horns everywhere... yeah, I was digging it. The Texas-shaped swimming pool was unfortunately covered over, though I hadn't planned on going in, anyway. And the smell of the steakhouse in the parking lot... *droool*. I reasoned there was nothing wrong with a little downtime in the room; that was part of being on vacation just as much as the adventuring was.

Laundry done, I headed back across the parking lot and past the hotel courtesy cars—and, naturally, this being The Big Texan and this being Texas, their courtesy cars were Cadillac stretch limos with steer horns on the hood.

I mean, duh.

I got to the front and asked for a seat, and the kid at the host stand was great: earnest and donning a cowboy hat, Bolo tie, checked shirt... He looked like he could've played for the Houston Toros against the California Bears in the Astrodome in *The Bad News Bears in Breaking Training*.

Naturally, I was encouraged to visit the bar while waiting. Well, alright!

I got a large Pecan Porter brewed onsite and ended up bullshitting for a bit with a couple of guys sidled up to the bar, who were driving cattle down from Iowa. This put Bing Crosby's 1941 version of *Sioux City Sue* in my head ("I drove a herd of cattle down, from old Nebraska way, that's how I came to be in the state of I-oh-way"), but I refrained from belting out a chorus. These were nice guys doing honest American work balls-out.

After that, I walked around the gift shop (of course!) while waiting, ogling the gelato and pies, etc.—and almost got turfed in the nuts by kids running amok between the rhinestone skirt racks. Thanks, Junior; you almost got a 22oz stein dropped on your head.

As is standard for me, I gathered some observations during this wait. Scene of the Wait I: a bleach-blond mid-eighties real-estate photo type lady with a Corona in one hand and a Bud Light in the other frantically waving her party down (with her Corona hand): "They cain't seat us unless our full party's here!" Scene of the Wait II: a scrawny Baahstin kid in a backwards Bruins hat and a full sweat walking past shaking his head. Mid-eighties real-estate photo type lady: "Did y'all finish?" Baahstin: "Nah, that was wicked tough!" Another 72oz steak challenge fail.

In the end, it was a 45-minute wait for a table for

one—and then I was seated in a booth that would've held eight comfortably. This is why I'm not in restaurant management.

Onto more important matters, however: I went with a 16oz bone-in ("The Duke's Cut") steak, beefsteak tomato with red onions and Texas rice, and it was absolutely *delicious*. *And* I had leftovers for breakfast. And to add to this, during my feast, an old cowpoke with a git-tar and one with a fiddle walked around singing bluegrass, which was adorable and perfect. I was one of the only souls in the joint not wearing a cowboy hat, 2,062 miles from home, totally out of my element, and loving life.

After dinner, I crawled into bed and pulled out both copies of *Travels with Charley* I'd brought with me. I read Steinbeck's description of Stonington on Deer Isle, Maine: "The town very closely resembles Lyme Regis on the coast of Dorset..." I'd never heard of Lyme Regis, Dorset, England, at the time, but I remembered reading this for the first time when I was twenty-two and filing away both Deer Isle and Lyme Regis as places I'd like to one day visit, in addition to Amarillo, Texas (another stop along Steinbeck and Charley's journey). Andrea (my wife), as it turned out, had visited Lyme Regis before we'd met, loved it dearly, and wanted to one day take me for a visit. And now, here I was in Amarillo, Texas, reading about Lyme Regis six years after we visited Lyme Regis together, sporting the very same copy of *Travels with Charley* that I'd owned *and* taken with me to Lyme Regis—which was also the same copy that

I'd acquired and pored over at twenty-two.

It then occurred to me that I'd now visited many places that I'd once only dreamed of visiting—and not just on this trip (although I'd certainly done well to put myself in several images I'd long had in my head on this trip so far), and that was because I'd allowed myself to just *go* for it. Not bad, Westbye, not bad.

I was also thinking of Mikey Dee (he'll enter our story a little later): how much he would have loved The Big Texan and how much I wished we could have been together for this experience—or at least to have gotten together to bullshit about it after the fact. I thought of Mikey seeing me now, nearly 20 years after he'd known me (albeit just for three months) and wondered what he would have thought. I'd like to think he would have been proud at seeing me getting my shit together and getting busy living rather than get busy dying, and I don't think this is too far off.

Well, that's it for Amarillo. I'm sure it's a great town, and I'll get back to it, as I will for sure get back to the rest of Texas—but for now, this was a great taste, and I could now never again say that I'd never been to Texas... and I was very happy about that.

CHAPTER 5
UMA AND BERKLEE DAYS

I WAS NEVER MORE CULTURALLY awake and alive than I was during my four years at UMA.

On the surface, the University of Maine at Augusta was not much more than a sleepy community college hub campus in the University of Maine system—but oh, the treasures that lie beneath the surface. Immediately upon my arrival in September 1991, I started absorbing the jazz history and theory lessons of the esteemed Thelonious Monk scholar Gary Wittner, began sucking in the ear-training wisdom of Chuck Winfield (who played trumpet with Blood, Sweat & Tears and Barbara Streisand on Broadway), and gave in to the brilliance of Professor Don Stratton (one of the most profound influences I've ever had the privilege of being around). I studied Latin percussion with Alberto Del Gado, who was in the original Skitch

Henderson *Tonight Show* band; I took guitar lessons from Gary Clancy (who produced The Joe Perry Project and played with Tiny Tim), Tom Hoffmann (who toured the world with his trio), and Bob Thompson (who played on countless Maine TV and radio commercials from my youth). I sat in with visiting clinician Eddie Gomez (who played bass on numerous Bill Evans Trio records) and with Milt Hinton (who played bass with Cab Calloway and Dizzy Gillespie, along with the Jackie Gleason and Dick Cavett orchestras). I played in student-teacher ensembles every semester, sharing the universal language with my fellow amazing players, and every semester, I was instructed to get a band together and play a song in Jewett Hall for Recital Lab. Often, this turned into a last-minute-miracle affair of finding anybody who was available, picking a standard at random, and sight-reading live. And it always turned out great.

For four years, I lived, breathed, *became*, jazz. And at the same time, I was playing the Augusta circuit in a Grateful Dead/Phish/Frank Zappa/etc. cover band, so I was seriously oozing chops.

The knowledge that I absorbed during those four magical years at UMA stays with me still. I was a shit student academically, but regardless, it was a full-on mind, body, and soul immersion in the American songbook, and I now can't imagine my life without it.

It was also around this time—on the night of Tuesday, June 14, 1994—that my sports passion returned and it all came home. On that night, my dad's Rangers *finally* won the Stanley Cup for the first time since 1940, and we listened to it together. I was twenty-one and pissed at the world, but nothing could get in the way of me, my dad, and my radio. I tweaked the dial until I found Marv and Sal, those voices rising from deep in my DNA together again, and we listened passionately, hanging onto every play. And when Mark Messier held the puck in the corner for the final seconds and Madison Square Garden went ballistic on my boom box, we were together again for it. My dad stood up, stuck out his hand, and said, "Well, congratulations!" and went to bed. But I could see it all in his little smirk: the joy of *finally* winning in his lifetime, and the perfection—the almost-cinematic wonder—of our listening to it together on radio.

By the time graduation started looming on the horizon, I realized that I was slightly lacking in academics, and I was also completely burned out—so I took a semester off and transferred to my dream school, Berklee College of Music, Boston, in September 1996.

"*Ich bin ein Masshole!*" were the words I uttered aloud as soon as I passed the *Welcome to Massachusetts!* sign on I-95 as I drove to my dorm at Berklee College of Music in my parents' 1995 Hyundai Elantra on Sunday, August 25, 1996. I was about to turn twenty-four, Poe's *Hello* was playing on the radio from 104.1 WBCN Boston, and my world was about to change forever.

It was a hot, muggy morning. I dropped my stuff off in my room—on the eighth floor of the dorm at 150 Mass Ave., on the corner of Massachusetts Ave. and Boylston St.—sat at the desk I'd claimed as my own (first come, first served!), lit up a smoke, and opened a bottle of Coke I'd bought on my first of many Store 24 runs. I had a view of the air shaft and, above it all, the Prudential building and, behind it, the John Hancock tower. *I'd fucking* made *it*. Then, I drove back up to Portland. My parents met me, we grabbed lunch, and they dropped me off at Trailways, where I took the bus back down to South Station and caught the T (Massachusetts Bay Transit Authority subway lines): Red Line to Park Street, and then the Green Line to Hynes Convention Center.

By then, my roommate, Soon, who was from Seoul, had arrived. We tried chatting a bit through the language barrier, but we mostly unpacked in silence.

Not long after, my other roommate, Leigh Hassan, who was from Montreal, arrived. This was the moment when I met one of my closest friends to this day, a true friend who'd change my life and worldview.

That first night, our room became a gathering place—possibly in part because Leigh and I, wags and fast friends that we were, hung a sign on our door proclaiming, *WE GOT VAI'S ROOM!* As you can imagine, luring a bunch of eighteen-year-old guitar shredders with the false premise that we actually had the dorm room that guitar legend Steve Vai had once occupied did wonders for our social status. I remember lying on my top bunk, TV on, musicians congregating, the lights of Boston flickering, and feeling like all was right with the world.

That first week was a blur of hot days, endless nights, new friends, coffee, cigarettes (*tons* of cigarettes; I was up to a pack a day plus back then), 2AM runs to Store 24, meetings, orientations, and the usual minutiae of the first week of school. My love of walking through Boston also started here, as did my sense of isolation and disillusionment with Boston, and especially with Berklee. Berklee was the school of my dreams, but it didn't take long for the bubble to threaten to burst: I turned twenty-four in my first month at Berklee, and I was surrounded by seventeen- and eighteen-year-old prodigies from around the world. I was a really good musician, but I wasn't even close to their league. The demon screams started howling early. *I'm not good enough and I don't belong here.*

Then, there was the Wall of Fame outside the cafeteria. This wall was plastered with CDs from "Esteemed Berklee Alumni". The roster ranged from Quincy Jones (dropout) to Gary Burton (attended 1960-1) to Donald Fagen (Honorary Doctorate, 2001) to Aimee Mann (dropout). With this, the snapshot of Berklee I'd had in my head was being replaced with the reality before me: *Berklee was just a factory*. The books were cooked, the goalposts were on the twenty, and the real goal of the school was to make sure that the donations were rolling in. Or so it seemed at the time.

Plus, while I had certainly dealt with panhandlers in Portland, this was nothing even close to the scale of what I was presented with in 1996 Boston. For the most part, it was a respectful co-existence: I'd give if I could, and if not, I usually got a smile and/or a, "God bless you, anyway!" But with time, I started to run across a few more aggressive guys, and I started feeling like I had to be an asshole just to cross the street. Disheartening.

A saving grace, however, came in the form of the old Boston Garden, which was still standing. I often found myself walking to it (about three miles) before wandering aimlessly around the North End and back. I took many late-night walks around Back Bay, mostly along the Frederick Law Olmstead-designed Emerald Necklace Park that runs in the middle of Commonwealth Ave. My walks were solitary and cathartic, and *all mine*.

A few weeks into the semester, I got a job at Marcello's Pizza on Newbury Street. My boss, Moshen, was from Iran (he and his brother, Paul—yes, Moshen, and Paul— co-owned the joint), and he was a perpetual font of misery and fatalism. As soon as I walked through the door and into the empty restaurant, the litany began. "Briiiyan! My seeck beesnis! They are building *grave* for me back in Iran!" On and on. The only time he was ever happy was when he got laid or was going to get laid; then, he'd go on and on with dissertations about sundried tomatoes. "Briiiyan! You must eat sundried tomato! They make your deek hard for when you fahck beauteeful woman!"

I can't say I blamed him: when your business is dick, all you have is your dick. Or something like that.

I was a nervous kid (all those Hot Asses!) at the register, and I worked long hours making aesthetically dubious subs and pizzas for well-to-do insurance agents. I made bike deliveries all over Back Bay for extremely poor tippers, inhaled too many chemicals scrubbing tables, cut myself rather frequently (thanks to my non-existent knife skills), burned myself on the oven, and spent as much time as I could smoking in the kitchen and avoiding work entirely. I tried to avoid Moshen and his constant talk of his "seeck beesnis", but no soap: he was usually back there in the kitchen of his "seeck beesnis" smoking himself into oblivion.

I think I was making six bucks an hour, and some of that pay went straight to 12-packs of Rolling Rock, fifths of Jim Beam, packs of Marlboro Lights, and bad food. Largely, though, it went to books and CDs. I was constantly at Costello Liquors, but I was also constantly at Tower Records inhaling the stacks for new sonic and literary finds. Then, I was back in my dorm, avoiding it all. I slept through classes and generally coasted, uninspired and listless.

This doesn't mean I wasn't having a great time, though: Leigh and I had an open-door policy, and our room was a constant hangout joint. In among this crowd there was Jason Anderson from Baltimore (a beefy devotee of Pat

Martino and Ian McKay and, like me, a fanatic for Travis Bickle and *Taxi Driver*), Ajda Snyder, the "Turkish Queen" from Houston, and Christian Cambas, now an international DJ but then a scrawny little Greek whippet. Leigh played a Jackson guitar—a favorite with metal players—and Christian had a gorgeous Paul Reed Smith, a guitar that sells for a comfortable four digits. Christian used to burst into the room all the time yelling, "Oh! Oh! Oh, Leigh! Oh, Leigh! Can I play your guitar?"

Christian, who we named "DJ Fuggett" in a highly prophetic move, became *de facto* President of the Beverly Hills Society: every week, our room was the place for *Beverly Hills: 90210* and *Party of Five*. Meanwhile, Leigh himself was, and still is, one of the most unique characters I've ever known: a true Canuck and a master of the perfectly timed dry one-liner, always blasting Tupac and Biggie on 11 and frequently adjourning with Jason to our bathroom for a few hits of *The Chronic*. Leigh remains the only person in the world I've ever heard use the word "fuck" as punctuation. In Leighspeak, "fuck" could be either a comma or a period, although in Leighspeak enunciation, every declarative sentence sounds like a question. Example one: "I'm going to Store 24, fuck, to get a soft drink." Example two: "I'm going to Store 24 to get a soft drink, fuck." And again, when enunciated in Leighspeak: "I'm going to Store 24, fuck, to get a soft drink?" or "I'm going to Store 24 to get a soft drink, fuck?"

Never again, before or since, have I heard this.

Regardless, like I say, we had an open-door policy, so people were passing in at all hours of the day and night—and during the nights, poor Soon was in his bed asleep—trying to sleep. Can you imagine? A dorm room filled with copious underage drinking, cigarette smoke, and kids howling with laughter and listening to crazy-loud Tupac—and in the middle of it all, a sleeping Korean kid! What a bunch of inconsiderate fucks we all were! Leigh and I had a vision of Soon the moment he landed in his new room blasting Miami Sound Machine ("Come on baby, shake your body, do the conga!") and dancing with himself in delight, a disco ball spinning above him.

Strangely enough, he didn't return to our happy home for the spring semester. And we were sure about to miss him, because Leigh and I knew straight away that we had an issue with B. from Texas, Soon's spring semester replacement, when he said on his first day he moved in, "If you have any issues, just let me know. Don't get on my case about it, but let me know."

Yeah, that "don't get on my case about it" line? *Big* mistake, my man. He was a nice guy, but standoffish, and definitely a self-styled dandy, riding out the semester with the riffraff.

My walks became more and more frequent and lengthy at this point. It was an incredibly mild winter, so I took advantage. At the time, MTV was filming *The Real World: Boston* in an old fire house on Beacon Hill (the same fire house where Robert Urich's Spenser lived in the series *Spenser: For Hire*. I loved the show, but by that time, I was devouring the books. Robert B. Parker's Spenser taught me more about life and living than I could ever say), and so I'd often walk over there to see what was what. Never saw any filming going on, but there was always a crowd of drunken frat boys and sorority girls mingling outside, so it was still good entertainment every time.

It was also around this time that I realized I just couldn't hack restaurant work anymore, so I got a job as a telemarketer. Considering I was now moving to eight dollars an hour, this almost felt like a step up the ladder.

Little did I know that the psychological toll pitching credit cards would exact on me would be pretty intense.

Telespectrum was in Kendall Square, Cambridge, by the MIT campus. Monday to Saturday, there were three four-hour shifts available, and you could make your own schedule so long as you worked four four-hour shifts over the week and one on Saturday. And I could barely even handle the four hours.

Not all was lost, however: I was loving my time with my Berklee posse. Our room became a theater, never mind that the screen in question was my fraternal grandmother's early eighties 13" TV. Yes, we had the Beverly Hills Society, but with our VCR, we also had regular movie nights: *Taxi Driver*, *Kids*, *The Usual Suspects*, *Spinal Tap*, *The Decline of Western Civilization Part II: The Metal Years*, and *Kalifornia*, plus my collection of *Simpsons* episodes and bizzarro specialties such as *Lifestyles of The Ramones* and the 1988 Geraldo Rivera special on Satanism on VHS. Often, we would be up watching flicks until four or five in the morning, after which point I would excuse myself and take a walk around Back Bay in the gray, flowering, spring dawn. More solitary walks all my own, free of terms and conditions, in *my* town.

Leigh coined the sobriquet "Bizerklee" for our happy posse, and we developed an "M" gang sign (middle and ring fingers together, index and pinkie spread), flashed with the greeting "*Mass Ave. fo' life!*" And yeah, we lived it.

I wasn't completely comfortable with my newfound clique: the old, "What are you *really* saying behind my back?" mentality was hard to shake. But I was getting more comfortable with the reality that I fit in, at least with this group of friends, if not at my dream school and my dream town. All in all, a good period of my life.

After the semester ended, I moved into a room on 39 Rutland Square in the South End. It was the street of my dreams: low-slung walk-up brownstones, trees and landscaping in the middle of the street, wrought iron fences, and gas lamps. Beautiful. And my roommate was a Swede who was about to depart for a summer semester in Malmö, so the place was mine. Yet I had absolutely no money and no idea how to take care of myself: my "diet" for a day was often two packs of Marlboros, a good stretch of a 12-pack of Rolling Rock or a fifth of Jim Beam, a Pop Tart, and a slice of peanut butter on toast. (My theory was that toasting the bread would kill off any mold I may have missed while scraping the rest off.)

I'd often assuage my poor diet by walking over to the old Samuel Adams Brewpub in the lobby of the Hotel Lennox in Copley Square. They had a great lunch special: brat and a beer for five bucks. I'd sit in the back, smoking like a fiend and writing in my journal (more on that in a moment) in anticipation of my brat. Lunch was always fabulous. And hey, one more for the road...

Often, I'd bail out of work and take an extended walk, sit on the front steps of the Boston Public Library, or head out to Revere Beach. Green Line at Copley to Government Center, then the Blue Line to the Revere Beach stop. I'd just sit on the sea wall staring at the breakers and trying to get my head together and figure out what the fuck was *wrong* with me; why I couldn't just be happy. Why I couldn't sustain happiness. And if I wasn't clearing my head at Revere Beach, I was at my bench in Copley. It's just before the lawn, on the Dartmouth side, facing H.H. Richardson's masterpiece Trinity Church and the old and new Hancock Towers. I'd often spend hours there, smoking like a fiend and trying to find clarity. Then, I'd walk back to my room and turn on the tube, blindly watching nothing.

During this period, I saw literally no one. I sometimes couldn't get out of bed. I'd call in "sick" at Telespectrum and stare blankly at game and talk shows all day. Or walk all day, if I could manage to drag myself out into the world.

Even still, in a way, I loved the independence: I loved only having a four-hour work shift, as brutal as that shift may have been; I loved not having a roommate and being able to set my own schedule, including staying up until the early hours writing and contemplating and taking a ten-mile walk around town if I felt like it; I loved sitting on my stoop with a cup of coffee at 2AM if I so desired; I loved being able to play jazz in the afternoon without having to factor in the musical tastes of anyone else; I loved being free in Boston at twenty-four, even if my life was completely ill-formed and lacking in foundation. It was *my* life in *my* town, after all, and that was good enough for me. Even if there was clearly something very big missing.

When I'd first gotten to Berklee, an unexpected development had arisen—one that would change my life: I started keeping a journal. This was something I'd always *thought* about doing (thanks, Grandma), but never actually had. I guess I felt the time was right, and was it ever: I dove in and became voracious and thorough, and, as a result, I have a definitive, tangible snapshot of my life from the age of twenty-four through to twenty-nine.

Rereading these dispatches now, at forty-six, has been seriously intense: I see the pain and isolation and undiagnosed depression all over again, but I also see the optimism and self-preservation that got me through those times and is, I see ever more clearly, getting me through my current midlife crisis.

Here's one of my earliest entries from my time at 39 Rutland Sq.:

> Boston
> 10:54PM
> Tuesday
> 5/20/97

> Feeling really out of sorts. Today: bailed work [ed: telemarketing] and slept in 'til two/three ish, walked over to Fenway to look for bleachers (no luck), back home, starving w/ bare cabinets and wallet, caged, frustrated, alone. I hate the September light (Too bright! Shadows too dark!), I hate the forecast of more of the same, just with more wind, I hate my loneliness, I hate the uncertainty. I hate hoping for something good to happen. All seems black, and I've got no one to help me through it. I've accepted the fact that I don't get second glances from any girls. What the hell is wrong with me? Goddamn loneliness and isolation. I'm heading for a life unresolved.

Yeah, okay, a bit melodramatic. Pretty damn naïve, too: several years later, I was at a coffee shop with my dear friend, Lexi, and she picked up on several girls who were checking me out. Reading signals has (clearly) always been a problem for me.

This next entry is raw and real, and it encapsulates where I was at the time. While the above entry clearly shows my depression, *this* entry clearly shows my self-preservation.

Boston
11:26PM
Saturday
5/24/97

Steady improvement. Probably temporary, but steady. Unsuccessful day schlepping credit cards, with a <u>lot</u> of pissiness from irate customers, but no matter as I'll still clear $500 pre-taxes on Friday [ed: the check ended up being $394.41 post-taxes]. Brigham's [ed: an old chain of Boston casual restaurants very similar to IHOP] fulfilled my craving for a gargantuan slop-dripping burger with fries. Nice service, the waiters all had that gleaming commercial smile. Nice to see that Lenny Kravitz looking guy with his kid, father and daughter having fun with dessert and a placemat. Came back to see the Sox lose in the 9th, nap, R&R, now. Tomorrow awaits. These visits [ed: Eric was soon to arrive for a trip to Fenway] are way too brief, but we'll make the most of it. Beautiful night for coffee on the steps, then sleep in.

Rebounding! Holding onto hope! And holding onto small moments of joy! In Eric coming down for a ballgame, I see myself holding onto excitement, happiness, and anticipation. In having a midnight cup of coffee on the steps of my beautiful apartment on my beautiful street, I see myself taking time to pause and appreciate what I have in the here and now. And of course, the opening lines are pure self-preservation: *it's getting better. I might crash again, but there is hope. Keep going.*

Here's an undated essay, of sorts:

I occupy one bedroom of Apt. #3 at 39 Rutland Square in the South End, overlooking the courtyard in between buildings. I own nothing but a 13" TV and a coffeemaker. All of my possessions—mostly books—are in garbage bags on the floor at the foot of the bed. From my bed I can only see the building on the other side, but from the little table in the kitchen the Hancock Tower and the Berkeley Building with her weather beacon are right there.

Rutland Square is the street of my dreams: low, three-story brownstones with high stoops, landscaping, and wrought iron in the middle. My roommate is a Swede studying abroad for the summer, so the place is mine. It's perfect.

Except that I'm paralyzed with undiagnosed depression, and I can barely get out of bed, let alone handle a four-hour shift schlepping credit cards. Most of my days are spent napping, reading in a cloud of nicotine, or walking around town aimlessly.

But I always come back to my roof. To get there I have to enter the open apartment upstairs. In their bathroom, next to their tub, is a wooden stepladder. I climb up, push open a corrugated glass window and shimmy through a suspect, splinter-ridden wood frame.

And then all of Boston is there for me, and the empty shell of my day-to-day existence erodes...

In August 1997, I ran out of money after bouncing too many rent checks, and so crawled back home to live with my parents in Maine. This was one of the most crushing blows of my life up to that time. Here's where I was at:

Boston
11:26PM
Wednesday
8/27/97

My last night in Boston races on. What the
hell can I possibly say? How long will it be
until I can come back to live my life on my
terms? Shit, fucking indecision. Had my last
Beer & Brat today, about to hit my roof for
the last time... hard ass time. I'm (mostly)
packed to hit a road that I don't want to take.
I'm optimistic that I will be back, but the
torpor will rule until that day. My last Boston
dateline.

Concord Trailways
I-95 North
Thursday
8/28/97

2:11PM:
On a bus again, but this time there is no joy
for the gigolo. Grounded, sucked into an
unwanted existence, like a TIE Fighter
pulled in by the Death Star tractor beam. I
died last night/this morning. Twelve hours

ago, I was somewhere between my bench and my roof. Now I'm here. Soon I'll be there. The Olde Town is about to say goodbye.

2:44PM:
Feel sick with longing. Took the wrong bus. I took the one that's moving.

3:50PM:
Gray sun Saco. I'm back. For how long? At what cost? Shit.

My world was ending, but I knew it was a temporary setback. Hope buried in hopelessness!

Whitefield, ME
11:56PM
Saturday
8/30/97

The transplanted Bostonian settles in. Got home at around 4:30PM on Thursday, Sox on the tube, reading with naps. Lots of pain lately; the horrors of leaving, drive down haunting on multiple levels, leaving... don't know. I'm just here.

A horrible setback, but I see the optimism here—the optimism of knowing that I would return.

A few weeks later, I hit the quarter-century mark:

> Whitefield
> 11:46PM
> Friday
> 9/12/97

> Well, it's my birthday. I'm twenty-five today. Happy Birthday to me. Once again, it's another day; the thought crossed my mind maybe 10 times all day. 14 minutes left: terrible day, can't keep breaking down. Where will help come from? Nothing to say.

Bleak, but understandable, considering my world had once again been crushed and I didn't have the coping skills to overcome this at the time. Well, I did, but I didn't allow myself to realize that. Classic HSP: I figured that every setback was fatal and that I'd never recover. As a matter of fact, I see HSP very clearly throughout that entry. And now, at forty-six, I realize how fleeting those feelings are.

Shortly after this entry, I got a job working the graveyard shift folding clothes at L.L. Bean—10PM to 4AM, I think. Not bad: easy job, 33% discount. I then spent New Year's Eve 1997 with a friend of a friend in Boston, and the wheels of my return started rolling: I went from folding clothes at L.L. Bean in Maine to folding clothes at Talbots on Boylston St. in Boston on New Year's Eve and January 2. Progress! A friend of a friend, Lisa, let me crash at her place in Brighton for a few days, and things were seriously starting to look up.

Brighton
12:40AM
Saturday
1/03/98

Uncertainty is the theme, but all will even out in time. Amazing to be back home again. Hasn't really sunk in yet, but it's like I never even left. All those months of agony in Maine are over. I served out the term, and the magnitude of my return is not lost on me. All of my spots have taken on a newfound significance, still alive, still here, way more appreciative, ready to continue the growth. I was saying the same shit a year ago, but I'm so much more aware and stronger now. All of the setbacks have made me so much better, wiser and stronger. Westbye is back.

1:36AM:

Addendum: Christ, I'm so fortunate. I'm here (receiving what I would give) instead of fighting the cold in front of the library, cared for. Lisa, yr the shit. It's still kind of hard but I understand: I <u>would</u> do the same thing in a heartbeat. Just be cool and don't keep going down the road of I'm-not-worthy gloom and doom. That's not me anymore. No work tomorrow: I'll get a room and savor my Olde Towne. Full circle again, and way better the second time around.

One of the guiding principles of my life emerged here in print. For most of the first half of my life, I felt guilty over people doing things for me because I usually wasn't in a position to reciprocate, and I tended to put price tags on the generosity of others—yet here, I realize that if the situation were reversed and *Lisa* needed a room, I would absolutely provide one and never even *think* of expecting anything in return.

This presented a transformative lesson for me: take your gifts humbly and pay it forward whenever and however you can. Example: once, in the summer of 2000, when I was really struggling, Lexi, who was making good money in a corporate gig, spotted me $100. To me, at that time, this might as well have been $10,000. I wasn't in a position to repay, but I never forgot that act of generosity, and ever since then, I've done whatever I possibly can to pay it back, whether picking up the check at dinner, slipping a friend in need a few bills, paying for the car behind me at the Starbucks drive-thru, or just checking in on a friend to see how they're doing. Good karma begets good karma.

Another guiding principle of my life has also emerged here: self-evaluation and change. I was aware that I could come off as self-deprecating and self-flagellating, and I knew I wanted to purge that from my system. In other words, I wanted to make a conscious effort to overcome myself. And now, two decades of change later, I see how far I've come in that respect.

Anyway, to return to our narrative: my triumphant return to Boston was cut short, but I wouldn't change this setback for anything, because I lived through a once-in-a-lifetime historical event: *The Ice Storm*. It was as a result of this phenomenon that I, having travelled to Maine on January 6 due to financial difficulty, ended up having to delay my return until mid-February. Here's an undated essay about it.

The Ice Storm.
String those three words together around anybody who lived through it and watch the cringes and shudders. It was catastrophic, deadly, and destructive on a scale previously unimaginable. It came on suddenly on a

balmy day in January 1998, and it threw our world into primitive chaos for weeks afterwards. You had to live through it to believe it.

I was in Boston, trying to get home to Maine for a few days. January 6th was warm, with a light rain. There were rumblings that it would get colder, especially up north, and ice might be a factor. Little did we know.

I talked to my dad before getting on the bus, and he suggested I get to Portland, get a room and he would pick me up when he could: things were getting bad up north as the temperature started to drop. The entire trip was a cacophony of rain and ice, increasing in intensity against the metal roof of the bus as we inched northward. This was the sound of impending disaster.

I got a cab and headed for the Swiss Chalet in Westbrook, two miles away from the bus station. I checked in and would remain trapped in my room for the next three days. And I was one of the luckiest ones in town.

Power was lost immediately. The weight of the ice on the trees and power lines caused a swath of crystalline destruction from New England far into Quebec. Power transformers were crushed and crumbled, wooden electrical poles were snapped like toothpicks, and entire forests were sagging and begging for mercy. And roads were completely impassable.

The Swiss Chalet had power, so I hunkered down, escaping only to eat at the adjacent Denny's or to skate across Brighton Avenue to the Shop 'n Save for beer and smokes. Literally, skating in the middle a major thoroughfare in my hiking boots.

Finally, after three days, the roads were cleared barely enough for my dad to get me. My parents had lost power at the beginning of the storm, and now I was joining them. It would be another eight days before I would know electric light and power and bathing water again.

For eight days the power company worked 24/7 to get electricity restored, and crews worked 24/7 to get the roads cleared of fallen power lines, trees, and other detritus. Still the cold held on, and the omnipresent ice glared in the sun, and even in the dark.

We could occasionally get into Gardiner for provisions, but with no electricity, it was mostly non-perishable, easily disposable fare. I choked down cups of Nescafe Crystals brewed on the woodstove and dreamed of three squares and a hot bath.

My friend Dana, a Korean vet who lived in a cabin in the woods, had given me an Army-issue winter coat that he had worn during the Battle of Inchon. It is still the warmest garment I've ever had, and I wrapped myself in it while hovering beside the woodstove over those eight days. I also warmed myself with nips of Jim Beam, and wished I had a hound dog to sit at my feet and complete my Jack London fantasies.

And then it was over. Power was restored, life went on and suddenly it was summer, then it was a year later, then five years later, then ten. But nobody who lived it will ever be the same, and we will never take a day of normalcy for granted. If you survived The Ice Storm, you know. You had to live through it to believe it.

And here is a dated journal entry from the time:

Whitefield, ME
2:13PM
Thursday

1/15/98

Christ, all I need now is a goddamn hound
dog lying on the floor. Day 8 without power
finds me in front of the stove huddled in my
Korean jacket. The Jim Beam was nice. The
empty-stomach-induced retching was not.
Think I'm going insane. Cuddles the cat is on
my lap, hampering my writing, snow is
coming. I'm still here, freezing and waiting.

Power was finally restored on January 24, and normalcy
slowly returned. But, of course, nothing would ever be the
same again.

After this unexpected detour, in February 1998, I took
Trailways down on a Friday, got hired for a job in a call
center for a major insurance company, got a copy of the
late and great *Boston Phoenix*, and found a sublet in
Coolidge Corner, Brookline, right behind a Trader Joe's.
The job started Monday, so I spent Saturday refilling a few
garbage bags with my books, CDs, and clothes, and got
ready.

On Sunday, my parents drove me down to drop my
stuff off at my new home. They were, as they told me later,
a little unnerved, and I soon found out why: I'd just signed
on for three months of life with a crazy lady.

Malinda greeted me and led me to her basement lair.
She was in her mid-fifties, dressed all in black (like she'd

just come out of a rice paddy), and very far removed from any African lineage she may have had, yet her apartment was choc-a-bloc with African masks, sculptures, etc. ("Oh, isn't this piece so quaint? Exquisite!"), beat-up furniture that, as I quickly learned, must *never* be sat on (endless pieces that proclaimed what an *artiste* she was), and every form of organic healing root and potion in the kitchen.

My room had a transom window that looked out onto a thick wall of shrubs, a futon, and a desk... and that was it.

After "unpacking" that first Sunday, I headed back into town for a Guinness float at the Deli Haus in Kenmore Square, and, feeling a bit put off by my new domestic overlord, I decided to walk back so I could increase the time away from her.

The walk was about two miles, and as it turned out, it was a precedent-setter.

My new job was in Quincy, so I caught the Green Line at Coolidge Corner and then the Red Line at Park Street— and then took a *long* ride over Dorchester Bay to Quincy Center.

The job was an utter mindfuck: two weeks of training in which we had to memorize a 70-page script of legalese regarding the settlement of a class-action suit brought against the company. Long story short: agents advised clients that dividends could rise, but kinda sorta didn't mention that dividends could also fall. And this was apparently a problem: as soon as I logged on in the morning, more than 200 calls awaited in queue, and the deluge of pissed-off clients began.

After work, I got off the Red Line at South Station and walked the four-plus miles back to Brookline, stopping off for bad food and any other available form of procrastination along the way. It was better than being stuck in my basement cell. So long as I lingered on the streets, I didn't have to worry about walking on the carpet too loudly, shielding my reading lamp from the window, reading all of Malinda's post-it note jeremiads, or having her carob, ginseng, and St. John's wort brownies.

And so, every night from February to May, through snow, sleet, freezing rain, and sun, I walked these four-plus miles home. Of course, the health benefits of this were counterbalanced by endless cigarettes and cheap fast food and beer, but still, I'd take my time, stop into Tower Records for books or Planet Records in Kenmore Square for CDs, and occasionally find myself lining up at the ticket booth at Fenway for a bleacher (you could do that back then). Long, solitary walks through the blooming spring of my beloved Boston, all on my own.

Here's an undated journal entry from this time:

> I'm subletting a basement room from a nutcase in Brookline and working at a call center in Quincy. It's ten miles from Quincy to Brookline, and six miles from Quincy to South Station. Every night, no matter the

weather, I get off the Red Line at either South Station or Park Street, grab a bite and walk the final four miles back to my room. This is how desperate I am to not be "home."

I usually make it just before curfew. Yes, I'm twenty-five and my roommate has imposed a curfew. Her paranoia is such that I have to make my sofa bed, hide all my possessions, and pull the transom shades every morning before leaving, lest the superintendent see me and snitch her out to management. Never mind that she placed her rental ad in the not-exactly-covert Boston Phoenix, and never mind that the super knows I'm there and that we've swapped nips of Old Grand Dad and stories about what a nutcase she is.

This is my life. This is why I prefer walking four miles in a downpour or a blizzard or an arctic gale to being home in my room.

My walks are solitary and free of terms and conditions. From South Station I walk up Summer St. to Park St. and the Boston Common, so named because the sheep paths that became the streets of Boston originated from this common grazing ground. I walk through the Common and across Charles St.

to the Public Garden, where spring flowers will soon bloom. I walk Commonwealth Ave through Parisian Back Bay, enraptured by the brownstones, the park in the middle of the Ave, the old gas lamps.

In Kenmore Square I arrive under the flashing Citgo sign. I head upstairs to Planet Records and buy a grab bag of CDs. I buy some Tremont Ale at the basement Kenmore Liquors and wrap the bottles in my backpack. I examine the menu at the Chinese Pizza place and think better of it.

I continue on Comm, past the stately Buckminster Hotel and on to Boston University territory, where the Green Line trolley emerges from the underground of Kenmore Square Station in the middle of the avenue. Past school buildings and dorms and the Paradise Rock Club, where I dream of someday playing. Past the site of what was once Braves Field, where the Boston Braves hosted Jackie Robinson, Stan Musial and more of my idols. I dream of crowds in pearls and fedoras and streets clogged with Packard's and De Sotos.

I continue past Temple Israel and to Coolidge Corner. Almost there. I buy some pistachios at Trader Joe's on Harvard Ave,

then slink downstairs to retire for the
evening. I flick on my desk lamp, crack open
a Tremont and read and write and drink in
dark solitude, like a WWII blackout.

I'm home.

In May of 1998, I finally got out and found another sublet
with my buddy (still to this day) Chad in Everett. Freedom!
And Everett was far enough out that even if I wanted to, I
couldn't walk back home. Things were looking up!

From there, I worked my temp jobs and continued my
solitary path, and on Friday nights, I was frequently drawn
to Harvard Square with my journal.

Harvard

Evening

Friday

10/23/98

8:05PM:
Harvard again. I'll keep on standby mode,
just in case something hits. Kind of limited
action tonight, surprisingly low Friday
volume. I would've expected more with All
Hallows Eve impending, but it is early. <u>Very</u>
October. I'm in a real good life spot right
now, but having a hard time finishing things
off, finding consummation. Maybe I'm

pressing a bit, but no action comes without force. I'd rather push than remain idle. The moment the drive stops, the atrophy begins. To push myself is to find my limits... and then to go beyond. Random bullshit musings going nowhere, but good to catalog my thoughts. I must get my shit together. Couple of bands fighting for airspace in the harvest chill. I sure don't miss outdoor gigs in New England October. Miss playing out like crazy, though. Good hacky war going on in front of me. Makes me feel old, like I've missed out on some opportunities. Better late than never, but I wonder where I'd be now if things were different. A lot of repeat offenders out in the square tonight. I guess it's the Friday thing. Chuck the books, make a few calls, bum a smoke, drown in coffee, see what happens. American-style disenfranchised youth, roll on. Always hurting for cash, but the great American pastime of hanging out is always free. Show's usually worth it, too. Incoming! We have hacky fire! 20 points for my coffee cup. Am I old enough to consider myself aging? Young enough to pull off being a scenester without looking too old? Christ, this is a fucked-up age. Sixteen and twenty-six must be the hardest. Twenty-six is a total middle ground with no definitive answers. Sixteen you want to be twenty-six and vice versa. I'm managing, but with a good amount of bullshitting. I'd imagine that with thirty comes acceptance. Hope takrist I make it. Hope I don't go down in flames, done in by my vices. I've been doing really well lately, though. It's all I can do: effort = results = pride in progress. The Mix-98 band [ed: Boston radio station playing "the hits of yesterday and today". The band in the square that night wasn't officially sanctioned by the station, but their setlist skewed toward the usual Mix-98 fare, so...] has called it quits, as the hacky circle ebbs and flows. It's noticeably cooler now. I've been here 50 min. Same goddamn spot! Time to warm up a bit.

9:07PM:
I go for a piss break and my spot is commandeered! Little else has changed. I'll give Harvard a little bit longer. Hard to write with gloves on! The Mix-98 band has returned and is now doing "Sympathy for the Devil." Just a matter of time. I'm surprised that there's been no mass chorus of *whoo-*

whoos. Lemme hear ya, Harvard Square! The Square is presenting nothing new. This is enough...

Clearly, I had no shortage of fodder around me.

> Park St. Station
> Night
> Friday
> 10/23/98

10:48PM, waiting for a Lechmere Train. Stunning blond on the Green Line. Understated class. She is alone, reading in solitude, radiant. Then she goes for the pick. Full nasal penetration, probing, digging. She pauses, rubs, snorts, then proceeds to dig again, her press-ons collecting the treasure. Shit, you think you know someone...

DAY FIVE

MAY 12, 2019

Amarillo, TX, to Gallup, NM: 424 miles.
Time Out: Checked out of The Big Texan around 5:30AM CST.
Time In: Checked into El Rancho around 6:00PM MST.

O N DAY FIVE, I FORGOT all about the Cadillac Ranch, and I forgot all about the change from Central to Mountain Time. Had I remembered the latter, I might have remembered the former. But turns out I just have to come back instead...

It was still dark when I blasted out of Amarillo, and as I drove, I watched the sun rise behind me over the Panhandle. And even though it was closed, I hit Mission I: Midpoint Café in Adrian, which lay 50-odd miles beyond Amarillo. No ugly crust pie for me today, but I did get something I could never buy while there: the opportunity to stand at the geographic center point of Route 66 in the still, Texas dawn, with nobody around for miles. The tangibility of this journey, the tangibility of the America I knew and didn't know, really hit me here, as did a very real sense of accomplishment: I'd completed 1,139 miles by myself. All the evidence pointed at the fact that I could most definitely make the next 1,139.

In that moment, I thought of the Bob Mould line in the Sugar song *Hoover Dam*:

> *Standin' on the edge of the Hoover Dam*
> *I'm on the center line, right between two*
> *states of mine*

And then I thought I might start crying and/or shivering, so I got back into Rose and cranked the heat...

Back on the road, I headed for Mission II: Tucumcari, which lay 70-odd miles down the line. On this journey, I crossed the border into New Mexico, the rising sun glinting off of 18-wheelers all the while, in turn causing the trailers to seemingly burst into flames on the open highway. The feel of the southwest was getting stronger with every mile, and eventually, to the south, I saw Tucumcari Mountain come into view—and with that, I'd suddenly put myself in another image that had long been in my head.

The mountain guided me into town, and suddenly, I was on the strip.

Let me say up front that there ain't much to Tucumcari, New Mexico, on a Sunday morning—yet I could feel what it had once been and what it had the potential to someday be again.

Tucumcari Tonight!: that's the song and slogan of Hotel Row, which is comprised of The Blue Swallow, Motel Safari, The Pony Soldier, The Palomino, The Apache, The Aztec... they're all still there in one form or another. Nothing may be left of The Pony Solder but the sign, but that's enough. Meanwhile, Motel Safari has been restored, as has The Blue Swallow, and both are magnificent. TeePee (or is it TePee?) Curiosity is also still going strong. Standing on the strip of a chill Sunday morning, it's hard to envision what Old Tucumcari was like—but step back and let the frame develop a bit, and it's all there.

That said, it wasn't quite what I'd imagined: I'd seen a lot more dust in my mental image, and, naturally, a *whole* lot more people, but it appeared that Tucumcari was holding her own, rolling with the changes and nowhere near close to death, unlike far too many towns that have been decimated by Walmart and Chili's, among the other detritus of our American nodes.

So, there I stood on Route 66 in Tucumcari, taking in the chill of the morning and thinking of myself at twenty-six in 1998 Boston, listening to Better Than Ezra (as you'll see in the Appendix, their debut album *Deluxe* was a go-to then, and the song *Coyote* mentions Tucumcari. I'd never heard of it, but filed it away, like Lyme Regis) and dreaming of Tucumcari... and it occurred to me that I was *actually standing on Route 66 in Tucumcari*. I'd *made* it: I'd put myself in another picture I'd long held in my head. That big, dumbass grin came back and spread like wildfire.

On to Albuquerque! 175-odd miles to go. But first, fuel and caffeine (same thing, really) at the Pilot station in Santa Rosa.

Just as I started heading back to Rose, I made a new unlikely friend: a precious gray kitten! It wandered over and reared back for scritches, which I was only too happy to provide, though I was worried about the poor thing, and so tried to grab it to bring inside and see if anyone was taking care of it—but no soap. Still worried, I went back in the store and asked about the cat, and the clerk said it was fine—well-fed and -looked after. So, I came back out for a few more scritches and said goodbye, sad to not have my new friend along for the rest of the way.

Next up: an ADD stop at Clines Corner. I remember also seeing Clines Corner in *Route 66 Lost & Found: Ruins and Relics Revisited*, and here I was, standing in the parking lot of yet another place about which I'd said, "I'd love to see that one day." This 24/7 travel center had been operating in its namesake town since 1934, and it was *still* going! In addition to the requisite Subway, the gift shop had tons of homemade fudge and red and green Chile sauce, as well as other local wares. It was so refreshing to see such unique fare; localism ain't dead yet! It was also here that I saw a guy who'd also been at the Pilot station in Santa Rosa a mere hour earlier, and in that moment, it really hit me how connected we all are on our respective journeys. We may all have different destinations, goals, and plans, but we're still all on the journey to "somewhere" together. Our paths cross and diverge, but we're all one and the same, together in our America: we share the roads and we share the land (cue up The Guess Who!).

I didn't see that guy again, and I'll never know his story, but it was still nice to recognize a fellow traveler along the way—and besides, this bit of mystique meant I had plenty of contemplation fuel for the hump to Albuquerque 60 miles down the road.

Albuquerque: officially established in 1706, but it's a lot older than that. The Rio Grande Valley was inhabited by Native Americans for thousands of years, most notably the Pueblo people, an extremely advanced civilization and masters of arts, crafts, ceramics, and masonry. Spanish Conquistador Francisco Vasquez de Coronado arrived at the Pueblo of Zuni in 1540, where he encountered the Tiwa people, who at the time had a trade network spreading from Mexico to the Great Plains. It was in this that the new arrivals found economic opportunity. With that, Don Francisco Cuervo y Valdes became provincial governor in 1706 and established the garrison that would soon become Villa de Alburquerque (named after the Viceroy of New

Spain, the Duke of Alburquerque: the superfluous "r" was dropped somewhere along the way) near the Tiwa pueblos. New Mexico came under Mexican rule when Mexico won their freedom from Spain in 1821. El Camino Real (the Royal Road) connected Mexico City to Albuquerque, while the Santa Fe Trail connected Albuquerque to the east.

In a word, Albuquerque was booming—and shortly thereafter, the Atchison, Topeka and Santa Fe arrived, Route 66 followed... and you know the rest.

(Yes, I did just blow through 313 years of American history in less than 200 words. Life is short, and so is the focus of this book.)

Now, I mentioned previously that I was meeting a friend, but I was actually meeting my wife Andrea's best friend, Alex (though we were also friends, having been connected via the almighty Facebook for a while). I was now meeting her for lunch in person, and felt ever so slightly nervous. Alex was fighting cancer, and my heart had gone out to her from a distance for some time now—but now, we were going to hang in person and in real time. I knew she had a good gallows humor similar to mine, so I wasn't *too* worried about saying anything untoward, but still... No pressure!

Driving into Albuquerque was an utterly foreign experience, all the highway architecture (bridge overpasses and retaining walls and light poles) in adobe with native art filigrees in turquoise. Beautiful and alien and welcomed.

Because I so royally screwed up the timing, I arrived in Albuquerque somewhere around 10AM (and yes, I missed The Musical Road of Tijeras in the process. Oh, well), meaning Alex was not quite ready yet—and so, at her recommendation, I headed over to The Owl Café, where I spent a good 45 minutes people-watching the Mother's Day crowd. And this suited me fine; being somewhat of a wallflower, people-watching is one of my favorite activities.

After that time had elapsed, she arrived, and we hugged profusely and settled in for grub. I instantly felt at home with a kindred spirit, and, in her warm company, I got my first taste of New Mexican green Chile sauce with beans, and I was *loving* it. I also ordered a small cup of the tortilla soup with green sauce (I'd had a fine-but-whatever breakfast of French toast and sausages at Annie's in Santa Rosa, and so wasn't desperately hungry)—and from there, the conversation began in earnest. And it didn't stop for many hours.

After some time, Alex suggested I leave Rose at The Owl—and, with that, she drove me around Albuquerque in her battered pickup festooned with dog hair. We took a spin along Central Ave. (a.k.a., Route 66) through downtown, with Albuquerque Rapid Transit (ART) buses weaving in and out from stations in the middle of the strip. We drove through Nob Hill and passed by the University of New Mexico campus (which I recognized from a shoot-out on an episode of *COPS*. Alex wasn't surprised in the least). We cruised 66 past the KiMo Theater, the Lobo Theater, Duran Pharmacy, and The Dog House Drive-In, and I felt that renewed sense of "I'd love to visit that someday" throughout.

After some time, we parked for a walk around Old Town, and it was magnificent—a completely foreign America: adobe and tile mosaics; stucco and turquoise and cacti. We also saw the Chapel of Our Lady of Guadalupe and the Portal Market, where local artisans offer their handcrafted southwestern fare, and strolled past the bandstand where flamenco musicians play.

Another world, for sure.

After a quick freshen up at her adobe house, we headed for the Sandia Peak Tramway... where we found the tram was shut down due to a lightning threat—but, after a few minutes, the all-clear was given, and we queued up for the ride.

The Tramway is an absolutely amazing experience: a 2.7-mile ride up the Sandia Mountain chain, rising to 10,378' atop Sandia Peak in the Cibola National Forest. The view of Albuquerque *et al.* is stunning, and I will remember this jaunt evermore, especially since I hadn't been planning for it. Life falls out of the sky...

One of the guiding tenets of my life is to laugh at what scares me. This gives me power over the fear and allows me to be human while I overcome my setbacks. I've utilized this defense against my depression and anxiety for years. Anyway, during this excursion, I was so grateful that Alex got that, and, as predicted, there were many moments of gallows humor along the way ("Oh, just because you have *cancer*, you think you can..." "Why are you slacking? You got *cancer* or something?"). I don't for one second mean to suggest that this approach will work for everyone, but it certainly worked for us, and I'm grateful for that, since it meant she was already on my wavelength! We also threw out *Simpsons* references and sang choruses from Depeche Mode, *My Little Buttercup* from *The Three Amigos*, and *Springtime for Hitler* from *The Producers*—and there was a shit-ton of hyperventilaughing (just go with it, okay?) along the way.

I met a friend I care for deeply, and we truly connected in real time. There are few greater gifts than that.

Onto Gallup! 138 miles to go.

Alex described Amarillo and Gallup as the two most boring towns in the world, and I can see where she was coming from—though I didn't mind this, as I was anticipating downtime at both spots. I grabbed a large Dr. Pepper, bailed on Albuquerque while listening to the NBA playoffs, and balled the jack on I-40.

The feel of the southwest grew stronger and stronger as the late afternoon sun elongated and spread: the Sandia chain; Mt. Taylor and the Chuska Range to the north; the Zuni Mountains to the south; mesas and steppes along the highway like I'd never seen before. I thought of how just over 24 hours earlier, I'd been in rural Oklahoma, still in the east, and how utterly foreign this American landscape was in comparison. It was a completely different world—one I'd never seen with my own eyes—yet here I was. This was not my day-to-day world at all—far from it—and I welcomed the change: fresh view, fresh perspective, a new slant.

Two-plus hours later, I was in Gallup.

I couldn't wait to get to the El Rancho Hotel: it was built in 1937 by the brother of D.W. Griffith (who's always referred to as "the brother of D.W. Griffith", never by name; perhaps nobody wants to draw any more attention to the Klan-loving racist who shit out *The Birth of a Nation* than necessary, and I certainly applaud that choice) as a production base for all the Westerns being filmed in the area. Employees were trained by the famed Fred Harvey company, and the hotel boomed until... wait for it... I-40 opened and siphoned traffic away from Route 66, from which point the hotel fell into disrepair. Not to worry, though: Armand Ortega, patriarch of Ortega National Parks LLC (the family operation that runs concessions and spearheads preservation efforts at a myriad of national parks), bought the property and restored it to its former glory. Guests throughout the hotel's storied history include Lauren Bacall, Spencer Tracy, Jackie Cooper, John Wayne, and Claude Akins.

I must say up front that I am a fan of Claude Akins.

When I was a kid, one of my favorite shows was *The Misadventures of Sheriff Lobo*, and when we visited

Orlando, I always wanted to eat at Perkins Restaurant because I was sure that Deputy Perkins (Miles Watson) ran the joint and that he and Lobo would be there. I love Lobo and Claude Akins and his long career in Hollywood with the likes of Sinatra and Donna Reed (*From Here to Eternity*, fachrissakes!).

When I checked into El Rancho and got to floor three, I noticed that in addition to a plaque with the room number, there was a plaque stating who had stayed in said room before—and, when I saw the room Claude Akins had stayed in, my heart sank. Why? Because all I could think of was the *Simpsons* episode "Krusty Gets Kancelled" in which the Krusty the Clown show is canceled and replaced with, well...

> [MAN 1] Krusty, we're from the network. Uh, we have some bad news: I'm afraid your show's been canceled.
> [KRUSTY] Oh, I thought this would happen. I just hope you replace me with something as educational and uplifting as I tried to be.
> [MAN 2] Actually, it's a hemorrhoid infomercial starring Claude Akins.
> [KRUSTY] Can I play hemorrhoid sufferer number one? "Ooh! Oh, that hurts! Ow! Oh, is there no relief?"
> [MAN 1] I don't think so. (They start to walk off)

[KRUSTY] How about one of the "after" guys?
"Aah. Ohh, that's better. I can ride a bike
again!"
[MAN 1] Sorry...

So, when I saw Claude Akins on my door, I thought to
myself (insert Luke Skywalker voiceover here), *Nooo!*

As it turns out, I was on the wrong side of the hall and
had actually gotten the Rita Hayworth room. So much for
Lobo and his apocryphal 'roids!

I spent a few minutes in Rita's room rewinding *Pal
Joey* in my mind before heading downstairs for the
restaurant. It was loaded with what were obviously Route
66 warriors, and I loved being in their company, even
without interaction (not really feasible, me being solo at a
four-top, not that I was really seeking it out by this point).
My server was an incredibly sweet older lady with a heavy
Chicano accent, and as she greeted me, I felt that big,
dumbass grin spreading again. I was a long-ass way away
from Maine. I ordered The Duke's Favorite margarita and
the Armand Ortega (sliced sirloin on flour tortilla with red
Chile pequin or green Chile; I went "Christmas" and
ordered the red and green Chile). Steak two nights in a row.
Only on vacation. I've never been able to roll a burrito, but
delicious is delicious regardless of form, and I was loving
my New Mexican Christmas bastardizations.

From the restaurant, I strolled into the 49'er lounge
and sank a few while watching John Lester pitch at Wrigley

on the bar TV. It was a far cry from Errol Flynn's days, but it was still great to be there. *Things happened here.* Spanish pop on the juke and no interaction, but still, memorable. Besides, it's not often one can say they've been in the same room as Bogart! Though while in the 49'er, I admittedly started to feel a little down: I started thinking of my server (tangent: what a fucking horrible term. I'm not a king in need of "service". Degrading) and the fact that she probably worked twice as hard as I ever have in my life, sent what she could home to her family, and kept a perpetual smile on her face.

I wanted to go back and give her a big hug.

I then thought about my earlier characterizations of my former co-workers ("The Mood", "Snorts", *et al.*) and I felt like utter shit.

The thing about a toxic environment is that, like a deep depression, you don't realize how bad it is and how much it blackens your own thoughts until you can pull yourself out and step away from it. I can, I realize, be a judgmental asshole, and I'm not proud of that and know I need to work on it. This wasn't how I cared to present myself, much less how I cared to be.

I was also feeling wistful here because I realized that a few hours earlier, I'd made my second crossing of the Continental Divide in (the fortuitously named) Continental Divide, New Mexico... and I'd missed it at the time. I'd wanted to celebrate the crossing, but I totally blew past it.

And, my brain being a nonlinear ADD garbage dump, I was *also* thinking of Merriweather Lewis, Commander of the Corps of Discovery.

I thought of a segment from Ken Burns' *Lewis & Clark*, in which Lewis wrote a journal entry on the Continental Divide—something around his birthday and "living for the good of man". Or *something*.

A few swipes on my phone and I found it: on August 18, 1805, his thirty-first birthday, Lewis sat at the upper end of the American Continental Divide and wrote in his journal:

> I had in all human probability existed about half the period which I am to remain in this Sublunary world... I had as yet done but little, very little, indeed, to further the happiness of the human race, or to advance the information of the succeeding generation. I viewed with regret the many hours I have spent in indolence, and now sorely feel the want of that information which those hours would have given me had they been judiciously expended... I resolved in future, to redouble my exertions... to live for mankind, as I have heretofore lived for myself.

President Jefferson wrote of Lewis' "depressions of the mind", and it astonishes me how a man who was clearly a manic depressive managed to pull himself together in the service of such an impossible journey as commanding the Corps of Discovery in the exploration of the Louisiana Territory. I suppose Lewis is something of a spiritual guide for me in that sense: you can clearly see the depression and self-flagellation in that journal entry ("indolence"? Seriously?), and in this moment, I found myself thinking hard about the second half; about living for mankind. Yeah, I could be a shiftless asshole, and I wished to be neither (i.e., shiftless or an asshole) anymore—and I wanted to do more to help others and make a positive difference in this world. Like I said at the beginning of this book, I was trying to find my calling on this trip, and maybe, just maybe, I was starting to hear something at this point...

Still rather melancholic and wistful, I strolled into the lobby, humbled but optimistic, and spent a few minutes walking around snapping pics of signed eight-by-tens from Bogie, Ava, William Bendix, Lee Marvin, Jimmy Stewart, etc., and called it a night.

Back to the room where Rita Hayworth once slept. I felt quite pleasant with that ghost in my room. And, presumably, the fact there were no spectral hemorrhoids.

CHAPTER 6

MY BRIAN WILSON YEARS

I THINK OF 1997–99 as my Brian Wilson years. Like the Beach Boys legend, I spent far too much time in bed with crippling mental health issues. Unlike the real Brian Wilson, however, I wasn't hoovering mounds of Peruvian blow with hot-and-cold chicks in my bed and recording *Pet Sounds*. Instead, I was living a life of temp jobs for pennies on the dollar (when I could find and hold them), clouds of nicotine, and bad food. (As we've established, most of my income went on cigarettes and replenishing the piles of insufficient funds fees in my bank account.) I had a disconnect from my friends and family and from life. I was always staring, braindead, at game and talk shows, wondering what the hell was wrong with me. And, of course, not having insurance made it kinda difficult to *actually* figure out what was wrong. So, I endured.

I basically had nothing tangible to my name during my twenties: no furniture; no possessions... At 39 Rutland Square, the bed came with the room. I had my paternal grandmother's 13" TV and my books and my CDs in garbage bags on the floor. When I lived in Everett, MA, a friend had a job cleaning dorm rooms and scored a "gently used" mattress for me, which of course I set up on the floor. Floor, mattress, fitted sheet, top sheet, and the comforter I'd had in high school. That mattress and my grandmother's 13" TV were lost when I fell behind on my rent and the landlord locked me out.

So, what was my love life like during my Brian Wilson years, you ask? Pretty much non-existent. I carried on a long-distance relationship with somebody I had no business being in a relationship with, no matter the zip code, for nearly two years, because neither of us knew how to say we have nothing in common and this isn't working. She'd visit every other weekend, and during these visits, we would... well, we would be together and be apart at the same time. No real connective tissue between us. But we didn't know how to say it.

I never looked for anything else during this time, though the relationship finally ended when she told me she couldn't decide between me, her other boyfriend, or her girlfriend.

Before that relationship started and after that relationship imploded, I tried going the personal ad route.

This led to:

- Extreme maintenance and subterfuge trying to get the phone bill before my roommates—and major embarrassment if/when I failed and had to cop to making "900" calls.
- Calls answering ads in which I would say something utterly stupid and not receive a return call.
- Calls replying to *my* ads in which I would say something utterly stupid and not receive a second call.
- First dates in which I would say something utterly stupid and get a, "Uh... maybe," about a second date, followed by radio silence.

I also tried the bar route often, and frequently found myself sitting alone, hoping someone would come up to me because I was too paralyzed with shyness and awkwardness to approach anyone else. Note that I had no skill with reading signals, so I had no conception of whether or not a given girl was checking me out. Plus, I'd sometimes place one call too many after receiving radio silence, thus leading to further rejection and humiliation.

So yeah, I was far from having my life together. Case in point: I used to wash my clothes in Snuggle because I didn't know it wasn't detergent (I just liked Snuggle is all). I had few friends and suspect social skills. I was basically a steaming pile of mess. But I knew that eventually, I'd get myself together and make something of myself. For now, though, I needed to live out my Brian Wilson years, and these proved to pretty grim times. I was rail-thin from smoking like a fiend and eating little more than peanut butter sandwiches, peanut M&Ms, PowerBars, and fast food. Wednesdays were great, however: the McDonald's at Government Center had $0.39 cheeseburgers. I could *eat*!

Most nights, I'd eat out because I couldn't cook and I usually had a bounced check on my record at Star Market. Oh, the joys of walking a mile to the store in sleet or freezing rain, slinking up to the customer service counter with my INSF letter, and having the clerk bellow, "Ah, ya bounced one, ah?"

Dignity? What?

Wednesdays were also the days I bought bags of coffee at the Green Mountain stand at Downtown Crossing because the kid who usually worked Wednesdays didn't know the prices and I could get a pound for $6.99, or sometimes $5.99—a nice haircut off the usual $9.99.

Not proud of it now, but I did my best as I was equipped at the time.

I tried cooking a few times, and the culmination of my incompetence was the night I fucked up dough-in-a-can.

I repeat: I fucked up dough-in-a-can.

To elaborate: I decided I didn't want my usual DiGiorno frozen pizza, and wanted to try making one. Apparently, I didn't have any bounced checks on my record at Star Market at that time, so I bought myself sauce, a bag of shredded cheese, and a Pillsbury dough-in-a-can—and, with that, I brought my ingredients home, excited to finally become a gourmet, opened the can, plopped out the dough, rolled it out... rolled it out... and tore a hole in the dough.

Basically, I couldn't figure out how to pinch the dough back together, so I just kept rolling it out, trying to squeeze it back together... but no soap.

Turned out I'd be earning no Michelin stars that night.

I must've given up and ordered yet-another sub, because once you fuck up dough-in-a-can, believe me when I say your culinary aspirations are pretty much dashed. (Tangent: I was thinking of this ignoble incident when I—much later—was improvising a linguine with bacon and caramelized shallots. Once again, I have triumphed over trauma. We continue...)

Basically, at this time, I bounced around (like my checks) from roommate to roommate and job to job, obsessing over classic jazz, American punk, Charles Bukowski novels, Kerouac stories, COPS and Red Sox baseball, Bruins hockey, Celtics basketball, and Patriots football all the way. In the spring of 1999, I had pneumonia for seven weeks because a) I couldn't quit smoking and b) I didn't have insurance. On my second day of my data entry job at an insurance company, my new boss pulled me away from my non-infected co-workers and said, "Uh, you *do* know that you can go to the emergency room and they'll bill you, right?" Nope, didn't know that!

That job was great, actually: I was on the 56th floor of

the tallest building in Boston with a view running from Copley Square to Beacon Hill to Logan and the open Atlantic beyond. Great job for daydreaming—which I did often.

At Work
56th Floor
Boston
8:42AM
Wednesday
7/07/99

Crystal morning looks like September after the heat breaks. Atlantic shimmer blinding. 51 ½ hours until we hit the 'pike [ed: the girlfriend and I were planning a lifelong dream trip for me: Cooperstown, NY, and the Baseball Hall of Fame. We didn't make it. But I've been many times since], Sox 3 games out, Nomar and Pedro cruising. The grass on the Common is coming back after the rain. Life in the Hub goes on.

My depression carried on for all these years. As seen in the above journal entry, I was able to appreciate beauty, but sustaining such joy was outside of my capabilities. On my walks, I'd often find myself crossing the Massachusetts Avenue

Bridge over the Charles River and counting the Smoots on the sidewalk. The bridge is also known as the Harvard Bridge, and it leads directly to—wait for it—MIT. (Fun fact: one October night in 1958, a group of Lambda Chi Alpha frats decided to measure the length of the bridge using the most convenient available implement: a five-foot seven-inch Lambda pledge named Oliver R. Smoot. They laid Mr. Smoot on the sidewalk on the Cambridge side and started measuring, coming up with a final distance of 364.4 Smoots + one ear. Mr. Smoot later became Chairman of the American National Standards Institute and then President of the International Organization for Standardization, and the Smoot henceforth became an official unit of measurement. The Smoot lines, measured off in ten-Smoot increments, are freshly repainted every year, including the Halfway to Hell Smoot with the arrow pointing to MIT in the center of the bridge. This was my spot.) Behind me, close enough to touch, were the light towers of Fenway Park and the famous Citgo sign; ahead of me, the sweep of the Charles and the dome of MIT. I would stop "Halfway to Hell" and lean over the rail just a bit; just a glance into the murky brown current rushing by below.

I knew I could never do it, but the thought was there. How quick would it be? How painless?

The thing is, I knew it would be painful for others, and I knew that things would eventually get better for me, so I always kept going. Forward. Self-preservation. My depression carried on, but my self-preservation streak always won out. And by 2000, this very streak led me to discover MassCare, a program for low-income residents of the Commonwealth without insurance, and I signed up. From here, I started seeing a shrink at Mount Auburn Hospital, was *finally* officially diagnosed with depression, and started taking Zoloft—and everything eventually started to get better.

Clearly, my life in Boston in my mid- to late-twenties was, in many ways, a mess, but it was a formative period nonetheless, and I rose from those ashes.

Here are a few snapshots of my life from that time.

South Station

My feet in lockstep: the song of the morning. Jackboot corporate march, navigating another detour around ever more construction. My fellow commuters and I, lockstep to offices, feet pounding on the stairs, echoing into the day that will not be free for us. I hate the station in the morning. Hate the Red Line platforms, and the stairs and the detours, the smell of mud and welding sparks, the sound and feel of concrete-busting drills and ball-busting foreman. Plywood barriers, vinyl tarps, broken PA announcing broken trains. Cold concrete of the walls, always the hint of a rebar about to pop out and always a drip of water from the ceiling. I hate the broken station, hate the broken morning.

Until I reach the top of the escalator and emerge in the station proper, under the giant clock, like the old destroyed Penn Station. The light pours in from the floor-to-ceiling windows in front of the tracks, and I'm suddenly liberated from the bowels of commuter hell and gently placed in a grand civic institution and a distant era. I smell coffee from Rosie's Bakery and croissants from Au Bon Pain and fresh flowers. I peruse the stacks of the news stand looking for a book instead of heading for work. I am stimulated and liberated, and the day is new.

After work my head pounds from the day. I return, buy bad food served in cardboard and Styrofoam and find a table in the grand concourse, not wanting to go back to the subway and back to my room and roommates. The voice of the conductor booms through the station, in the most wonderfully enunciated, stilted English I've ever heard.

The PROV I dence local...with stops in... CAN ton... MANS field... AT tle boro... and ... SOUTH... AT tle boro... now boarding on... track... niiiiiiiiiiine

All around the sounds of suitcase wheels, and the good hustle of fleeing from offices and heading home. The automatic doors open to the tracks, and puffs of frigid air hit my table. I don't want to go home. I don't want to go back down into the depths to the subway. I linger, observing, taking it all in.

It is the late 1990s, yet I am sitting in a magnificent temple of rail travel. Like all of Boston, a modern throwback. It's 1998: it could be 1988, it could be 1978, it could be 1948. Rail travel is the constant. This show is better, more noble and fulfilling than anything on television. The show does go on...

I linger, observing, taking it all in, and then descend the escalator to the subway, already looking forward to doing it all over again in the morning.

Cast of Characters

I: The Barker

Summer St. and Melcher, just over the bridge into South Boston where I catch the shuttle bus to the warehouse and my data entry job. That's where The Barker sets up. Sandy brown hair, scraggly beard over a face that looks like the moon, voice shredded from years of unfiltered smokes and yelling over traffic. He has his own signature call, like a home run call.

> *Globes and Heralds!*
> *Times and Wall Streets!*
> *Buy a newspaper!*

It's August 1998, the final days of a roaring hot summer, just before the humidity breaks and the bite of World Series weather settles in. The world is abuzz with McGwire and Sosa and Maris. Every day The Barker has my Herald ready and as I approach, he says, "Got another one yesterday!" I don't need to ask what he means or who he means: the McGwire home run chase is *the* news. As the season ends and the unbreakable 61 is about to fall, The Barker starts to ask, "Ya goin' to the game today?!" I return his ribbing with ribbing, and we banter until my shuttle bus arrives. Just a minute, two minutes, four minutes. Nothing more.

Nothing more, but The Barker is my everyday man, my regular bit player in my daily Boston drama. And even though the protagonist starred in another great baseball city 1,500 miles away, The Barker brought the news home and made the greatest season in the greatest game a Boston association.

II: The Biker
I hear him long before I see him.

In the early morning of Copley Square, having been up all night writing and drinking coffee, I'm sitting at my bench. The great lawn spreads before me, saturated with dew, and beyond is H.H. Richardson's Trinity Church. The city is still and soft, safe for the flutter of pigeons and the thunk of a stack of newspapers dropped on the sidewalk.

I hear him approaching on Boylston St. from the Common. His cry is somewhere between a "WHOOOOOOP!" and a "YOOOOUUUUUUUP!" and he repeats it several times per block. Suddenly he is in view, riding his wheelchair bike like a Big Wheel, orange safety flags flapping in the dawn.

He always wears a gray hooded sweatshirt, and the effect, along with his beard, is like a medieval warrior bedecked in chain mail. He is now on my block of Boylston, between Clarendon and Dartmouth.

"WHOOOOOOP!"...

"YOOOOUUUUUUUP!"...

He passes and continues on toward Mass Ave and the morning continues to brighten.

III: The Vendor

Her flower stand is at the front of the food court in the Prudential Building mall. She's always setting up as I'm passing by, usually on my way back to my brownstone to call in "sick." Jet-black hair, with a Cramps patch on her bag. I like The Cramps, so therefore we'd have a ton in common and we'd get along and fall for each other—if she'd only stop me and say hi, right? Maybe this morning? Maybe tomorrow...

IV: The Bride

Chill October Friday nights bring me a paycheck and a weekend of solitude. I often find myself drawn to Harvard Square, writing and watching the kids. I take note of the clock under the CAMBRIDGE SAVINGS BANK sign and start my dispatches on CSB Time. By the time I leave for the evening, my notebook is full of observations, ashes, and coffee stains.

The best nights are when I see The Eight Foot Bride of Harvard Square. She is a vision of spectral beauty. Black bob wig, porcelain white skin and wedding dress and gloves. She. Does. Not. Move. No movement at all until you drop a donation, at which point she subtly, oh so subtly, hands her donor a flower. She is tranquility in a sea of creeping gentrification, creeping menace, and choking diesel clouds. She is the center of the square.

[ed: Later, after I find success as a Boston musician and find myself in the process, I learn that the Bride is Amanda Palmer, leader and visionary of The Dresden Dolls, and that we have many mutual friends. But I still see her as the beautiful Bride and myself in awed solitude before her.]

V: The Writer

I moved to Boston when I was twenty-four, September 1996, to attend Berklee College of Music. I was alone and very green, with surprisingly limited life and social skills. I stayed for nearly six years, leaving when I was twenty-nine, engaged and a self-made musician and writer. I failed spectacularly as a restaurant worker and delivery boy, failed miserably schlepping credit cards, did very well in the lucrative field of data entry and survived many periods of being "in between positions." I bounced $300 rent checks and slept on floors and wondered if I'd ever amount to anything. I came of age, I made friends, I made myself. I lived dreams and paid forward whatever I could. Boston made me. Boston and her people and her civic institutions. And her characters. These are just a few I met along the way.

At Fenway

It begins as a notion in the afternoon.

I'm deskbound at a call center, listening to irate and distraught insurance policy holders and informing them of their limited rights under the settlement of a class action lawsuit for $11 an hour. I have a 70-page script of legalese before me, and not one page bridges the gap between the answers that exist and the answers they want. I feel like a monster, and I want to visit every last caller and kick puppies in their presence, for all the good I'm doing them. 200 calls in queue throughout my floor. No let-up.

The *Globe* sits on my desk. I scan the box scores from last night, the news and notes, the predicted starters for tonight.

Hmm... maybe...

I step out of the air-conditioned nightmare into blissful east coast summer humidity. Gonna be a beautiful night, the kind you want to be outside for.

Maybe...

On the train, I grab a seat on the left so I can get a view of Dorchester Bay and the rainbow mural on the Boston Gas Tank. It's the largest copyrighted piece of art in the world, and it's a reproduction from the demolished original tank. Supposedly the artist painted a profile of Ho Chi Minh in one of the rainbow bands, but I can't see it. Maybe that's intentional. If I can, I'll grab a seat on the right as we approach Charles St.

so I can take in the view of Boston when the train crosses the Longfellow Bridge.

If I'm still on the train, that is...

Yeah, why not? Ballgame tonight.

At Park St. I abandon my commute and switch to the Green Line. The buzz in my stomach grows as I get closer. Five stops away.

Boylston, Arlington, Copley, Hynes Convention Center, Kenmore Square.

The train is packed. Game night crowd. I get off at Kenmore, hit the top of the stairs and step into an electric summer carnival.

The Vet who plays Hendrix tunes (right-handed) is set up, case open for donations. Unlicensed vendors sell woefully cheap t-shirts, caps and pennants, and the *Boston Baseball* hawkers do a brisk trade. I love their scorecards, so I hand over a buck for a copy. A kid plays the drums on an array of plastic buckets and salvaged industrial parts. Rocker kids heading to see the latest and greatest bands at the clubs on Lansdown sneer, and I pass them by and rejoin the game crowd.

The Citgo sign does its synchronized neon dance across Commonwealth Ave. The sign—removed from its regular spot on top of the left field wall on a television screen—takes on an entirely new persona: a night watchman for the square, guardian of the gate to the suburbs, all-seeing electric eye of Back Bay. It sits atop the Boston University Bookstore with no context, a relic from a distant era, now risen from darkness after the 1980s energy shortage. It is cheap and vulgar, and beautiful and perfect. It is Fenway, it is Boston.

The game day crowd veers left onto Brookline Ave and approaches the bridge over the commuter rail tracks and the Mass Pike. And suddenly there is Fenway. The lights on the towers slowly turn on and John Fogerty plays on the PA. I look left and see the pike, the Prudential and John Hancock towers and all the lights of downtown dancing in the early twilight. I look ahead and see pre-game revelers streaming out of The Cask and Flagon.

Another bucket drummer is set up on the corner of Brookline and Lansdowne, and the air is heavy with the blissful smell of sausages, peppers, and onions. A batting practice ball clears the wall and bounces on Lansdowne, and a group of kids with gloves chases down their treasure. The buzz of excitement in my stomach is out of control.

I get in line at the ticket office on Yawkee Way and scan the huge seating map. Outfield Grandstand seats available. Score! I buy one, head back outside and enter through the turnstile at Gate A.

Into the dark, down the ramps under the grandstands behind the plate. It is cooler and dark in here, with peanut shells crunching under every step. T-shirt stands, beer stands, chowder stands, Fenway Franks and ice cream helmets. I buy two dogs, smear on Gulden's mustard and head up the ramp.

And there is the field, the wall and everything I've dreamed of all winter. The sun catches the edge of the roof above the right field grandstands, casting a glow across Fenway. The organ plays, the whites of the hometown team uniform pops, the kids go crazy. I take my seat under the roof, scarf my dogs, and fill out the lineups on my scorecard.

This is the oldest part of the park, with wooden slat seats that may date to the first game in 1912. The seats face center field, thus I have to crane left to see the mound and plate. They are narrow and hard, and there are poles in my line of vision. Because of the roof I can see nothing above the wall in left. And yet they are among my favorite seats in the house, just because of this coziness and feeling of originality.

A game at Fenway is a collage of a thousand moments that I treasure:

The pause just before the pitch. The pitcher holds the ball, just before the windup. The batter finishes cocking the bat and settles in his stance, ready, waiting. Infielders stop fidgeting and crouch in position like soldiers at attention. It feels like the air has been sucked out of the park. Then the tension is broken with the pitch...

The moment when the BALLS and STRIKES lights on the scoreboard snap off. End of inning, end of rally. Finality. Turn the frame, go get 'em next time.

The slant of the sun across the field, and the approaching night.

The cry of the vendors and the linguistic joy ride that results from a heavy Massachusetts accent. HEY, HUT DUGHS heeeAAAHHH! FRESH POPPED PUP KAHN HEAH!

The feeling that *somebody sat in this very spot and watched Babe Ruth hit.*

Somebody sat in this very spot and watched Ted Williams and DiMaggio. The connection to that history and the history of Boston just outside the walls.

The final out and the exit from the park to a changed world.

Night has come and I wish I had a coat. And I still have to get home. But I have spent the night at Fenway Park, and for a few hours I have left the day, the call center, the irate and the distraught and the trappings of the real world behind. It begins with a notion in the afternoon and ends with the warm glow that comes from a surprise gift. I go home with the feeling that there is nowhere else in the world I would rather have been, and no greater adventure than the one I had getting there.

Curious Liquids
Boston
Early Afternoon
Sunday
8/22/99

I'M GOING RAPIDLY FAR IN THE DIRECTION I DON'T WANT TO GO, AND SLOWLY NOWHERE IN THE DIRECTION I

DO WANT TO GO. LET'S PULL A U! THERE ARE NO TRAFFIC COPS ON THE ROAD OF LIFE.

There it was, fixed in the tangible form of my journal in bold, all-caps handwriting; a clarion call to revolution. My midlife crisis at age twenty-six—or should we say quarterlife crisis?

It was one of the first days of the ending summer that hinted at football rather than baseball, and I was in the basement of Curious Liquids Boston with a latte and journal in front of me.

As it turned out, I actually *wasn't* going rapidly far in the direction I didn't want to go in—things have a way of making sense in retrospect—but, of course, I didn't know that yet; all I knew was that I'd been working 50-plus-hour weeks doing data entry as a temp for the insurance company. My boss seemed to like me, and there was talk of moving me to a permanent position. But, as it would turn out, all the talk was thin, rapidly melting ice.

Curious Liquids was a lovely coffee shop directly across from the State House on Beacon Hill. (Don't go looking for it; it's not there anymore.) The liquids weren't *curious*, exactly, but they were damn good, and there was a stone basement room that felt like an extremely cozy medieval dungeon. I tended to gravitate there on Sundays, when I could kick out on a leather sofa and while away a few hours, writing. I wrote the line above as part of a larger journal entry, and I remember staring at it for a while after I'd written it. Epiphany time! I didn't hear a *hallelujah* chorus, and no sirens, disco balls, or confetti emerged from the ceiling, but I felt a change, and I knew this would be an important moment in one year, five years, ten years; that I would remember it.

So, what direction did I *not* want to go in? In a word, corporate life: button-down, soul-sucking, divide-and-conquer nine-to-five. What direction *did* I want to go in? I wanted to play in a working band again, but bigger than I had before. I'd last played the Augusta cover scene, but I'd have rather drunk hairspray than play *Sweet Home Alabama* for a room full of toothless, backwoods drunks ever again. No; I wanted to play originals in Boston, one of the greatest scenes in America. But I was an outsider, and I needed an in. So, what kind of "in" could I create for myself?

I also wanted (maybe) to write. I'd thought of writing more than a bit—not hard to figure out, considering the rate at which I spilled my guts into my journals!

Then, I had a lightbulb moment: the writing in some of the fan 'zines covering the Boston scene was pretty atrocious. *Maybe I could do that,* I thought. *And, if I'm a writer, it'll be easier to overcome my painful shyness and start circulating among musicians.*

I left Curious Liquids that day and immediately went looking for a copy of *The Noise,* one of the longest running and most prestigious 'zines covering the Boston music scene. I'd never even written for a high school newspaper, and I knew nothing about word count or editing or anything, but I thought I could at least write a little better than some of what I'd seen. So, on Friday, September 10, my temp position with the insurance company ended, marking my descent into instability and depression. But I had a viable reason to hold onto hope this time. The following entry chronicles this time quite nicely:

Everett
8:24PM
Thursday
9/23/99

The sun has set. The elongated harvest moon ascends to the night watch. Summer is gone, literally, figuratively, spiritually. I really felt it today. Brisk, crisp, invigorating. Autumn crawls in from the north. Another nowhere day on the job front. I'm trying to stay optimistic, but it's getting hard when I'm down to 1 box of rice, 1 box of mac & cheese, 1 loaf of bread and about $5.00. I'll deal. Made an unsuccessful venture into town yesterday for a copy of *The Noise*. Great to walk around my old Berklee stomping grounds in gray mist, and to be saved by $0.39 McD's Wednesday burgers (had 3). I felt compelled to watch tonight's sunset from the top of the hill [ed: Gledhill Ave, Everett, MA, which offers an amazing view of Boston in the near distance, or at least did 20 years ago]. Good idea. The dance of colors across the Boston skyline was hypnotizing; imperceptible changes by the minute, by the second. Landmarks eliding in and out of the diminishing light. I love the vantage point offered by the top of the hill. Tonight, it made me think of winter. Of possible upcoming days in Maine, of the days and nights spent on ice-storm induced Whitefield crust before leaving for Brookline, of more simple times. Patchwork memories in the rearview, unmarked roads on the horizon. Hate the uncertainty, but it might come to a prosperous end tomorrow.

After I wrote the above entry, I whipped together a few bogus writing samples and mailed them to *The Noise*. Several days later, the phone rang right in the middle of a riveting episode of *Sally Jessie Raphael* (or was it *Rikki Lake*?), and it was T-Max, publisher of *The Noise*. Upon picking up the receiver, I expected a polite "thanks but no thanks"—but no: I was suddenly a staff writer, assigned to cover *The Noise's* 18th anniversary show at The Middle East Club in Cambridge the following Saturday.

Oh.

Here's how I recorded this momentous occasion:

> Everett
> 3:36PM
> Tuesday
> 9/28/99

Hasn't really sunk in yet, but I'm about to become a published writer. Got the call this afternoon (from T-Max himself) that I'm now on the staff of *The Noise*. Unreal! Westbye the Hack becomes Westbye the Scribe. Beaming with pride, anxious to assimilate myself into the Boston scene. I'm trying to come to terms with my new reality. I'm unemployed, I'm starving, I'm destitute, I'm desperate, but I'm stoked! A far cry on multiple levels from two years ago. I'll take it.

DAY SIX

MAY 13, 2019

Gallup, NM, to Kingman, AZ: 332 miles.
Time Out: Checked out of El Rancho around 6:00AM MST.
Time In: Checked into El Trovatore around 4:00PM MST.

TODAY BROUGHT ONE OF THE most stunning experiences of my life.

I wanted to hit both the Painted Desert/Petrified Forest and the Meteor Crater in Winslow, but by the time I started out, my energy was flagging, and the thought of spending $20 and then $15 for two-plus-hour diversions was a bit much—so I played eenie, meenie, miney, moe, and Mission I became the Painted Desert/Petrified Forest.

Turned out I chose wisely.

I crossed the border from New Mexico into Arizona, past those amazing mesas, gasping at the American southwest unfolding before my eyes. I then got to the park gate at about 6:40AM, 20 minutes before it opened, and sat waiting in Rose while the sun climbed. Around 15 minutes later, cars started queuing at the entrance, and I joined them and handed over my debit card to a snap-brimmed ranger (I love ranger uniforms... mostly I guess because it indicates there are, indeed, still rangers, which means our national parks—our greatest idea—are still holding on, in spite of our best efforts to demolish them). The layout at the Painted Desert/Petrified Forest is basically the same as my own Acadia National Park on Mount Desert Island, Maine: at Acadia, you enter the park and follow the Park Loop Road throughout, pulling off for scenic vistas every few yards, seemingly, and the same was the case here: from I-40, you followed the park road southwest to Rt. 180, which got you back onto I-40.

First stop: Tiponi Point.

Some moments you just know, even at the time, will stay with you forever. And this was one of those: I got out of Rose and stood at the overlook in the soft, muted southwestern morning, not a soul around (save for the birds happily chirping at the new day), the view of the rolling mesas and buttes all my own.

The feel of summer vacation in America; road trips and memories.

I'd never seen the southwest like this, and it was a gut-punch of natural beauty and wonder. And it was *all mine.* I'll never get over these moments—not that I would ever want to.

I inched along the road slowly, taking in every turnoff: Kachina Point; Chinde Point; Pintado Point; Nizhoni Point; Whipple Point; Lacy Point; and crossed back over I-40 and onto the Petrified Forest: Newspaper Rock; The Tepees; Agate Rock; Jasper Forest; Crystal Forest; Martha's Butte; The Flattops... I spent about an hour and a half driving the 28 miles of park road feeling as if I were navigating a surrealist dreamscape. And as I crawled along, I took stock and prioritized.

In those moments, I realized how important preservation is—and that I would like to be involved in it. Okay, so I was already a big believer in preservation, but my views were reinforced tenfold along this drive. From the groundswell of appreciation and support I'd witnessed on this trip for Route 66 in general—as a physical mode of transport and as an idea and a spirit and a concept and a dream—to the neon restoration in Tulsa to the national parks along the way, I realized we are in an age where we're acknowledging what is important and what is worth keeping and fighting for. And we're realizing that the things we cherish are not mere commodities: they hold worth far beyond potential dollar signs. The Meadow Gold sign in Tulsa is invaluable because it has been part of the landscape of Tulsa for 80 years, not just because it sits on top of a building that can be destroyed and turned into yet another Best Buy or glass-and-steel condo; the Gemini Giant is invaluable because it has been part of the community of Wilmington, IL, for 60 years, not because you could sell it for scrap and put the money toward a cheaper new LED sign; and our national parks are invaluable because they are there, formed over millions of years by Earth, wind, fire, and water, not because you could drill and frack and squeeze an hour of oil out of the ground. The Meadow Gold Sign and Gemini Giant and Painted Desert/Petrified Forest are worth fighting for because they are there, and we need them.

In Ken Burns' 1981 debut film *Brooklyn Bridge*, the brilliant *New Yorker* magazine critic Paul Goldberger paraphrases architect Louis Kahn in his statement, "Great art is not the fulfilling of a desire but the making of a new desire. The world never really needed Beethoven's Fifth Symphony until he wrote it, and now we couldn't live without it." And in the same way, The Dairy Deelite could have planted a campaign sign in the grass announcing their opening, and residents of Wilmington, IL, still would have flocked there for a cone, but instead, they installed the Gemini Giant, and now, we can't imagine the Launching Pad without it; The Meadow Gold Dairy could have published a small newspaper ad for their products, and that would've been good enough, but they instead erected the Meadow Gold sign, and now, we can't imagine Tulsa without it.

The bottom line is, we can't imagine American life

without Route 66, and we can't imagine Route 66 without any of these icons. Because they are all there, and we need them.

I realized this all the more in this moment, as I drove through this foreign American wonderland, and I also felt a ridiculously strong call to help preserve the rest. We need to restore *all* our national parks to their original glory; we should try to save *every* fifty-year-old neon sign we can; we should celebrate Route 66 and ensure that it remains navigable and well-signed and vibrant; we should help out mom-and-pop businesses that are struggling under the crushing weight of shrinking profit margins in Big Box land. *This* is what we should be investing in, not tax breaks for new Walmarts.

I eventually got back onto I-40 and balled that jack, with thoughts of the Real America dancing in my head and Dokken on the juke, and I thought of how I would remember this experience for the rest of my life.

It was while I was thinking along these lines that I realized I was able to pinpoint the exact moment in my childhood when I realized how important it is to hold onto the moment: it was summer 1984 on Tacoma Lake, Litchfield, Maine. Since 1978, our family friends, the Moreaus, had lived on the lake, and we were frequent visitors: they had lake access, a dock, and a nifty little boat (a mustard-yellow six-seater). The Moreaus were often at the Homestead for cookouts, and we were often at the lake for aquatic downtime in kind. On this night, my brother Eric and our friend Rick, both two years my senior, as well as Rick's father Lenny and five-year-old brother Scott, were drifting on the lake, outboard motor cut off. The sun was starting to go down in summer pastels, and a low trail of smoke from campfires and charcoal hung over the lake. Surrounding the dead-calm water were perfectly manicured lawns, cabins, houses, dark woods, and gentle hills, one with an antenna that I always focused on; I loved watching the aerial light blink.

A wood-paneled cruiser passed us slowly, its engine making a gentle *put-put* noise that was perfectly befitting the serene moment.

We'd been cruising and playing, and now, we were just *being*, slowing down to take in the lake and the light and this gloriously perfect early summer evening in Maine. Jim Croce's *Time in a Bottle* was running through my head, and in that moment, at eleven years old, I had a revelation: *I get it.* I suddenly understood the feeling of wanting to lock important memories and hold onto them forever; I got the importance of holding onto these things—these esoteric moments—and keeping them safe.

Time is never immaterial. All we have is right now. Hold onto it. You'll need it later.

And now, cruising along I-40, I realized how much that memory was guiding my current journey.

But back to our narrative.

There were 250-odd miles between Gallup, NM, and

Kingman, AZ—but first, a quick ADD stop at Jack Rabbit Trading Post in Jack Rabbit, more for a pic of the *HERE IT IS* sign than anything else.

Jim Taylor opened the store in 1949, on the site of what might have been a Santa Fe Railroad depot. The name came from a statue of a rabbit Taylor happened to own, which he later decided to install outside the store.

The rabbit is still there, as is the *HERE IT IS* sign, which is faithfully repainted every few years.

Taylor proceeded to lease the store out, including to the Blansett family, who bought the trading post in 1967—and that family has been running it ever since.

I headed in and instantly felt a little put off by all the *DO NOT TOUCH* signs. I understood that kind of thing, but it still kind of rubbed me up the wrong way. I was a big kid; I could comport myself responsibly without going through toilet training, y'know? But whatever.

Next, I drove past the Meteor Crater (next time!) and was onto Mission II: Standin' on a Corner Park in Winslow, AZ. While it's a nicely done spot, I wouldn't detour more than 20 miles for it; truth is, there ain't much at all going on in Winslow, AZ. Oh, and as it turns out, the girl (my Lord) in a flat-bed Ford that slowed down to take a look at Jackson Brown? Yeah, as he admitted, she was actually in a Toyota pickup at a Der Wienerschnitzel in Flagstaff. "Creative license", they call it. Thanks for *lying* to us, Jackson Brown!

I cruised the rest of the way through Winona and

Flagstaff, which was the site of (miraculously) the only traffic snarl on the trip—*but* I was treated to the amazing Humphreys Peak and the Kachina Peaks on the way, and Flagstaff was also the site of the first Los Angeles sign: 465 miles, I believe. That really brought the trip home, and I sat in the bottleneck feeling that big, dumbass grin spreading yet again.

And then it was Seligman for Mission III: Delgadillo's Snow Cap.

Juan Delgadillo built a drive-in in 1953 out of scrap material from the Santa Fe Railroad yard. He parked a 1936 Chevy in the parking lot, sliced off the top, and planted a Christmas tree in the back—and yes, people noticed. Juan had a wicked sense of humor, asking his customers if they wanted cheese on their cheeseburger and offering "dead chicken" on the menu—and when he died in 2004, his family took over the business and continued his spirit of mirth.

In terms of pure fun, this may be one of the most memorable lunches of my life: it was crazy-busy at noon, so I parked way in the back and walked over, past the Dead Chicken marquee and the *Sorry, We're Open* signs. Spoiler alert: the left doorknobs—the ones under the *PULL* sign—don't work. I (eventually) got in via the right knobs and ordered a Bob Dog (short and fat, six inches) with "everything" (mustard, mayo, ketchup, relish, onions; "everything" on the burgers, per the menu, includes "mustard, mayonnaise, ketchup, pickles, onions, lettuce, tomato, and if you're lucky, the meat"), fries, and a marshmallow shake. The girl at the counter pulled out a regular soda cup and a ketchup cup and asked if I wanted a large or a small. "The small is a great deal!" she added. "You get free refills!"

Okay, I'm cracking up already.

I sat at a table in the baking Arizona sun, chuckling at the *KETCHUP... if you can* bin and at everybody else cracking up at this amazing American joint.

And, of course, I gorged on my 'dog and fries (with one smiley fry on top, always) and left with that big, dumbass grin leading me on. And outside of Seligman, I saw one of the biggest dumbass grin-inducing sights of the trip: a Burma-Shave jingle. The Burma-Shave shaving cream company started placing jingles—in the form of five-to-six sign verses—along national routes, including 66, in 1926. The series I was looking at was obviously a recreation (it was in great shape), but still! It read:

> (**Sign One**) Don't lose
> (**Sign Two**) Your head
> (**Sign Three**) To gain a minute
> (**Sign Four**) You need your head
> (**Sign Five**) Your brains are in it
> (**Sign Six**) Burma-Shave

This jingle was from the 1947 campaign, and the campaigns ran until 1963. What an amazing bit of Americana to drive by!

So, not much else to say for Arizona, other than a breathtaking drive through Navajo country. I got into Kingman (70 miles on from Seligman) in the afternoon and hit the front desk at El Trovatore. The receptionist was extremely knowledgeable about the hotel and its history, and gave me yet another who's-who list: James Dean, Marlon Brando, Marilyn Monroe, The Three Stooges... they didn't have the original registries, so they weren't quite sure who'd stayed in what room, but she gave me the James Dean room, and I'll just presume that he actually did stay there. And I must say, it was a very nice room: hardwood (or at least Pergo), refrigerator, James Dean posters, etc. The bathroom, on the other hand, was bewildering and a bit terrifying: vintage pedestal sink with mirror on the left and toilet ahead, and on the right, an ancient white porcelain tub with seafoam green tiles. The tub had some kind of cover over it, and the effect was like a coffin. Comforting! To the left of the sink was an archway with a shower curtain, and beyond that was a shower in a massive chamber that felt like a crypt. The floor and walls were all subway tile, so it also felt kind of like a giant coal pizza oven. Bizarre. I was getting Cask of Amontillado vibes, waiting to be entombed in my shower or burned alive and stuffed into the tub.

So, I left the bathroom.

I'd been given a few suggestions for dinner, but I wasn't very hungry after lunch, and I was kind of burnt out, so I just got back into Rose and drove around Route 66 and Beale Street aimlessly for a while. In doing so, I drove by the Arizona Route 66 Museum, and thought about it, but nah; not enough steam. I did see the Kingman Rt. 66 sign with all the directions, however (*E CHICAGO, IL 1805 MILES; W LOS ANGELES CA 274 MILES*, etc.) and the drive-through Kingman Route 66 sign. Great. Fine. Not much more by way of enthusiasm, however: by this time, I was pretty fried and beaten, so I headed back to the room (avoiding the haunted-looking bathroom) to look for grub options. Nothing was really calling me, so I just got back into Rose and drove around a bit—and eventually, I gave up, picked up some sushi from Safeway, and settled back in for the NHL playoffs.

Living it up in Kingman!

I had to head back out for a few nighttime shots of the neon tower sign and the roadside marquee, though:

E
L
T
R
O
V
A
T
O
R
E

It totally reminded me of the old sign on the Rt. 1 Brunswick of my youth:

M
A
C
L
E
A
N
'S

I felt a little choked up thinking back on that.

Back in the room, I was thinking of the trip thus far and my life at that moment. There had been no major mishaps so far: I'd made it halfway across the country by myself without incident.

Amazing.

And I had a job and a house and a lakefront camp and two paid off cars. God knew I was a long way away from bouncing $300 rent checks and fucking up dough-in-a-can! I'd gotten myself together—and that reminded me of an incident that changed my life for the better in the summer of 1997...

Leigh, Jason, and I were out in Harvard Square for some kind of hijinks. I was having some issues with cashflow (shock)—something like not being able to withdraw cash, or something—and I was pissy about it. Leigh at this point told me, "You're not taking control of your life." One, ouch. Two, he was right, and I *knew* he was right, and I knew he gave enough of a shit to be honest. I trusted Leigh was being honest because I trusted Leigh and I trusted he cared enough to bring tough love. And I took the advice to heart.

That may well just be the moment when I started to turn my shit around.

And here I was, in Kingman, AZ, on the trip of a lifetime. Well played, Leigh, and thank you.

A good end to an amazing day.

CHAPTER 7
ALIGNMENT IN THE CHAOS

FROM THE POINT OF MY being recruited at *The Noise*, I started writing live performance and CD reviews, and slowly but surely started circulating. I landed in several bands playing originals in Boston and recorded several CDs, and got a decent amount of airplay. And this led me to not only propel myself in the direction I *wanted* to go in, but to also meet a certain special someone: of all the friends I've made along the way, I've never known a life force like Michael D. Linick.

I was twenty-seven and older than my years when I met Mikey Dee. Mikey was an editor at *The Noise*, and I'd seen his name on thank-you lists in various liner notes. Bigtime Boston, at last!

Anyhow, I got an email from Mikey addressed to "Mikey's Pals" inviting me to a party at his apartment for his roommate Tina's thirty-third birthday. I was so painfully shy and socially awkward that I thought he might have invited me by mistake, so I called his office at the Planetary Group (where he was Director of Radio Promotions) at 8PM, or some such ridiculous hour, figuring there was no way he'd be there and that I could leave a voicemail.

And then he answered the phone.

Shit.

"Um, well," I stammered at his upbeat greeting, "I haven't been on-staff for long, so I just wanted to make sure that invite wasn't a mistake..."

"No way, man!" he said, amazed at my emerald green. "C'mon out!"

So, I shut off the demon screams and forced myself to take advantage of this opportunity. Life falls out of the sky and into our laps. I went to the party, and we became fast friends.

Mikey Dee was a writer, editor, DJ on WMFO Tufts, actor with Boston Rock Opera, radio promotions tsunami, and fierce advocate for the Boston scene. He was a lifeforce: a respectful Jew who devoured pulled pork from Redbones, a fanatic of all things Hollywood, and a delightful cad (his take on... subtropical interactions with Amazon redheads: "I'd pack a lunch and stay all day!"). He was out at live shows six nights a week, always front and center, air-drumming like mad and having the time of his life—every day except for Sunday ("It's a day of rest!"), when he'd be home making his famous breakfast bonanzas, doing the *Times* crossword, and generally chilling. If he didn't like your band, he'd play you anyway and say, "You *could* be great—*if...*" and if he loved your band, he'd use his benevolent pulpit to shout, "*Best band in Boston!*"

And he took *me* under his wing. *Me*! Who the fuck was I to get such friendly treatment from such an untouchable?

One night, I had the balls to say to Mikey that I, at twenty-seven, felt old. Mikey sized me up in a nanosecond and said, "You're what, twenty-seven? Well, I've got *ten years* on you, and I'm still rocking."

So subtle are these gifts so gently offered. The message was straight-up Andy Dufresne in *The Shawshank Redemption*: get busy living, or get busy dying.

That one throwaway line, proffered out of love on an unassuming night in the late autumn of our lives in 1999, changed my life and worldview. And God knows I didn't have much time to steep myself in his wisdom, in his lust for life: Mikey had a congenitally narrowed aorta, and in February 2000, he was scheduled to have a stent put in at Boston Children's Hospital. A quick procedure: one night in, and a few weeks of rest at home. No big deal. Only Tina called me at 4AM of that day, three months after we'd all met, crying, "Mikey didn't make it through the procedure!"

I was on the first subway to the hospital.

Three massive brainstem strokes. At age thirty-seven.

I'd arrived at the beginning of Mikey Dee's new life, and I was there for the first 36 hours of it, from the first utterances of the word "stroke" to the talk of "baselines" and "prognosis" and well beyond.

From that moment, a group of friends came together, dubbed "Team Dee", and we fought like hell and did everything possible to keep him fighting. Mikey's strokes had left him in a locked-in state—cognitively all there, but unable to speak or move—yet we did everything we could, moving him to Spaulding Rehab Boston and instituting Sunday Singalongs at Spaulding.

If you were at that hospital on any given Sunday during that time, you'd have seen anyone from T-Max (publisher of *The Noise*) to Boston rock mainstays Sean O'Brien, Linda Jung, Lynette Estes, Linda Viens, and Pete Sutton, to Boston Rock Opera founders Eleanor Ramsay and Mick Mondo, to Kay Hanley and Mike Eisenstein (from Letters to Cleo), to Gary Cherone (from Extreme and Van Halen), to Sir David Minehan (from The Neighborhoods), all strumming an acoustic and singing *Beatles* songs at eleven while our wheelchair-bound friend Mikey bobbed along internally.

No publicity; no big deal at all; just what we do for one of our own.

At first, I felt completely responsible for Mikey's wellbeing: I informed all of Mikey's pals of every millisecond of movement and every "blink once for yes, twice for no" movement. I wanted to be there every nanosecond of every day and never let anyone down, ever. I tried to be the rock for Team Dee, never mind the fact that I'd only known the guy for three months. After a while, however, Andrea came along and I distanced myself a bit from Team Dee, although my band played alongside 140 bands for the second round of the "For The Benefit of Mr. Dee!" shows in 2001, and I visited whenever I could.

Lesson learned: life is fleeting and transient. Don't take anyone or anything for granted.

By the time I got to Somerville, MA, in the spring of 2001, I was sleeping on the floor. It became a running joke—"I'm really tired. I'm gonna go to floor"—though my best friend, Lexi, lent me her twin guest cot at this time, and I was beyond grateful and amazed that she actually had *furniture*. *Spare* furniture, no less!

Then, by March 2001, the band was in Blast Furnace mode—absolutely cooking. We were preparing to record our second EP with Minehan, and we'd been selected to compete in the WBCN Rock 'n Roll Rumble. (Past alumni include Letters to Cleo, Powerman 5000, Morphine, Blake Babies, Mission of Burma, and 'Til Tuesday.) We were eliminated in the first round, but no matter; we'd still *made it*.

During this time, Lexi, my editor at *The Noise*, encouraged me to follow her lead and start blogging. She was doing it on a site called Diaryland.com, and I respected her writing and opinion like crazy (and still do)—so, I launched and connected with her and another mutual friend... who happened to be connected to a gal in Seattle. This mutual friend had run across Seattle Gal's blog via a random search for The Psychedelic Furs.

I started reading Seattle Gal's blog, and she returned my connection, and, after a few weeks of following one another, we started corresponding offline. And in April, I gave her a call.

We talked for three hours—and then did it again.

Sometime around then, Seattle Gal (a.k.a., Andrea) asked what I was doing over Memorial Day weekend. She had a severance package, and had never seen Boston.

So, on Friday, May 25, 2001, she stepped off her flight at Logan, and by Sunday night, we were discussing who would move where.

Boston won out.

(Fun fact: remember my mantra that life falls out of the sky and into our laps? Well, when Andrea was boarding at Sea-Tac that morning, the gate agent pointed out something rather unfortunate: she'd purchased a round-trip ticket *for the same day*—her *return* day. She whipped out her debit card on the spot... and purchased the last seat on the flight to Boston. Clearly, sometimes things are just supposed to happen. We continue...)

So, Andrea flew out for one more long weekend in July before, on Friday, August 17, 2001, I flew out to Seattle to pack her Capitol Hill one-bedroom into a ten-foot Ryder (we named him Mortimer) and head east. My first time on the west coast, first time in Seattle, first time seeing the Mississippi.

I think we'd arrived in Minneapolis by the time we learned each other's middle names. The endeavor went something like this:

Day One

I-90 E
Washington State
6:45PM PST
Tuesday
8/21/01

45 min outside of Seattle. The rain beats on and the Snoqualmie Pass waits to be conquered. The landscape is high and breathtaking, and I can only rely on the mind's eye to see beyond the lowering clouds. The rest of America lies in wait. We're finally on the road.

Made it to Moses Lake, WA near the Idaho border around 9:30, and found our first Motel 6.

Day Two

I-94 E
Montana
10:58AM MST
Thursday
8/23/01

Riding shotgun just outside of Miles City, MT. We conquered just about all of Montana in one dizzying stretch yesterday, and now it's Fargo to go. Film in the camera, Town Pump cappuccino for fuel, Big Sky stretching ahead as we push 70 in a 10' Ryder. The landscape is beyond breathtaking, and after endless hours, very boring. Hell of a lot of images along the way, though. Time will present itself for a thorough discourse in Fargo (which should be a world unto itself).

Motel 6
Fargo, ND
Night
Thursday
8/23/01

Oh ja, we made Fargo, youbetcha. Just got

connected to AOL, Motel 6 style, and all is amazing. Was I a bit too fried to update last night? After 15 hours in a Ryder, and at least 12 in Montana, yes, I was. We left Moses Lake at 7:35AM, wired on gas station cappuccinos, '60s bubblegum and '80s cheese radio. Idaho: beautiful at first, the downside of Lookout Pass, very steep and winding, nothing but Jesus radio—"a wholesome alternative to secular radio". Fucking boring, looks like the scenery at Big Thunder Mountain. Western Montana: Lolo National Forest, very green and hilly, trains passing under mountains <u>monogrammed</u> with the town name (A for Albertson). Missoula: Americana outpost on the flats. Target, Best Buy, Hardee's, a sushi joint. Lunch at Perkins: crewcut/mustache service with a flat laconic tang ("Ho's it gon' forya t'dey?"). Hot but dry, a soft haze looming above the vast plains and monogrammed mountains. Butte to Bozeman: The Rockies. Winding downhill through jagged peaks and scrub brush, the sun descending over the hills and far away smoke from Wyoming forest fires. As darkness fell on the way to Billings the quest to make Miles City was agreed upon...

Day Three

Motel 6
Roseville, MN
Night
Friday
8/24/01

I picked up the drive at a travel stop somewhere before Billings. Two things hit me at that outpost on the plains. A: I was totally out of place for *not* wearing a cowboy hat. B: Just how far from home I was geographically, mentally, etc. But it's good to have that kind of opportunity for a shift in perspective, and I'm certainly better off. I loaded up on cappuccino and prepped for the drive. We made industrial refinery Billings and crossed over onto I-94 E pushing 75-80-85 in Mortimer across the deserted night of Montana. Exhilarating, liberating. Construction delays, grooved roads, not a soul competing for highway space. Pulled over to see the stars, the Milky Way hovering brighter than I've ever known in the Big Sky night. Pulled into Miles City at 11:30 MST. Fucking unreal. 15 hours, three states, nearly all of Montana in one day. Total insanity on the plains. So, precedent set, we decided to conquer all of North Dakota in one day, landing in Fargo. Left Miles City around 9:30 and a full lifetime of found images. Today we saw The Badlands, The Grasslands, The Painted Canyon. There's not a single human word I could use to describe the scene, nor the way my life has been altered for the better. Nevertheless, I felt it in a hot wind blowing off the prairie. I'll never be the same, that's for shit sure. The land flattened out into grassland, and then a tangible line was crossed. Somewhere around Bismarck a body of water appeared, and the topography shifted into the eastern climes. The dry hot west was accomplished and done. Got to Fargo 'round 8:30 and set out for the Ponderosa. Oh, we got our culinary girth on. Took a stroll around Fargo, then back to the room with the North Dakota news.

Got to the Fargo Amoco this morning for fuel (gas and large cups of Seattle's Best) and I got two lines for a lifetime: to me, asking for directions back to I-94 E; (in a

perfect Coen Brothers accent) "You goin'
back Minneapolis wey?" and in the
background, a phone conversation; (also in
a perfect Coen Brothers accent) "Ooh, they
just *loved* the cheese curds!" THAT'S Fargo,
damnit.

Day Four

> Motel 6
> Amherst, OH
> Sunday
> 8/26/01

Crossed the border at Moorhead and on
through the bucolic Nordic farmland of
northern Minnesota. Lunch at Hardee's in
Sauk Center (another place I read about in
Travels with Charley when I was twenty-
two), got to the Motel 6 Roseville, caught the
260 bus downtown and I think it's safe to say
we both hit the same wall at the same time.
Got off the bus at 2nd St just after Saint
Anthony Falls on the Mighty Mississippi.
Cruised over to Nicollet Ave, First
Avenue/7th Street Entry, the club where
Prince, Hüsker Dü, The Replacements and

Soul Asylum put Minneapolis on the music map in the '80s, a little skyway action, and some frozen goods from Dunn Brothers Coffee, and... back to Applebee's! (Two Tequila Lime Chicken, Margaritas) We'll have to come back: too fried to get an impression other than it reminds me of New York and smells like thousands of dead pigeons and burnt popcorn. I don't want it to be like that but with the amount of time (or lack thereof), we'll have to make up for it down the road.

Day Five

Motel 6
Amherst, OH
Sunday
8/26/01

Saturday: Left Roseville in the gray morn', through MPLS/St. Paul to the Wisconsin border. Beautiful rolling farm country and lakes. And more beautiful rolling farm country and lakes. And more beautiful... Gray spits of rain and lunch at Perkins Tomah, surrounded by college football yahoos, a White Supremacist couple, and Jeffrey Dahmer (or the splitting image of him, working as a busboy). I drove through a tornado-spawning deluge in Madison, and our toll was taken by John Wayne Gacy's identical twin at the start of the Northwest Tollway [ed: banner day for serial killer lookalikes!]. Traffic around O'Hare, hopelessly lost getting to the Motel 6 Elk Grove Village. An hour wait for the Pace bus to O'Hare, 45 minutes on the Blue Line, and we were standing on Lake and Clark under the El, heading toward Wacker Dr. Over to State St. past the Chicago Theater to Michigan Ave in the shadow of the Wrigley Building and the Chicago Tribune Building. Crossed the river on Wabash and made our way over to Pizzaria Due. Chi deep-dish *in* Chi. Doesn't get much better than that. We both took turns nodding off on the train, a delirious sleep at the Motel 6 under the O'Hare flight path. Hopelessly lost getting back to I-90 E. I somehow managed to get us alive through Chi traffic, potholes and assholes on the Dan Ryan Expressway, and on to Indiana. There was a strong undercurrent of menace in the glare of the Indiana redneck who was staring down me and my maroon Chuck Taylors. Pleasant! On to Ohio.

Day Six

Farms, farms, farms, and tolls. Sketchy restaurants at sketchy rest areas, putrid looking mud in the carafe. Olde Tyme Shaker vibe: I hate Olde Tyme Shaker anything. Road burnout settling in as we pound across the rain-soaked heartland of our America. Original target for today: Buffalo. Revised target: Applebee's, Caribou Coffee and not-quite Cleveland. Hotel dryer is broken, and the funk from the tainted laundry bag ain't getting any better. But the end of the line is in sight and we're having the time of our lives, getting our groove on.

Well, the journal ends here, but from Amherst, OH, we made it to Utica, NY, stopping at Niagara Falls on the way. In Utica, we hit up another Motel 6 and ventured out to the adjacent Pizza Hut—and promptly crashed.

By this stretch, our four-hour driving shifts were reduced to two, and then one—and then, finally, we crawled back to Boston.

We arrived at my apartment in Somerville on Monday, August 27, 2001. The band was playing at House of Blues that night—but first, to check the mail.

There were two letters awaiting me:

1. An end-of-position letter from my temp agency.
2. A note from my landlord alerting me another payment had bounced. "Your rent being in arrears, your tenancy will hereby be terminated as of..."

So, we were *both* unemployed and facing eviction.

Welcome home!

DAY SEVEN

MAY 14, 2019

Kingman, AZ, to Santa Monica, CA: 335 miles.
Time Out: Checked out of El Trovatore around 7AM MST.
Time In: Checked into the Super 8 LAX around 3:30PM PST.

L AST DAY OF BUST-ASS driving. The last stretch! Next
stop: Santa Monica, the End of the Trail.
On the morning of Day Seven, I left El
Trovatore, hit up Beale Street Brews Coffee Shop,
wondering if I was actually in Memphis, and headed for
Mission I: Oatman, AZ, 28-odd miles down the line.

Little did I know that I was about to embark on the
most harrowing drive of my life: Sitgreaves Pass.

This pass through a gap in the Black Mountains on the
original Route 66 sits at 3,586' above sea level, and it is a

motherfucker—especially when you have no idea that it's coming! The first thing I noticed was that the speed limit dropped significantly... and then I noticed how close I'd come to flying off the side of the goddamn mountain—and by then I was on a gnarly hairpin. And then another, and another, and...

A little panicked, I slowed down to nothing and, for one of the few times in my life, considered praying. And then, I noticed occasional mailboxes. People fucking *lived* on this stretch of paved madness! Just... just...

After what felt like an eternity (but was probably only about 15 minutes), I was on the strip in Oatman waiting for a group of "feral" burros to arrive and wondering whether it'd be better to die in a fiery mountainside car wreck or be nibbled alive by a jackass. The front desk clerk at El Trovatore told me that the burros arrived like clockwork at around 8AM and leave at around 4:30PM.

I got to Oatman at around 7:45AM and parked, shaking just a bit. And then, once my nerves had calmed, I took in my surroundings.

Oatman, AZ, looks like an abandoned spaghetti Western set. There was one guy mucking out the dirt road and piling the bounty into the back of a Silverado. Well, that's encouraging!

I sat composing myself and counting superfluous apostrophes, wondering how I'd found myself at Big Thunder Mountain. And wondering where the hell the promised burros were.

8AM... no burros. 8:10AM... no burros. 8:15 AM... no burros. The little bastards were late! How dare they!

At 8:20AM, I was just about to bail when I heard an ungodly braying and, a few minutes later, saw a mangy-looking gray ass strolling into town in my rearview.

Okay, then! I wasn't going to hold their disregard for punctuality against them—so I drove a little closer and got out, and the one burro (gray/brown and trailing flies) wandered past to get some breakfast. After a few minutes, he wandered back over to the general store, stood on the porch, and then came over to Rose. I gave a few tentative scritches... and then the son of a bitch tried to get into the car.

Hells no! I was *not* about to be carjacked by a burro.

I had to give it a little swipe on the face, and eventually, he backed off—and with that, I counted my blessings (this morning was all about the Lord, apparently), jumped in, and slammed the door.

Good show, Oatman: thanks for the memories. Now onto Californ-i-a!

I cruised through Topock, crossed the Colorado river, and, 20-odd miles beyond Oatman, I was in Needles, California, home of Snoopy's brother, Spike. I already knew it from visiting San Diego, but California was still just a dream: the warmth; the softness of the air; the floral wonderland; the scent of citrus and eucalyptus everywhere... though it was also a special kind of nightmare, considering gas was $4.99 a gallon and a cool day in the Mojave was a relentless 95 degrees—and I hadn't gotten to LA traffic yet. I filled up, cringing and sweating, and headed for Mission II: Roy's Café & Motel in Amboy.

En route, the surrealness of my current reality hit me hardcore (again): *I'm driving through the Mojave.* Everywhere I looked were endless salt plains and Joshua Trees. An amazing sight.

I pulled off I-40 at Exit 100 (I think) and nearly drove right into a *ROAD CLOSED* sign. Damn! No Amboy! My heart sank a bit, and with that, I had no choice but to get back on I-40; I was meeting a friend for dinner in Glendale, and had to check in at the Super 8 LAX first, so time was a little tight.

Oh well. I'd be back.

But wait... what do I see? Exit 78! Open! Pretty much a straight shot to Amboy. Rock on!

It was here that I got tired of fading stations, and so I switched to my iTunes library—and turned out the gods of shuffle play were smiling down on me: the soundtrack of the Mojave now, to me, will forever be Swing Out Sister's *Somewhere in the World* and *Am I the Same Girl?* (yes, I am! Wait a minute... I mean...)—and for good measure, I even threw on the original Barbara Acklin version of *Am I the Same Girl?* (1968) and the original-original Young-Holt Unlimited instrumental version, *The Soulful Strut* (also 1968). I shuffled through more of my library during the remainder of that stretch of journey, of course, but I'll always associate those big, sunny pop hooks with the big sun of California now.

Life falls out of the sky and into our laps...

Roy Crowl opened a filling station on Rt. 66 in 1938 and later expanded with a service station, café, and auto court in the forties. Then, 1-40 opened in 1972, and Roy's business died overnight. Crowl's son-in-law "Buster" Burris had a nasty reputation for chasing off "undesirables" (like bikers and longhairs) at gunpoint, which kind of didn't help. Even still, Roy's crawled on, and later started being used as a filming location, including in the 1993 Brad Pitt film *Kalifornia*. (Yes, I thought of all our movie nights at Berklee.)

And maybe the funnest fact: the town of Amboy, CA, was put up for sale on eBay in 2003, but there were no takers. Not to worry, however: in 2005, Albert Okura, owner of the Juan Pollo restaurant chain and the original McDonald's museum in San Bernardino, bought the town for $425,000 in cash and set about restoring things. With that, the coffee shop and gas station reopened in 2008, and now, Okura continues to work on restoring the motel.

Preservation rules.

I pulled into Roy's (80 miles beyond Needles) and was instantly amazed: that beautiful retro-future arrow sign; the abandoned rooms at the motor court; the shimmering gray of the original Route 66... magical.

There were a few tourists taking pictures, of course, and I joined their ranks, though there were very few other people in Amboy, CA: according to *Los Angeles Times*, the population is four. By way of community, there's Roy's (which has been there since 1938) and a post office. That's it.

I headed into Roy's facilities for a leak, where I found a *NO POTABLE WATER* sign.

Well, it is the Mojave—and turns out getting water to Amboy is extremely difficult and cost-prohibitive for that reason. Even still, the gas station is once again open, and Albert Okura is known for building and preservation. A 2013 Kickstarter campaign helped restore the neon sign, and Harrison Ford supposedly flies his plane into Amboy to visit Roy's frequently. So, who knows? Keep an eye on Amboy is what I'm sayin'.

Regardless of lack of potable water, I was there—meaning I'd put myself in *yet another* picture I'd long held in my head. I'd arrived at Roy's after thinking I wouldn't make it—and, from Roy's parking lot (across the salt flats and the Santa Fe railroad), I saw the Amboy Crater, meaning I didn't have to go right up to it. Double winning!

After that brief pause, I kept on I-40 to Barstow, paralleling the railroad tracks. I skipped Elmer's Bottle Ranch (this time, anyway), and then, for the first time since Oklahoma City, I left I-40 and got on I-15. I'd spent four days with I-40 through five states and 1,214 miles, so yeah, I got a little misty leaving it behind: it was like letting go; a little death of a part of me. *La petite mort...* but, y'know, without the post-coital connotations of the term. Anyway, I will always remember I-40 fondly, and I can't wait to drive it again.

Onto Victoriaville and my first In-N-Out experience. Animal Style, at last!

It was quite good; certainly not the *greatest* burger/fries experience of my life, but very tasty—and the best part is that now, I can say I've gone In-N-Out! (That sounded kind of bad, which is probably the point...)

From here, I-15 stretched out through the Angeles National Forest, and the drive was pretty stunning: snowcapped mountains above the scrub grass plains; a gauzy, slanted sun; the landscape shimmering and barren. It didn't register at the time, but I was driving Cajon Pass, between the San Gabriels and the San Bernardinos—an amazing after-the-fact realization. Rancho Cucamonga, West Covina, El Monte... oops. I *think* I wanted to stay on I-15 through Pasadena, but missed an exit somewhere. Fortunately, my satellite overlord recalculated and got me on I-10 around San Dimas (naturally, I did a Bill & Ted "San Dimas football rules!" cheer to myself), from which point I crawled through downtown LA, through Culver City, and on to the end of the trail. Eventually.

I almost didn't make it to the End of the Trail sign on the Santa Monica Pier because I was on the verge of pissing my pants, and I nearly let it fly in the parking garage of the Santa Monica Place mall. I could already see the headlines: "A Maine man was arrested today for urinating in an upscale mall parking garage..."

I spent about ten minutes wandering the outdoor mall, desperately looking for a men's room, and, after I eventually found it, I *finally* crossed over to take in the sign and warm California sun.

I'd arrived. I'd made it. I'd done it.

The Big Adventure was done.

I stood before the sign, trying to let the frame develop, trying to comprehend the journey; the accomplishment; trying to find the words; trying to hold onto the feeling. But I had to wee yet again, so I scrammed back to the mall. Hey, at least I now know where the bathrooms are at Santa Monica Place!

I was very happy to have GPS here, since this got me to the Super 8 LAX via the back roads and PCH, through Venice and Marina Del Ray, a chill ride through a world that was entirely not my own. Along the way, I saw the iconic LAX Theme building, the 1961 Googie-style flying saucer that I'd seen in so many photos, and I also discovered the fantastic KXLU, Loyola Marymount University radio. I told you that college radio is where you find the best stuff! Their playlist skews to... everything, really: alt, trip-hop, Latin—a buffet table for the ears, and I could see it becoming a daily go-to at work.

Basically, I had a great, chill ride to the hotel.

I checked in... and soon discovered that my room was about 1,000' under the landing flightpath for LAX. Did you know that planes land at LAX every 45 seconds? Well, trust me, they do! The room itself was absolutely fine, but not quite soundproofed—a fact I was reminded of every 45 seconds. Fun! Regardless, I managed to crash for a bit, after which I proceeded to nearly clog the toilet (welcome to LA!) and freshen up for dinner with my bud Jess in Glendale.

My friendship with Jess is the damnedest thing, because we were both part of the Boston music scene at the same time, yet neither of us has the *foggiest* recollection of where/when we met. TT's? The Middle East? Other? Then again, I suppose it's nice to not have to play the, "Hey, I know you from... uh... yeah, that... *place* and... that... *time*..." game! Neither of us remembers, and we've been buds for over a decade, so who cares? Plus, we're both socially awkward misfits, which is always good company. Here's a text exchange we had beforehand to demonstrate:

> [ME] I'm nervous! Isn't that ridiculous? We've met—somewhere/sometime... and how long have we been in touch? Still... I'm fine after the first five minutes. Just have to get there. Just so you know if I say something really fucking weird or spill something all over myself.

> [JESS] Dude, you're talking to me: queen of

social anxiety! I say weird shit all the time and then obsess over what I said for YEARS!!! So, seriously. Let's hang out & be awkward together. It'll be fun!

I love my tribe. And now, it was time for some no-pressure fun! So, with that, I got back into Rose and crawled toward I-10. I drove past The Forum in Inglewood, which was absolutely awesome: I was eighteen when Magic Johnson retired and nineteen when Larry Bird retired, but for most of my preteen and teenage years, Celtics Lakers was a religion... or at least a cult. I grew up on the Boston side of the fence, of course, and hated the Lakers, but it was the kind of hate born of respect, and I lived and loved the rivalry. Basketball at its absolute best. Larry and Magic; Robert Parish and Kareem; Kevin McHale and AC Green; The Garden and The Forum. I knew The Garden, but had never seen the other side, and now, I had. And now, I was inspired to get a copy of *Fletch* on Blu-ray ("He's about six-five...with the afro six-nine...pretty good dribbler...").

I'm not a bad city driver, though I get zero opportunity for it in Maine. Even still, I've driven often in Boston and New York, and I'd handled Chicago, St. Louis, and Tulsa without incident on this trip. Hence, I knew what to expect with city driving: be aggressive and take your spots, and then be contentious—return the favor and let the other guy in.

That is, I *thought* I knew what to expect.

Turns out driving in Los Angeles flips this common courtesy on its head, body-slams it, and then kicks it into bumper-to-bumper traffic.

It wouldn't have been *quite* so bad had I known where I was going, but relying on GPS while in the middle of the act was, to say the least, stressful: when you're in lane two and GPS is saying, "In a quarter mile, stay in the right two lanes [i.e., lanes five and six] to merge onto…" or, "Stay in the center two lanes…" (what kind of madness is this where the center lanes are the exit?) and you try to merge doing 55 and a Lamborghini or Ferrari doing at least 80 whips around and nobody lets you merge… *Mommy! Very* frazzling.

Fortunately, I-10 is mostly a parking lot; thus, there *is* no merging during the hour-plus it takes to drive 15-odd miles.

LA traffic, you so cray-cray.

Jess had suggested Damon's, a tiki joint in Glendale, and I had no truck with that—and, mercifully, GPS got me there unscathed.

I walked in, we hugged profusely, and I sat down with my old friend and her boyfriend, Forrest, a lovely chap from the Netherlands with an accent flattened by college in Michigan. Only in LA. Well, only in Glendale…

We ordered Chi Chis (rum, pineapple and coconut, and *no* Hepatitis B, unlike the former American Tex-Mex chain of the same name), and I went with the brisket and pork combo platter, rice, and hush puppies. My God, so good... and once again, I had breakfast leftovers.

Conversation was great and endless; deep and shallow; and we were there a good two hours—by which time traffic was delightfully clear!

I cranked KXLU and floored it, because I could.

Back in the room, I nursed an ice-cold Tecate and relived the evening: I'd had a fantastic dinner with my friend, and I hadn't said anything utterly stupid (well, to my knowledge). And Jess was probably thinking the exact same thing and coming to the same exact conclusion. We'd both done great, and that ain't a bad thing! With that, I was able to let go of old anxieties even more than I already had. What a gift.

I also thought about the coming day, and it occurred to me that today was my sixth two-state day in a row: Thursday had been Illinois to Missouri, Friday had been Missouri to Oklahoma (with Kansas thrown in for good measure), Saturday had been Oklahoma to Texas, Sunday had been Texas to New Mexico, Monday had been New Mexico to Arizona, and today had been Arizona to California. And California and Illinois were the bookends—states I'd previously been to on either side of the six states that I *hadn't* yet visited.

Jesus, how often does one have an opportunity like that? It's a once-in-a-lifetime thing, if you're lucky (and I've been very lucky!).

That big, dumbass grin returned, and I fell into a

shallow sleep, counting not sheep but landings at LAX. Every 45 seconds...

CHAPTER 8

NAVIGATING A NEW LIFE

FORTUNATELY, ANDREA WAS MAKING A bit more than my $11/hour before she left Seattle, so she was able to cover my deficits—though we still started our new life by searching for temp jobs and sharing my borrowed twin cot and pillow (singular) in my apartment, which became known as the Crackhouse, since it was essentially a commune filled with a revolving cast of entitled stoner burnouts who we avoided at all costs.

Things were getting *real* old, *real* quick. But we held on and stuck it out together.

Two weeks later, everything was different.

I'll never forget the silence of that day: September 12, 2001. My twenty-ninth birthday (my first with Andrea). 15

days into our new life together, the world had changed forever.

The day before, we woke up (still unemployed) and went online. Then, we turned on the TV. Then, we didn't go anywhere for hours and hours.

I'd already previously decided that I was going to quit smoking on my twenty-ninth birthday—the first step of my new life—so I walked down to the corner store for my last pack of Marlboros, came back, sat on my porch on the second floor of my apartment, and chain-smoked myself into oblivion on that crystalline, gorgeous day in deathly silence. Nobody was talking about the TV images in the store or on the sidewalks, and there was no traffic down our street.

Finally, in the late afternoon, we went to the post office and then the Joshua Tree in Davis Square, where the big screen was playing CNN and the waiter encouraged us to drink up. "It's a National Day of Crisis!" And we did, in a silent, half-empty dining room.

The next day (my birthday), we took a Boston Harbor cruise. We stopped off at the dock bar first, where there were few patrons, and the ones that were there stayed glued to the tube, silently nursing their drinks. Then, we got on the boat.

The cruise to the islands is directly under the Logan Airport flight path. This means a Boston Harbor tour is often like a Mets game at the old Shea Stadium, with the LaGuardia runway a mere mile away. But this was different: there was not a sound. Of course, the FAA grounded all flights in the aftermath of the attacks, yet I'd taken many cruises before and was so used to the deafening sounds of takeoffs and landings directly overhead that I still found myself stunned at the silence that pervaded. No planes moving, taxiing, arriving, or departing. Dead calm. Dead silence. The kind of silence one hears only once in a lifetime.

On Friday, September 15, we walked seven miles from Davis Square Somerville to Copley Square Boston. At Davis, the compass in the square was completely covered in lit, melting candles.

We lit one and moved on.

At Copley, outside Trinity Church, the reflecting pool was completely shrouded in candles.

We lit one and sat in the early autumnal dark.

Silence, save for muffled traffic and one college kid, who quietly played folk songs on an unplugged Gibson Hollowbody.

The entombing silence is what I'll always remember. Shrouding, all-encompassing silence. Like the death-knell that it was.

I hope to never hear such absolute silence again in my life.

One day in the fall of 2001, while we were all still reeling and recovering, I picked up an issue of *Down East: The Magazine of Maine* at the newsstand at South Station.

Down East was a fixture in my and my grandparents' life, and picking up that issue made me miss home. That inspired me to take a look at apartment rentals in Portland—and they were (at that time, of course) ridiculously cheaper than Boston.

The wheels started turning.

Sure enough, in May 2002, we moved back to my home (Portland, Maine). During this time, my parents gifted us their white-with-red-interior 1995 Hyundai Elantra—the same car I drove down to start my Boston life at Berklee—and we used this to shift our stuff from Somerville to the Homestead—and, eventually, we walked into Roxbury and rented a U-Haul (named Penelope) and hauled the rest north.

Our first Saturday night in our apartment, I thought it would be appropriate to make a proper Maine dinner—so I made Maine red hot dogs. But I didn't steam them, as is proper, and they sucked. And our mattress collapsed.

Welcome to Maine.

We lived on State St. until we bought our house in May 2005. Before that, though, on July 6, 2003, Mikey Dee passed away. Official cause: pneumonia. Unofficial cause: dying (well before his time) of an unexpected stroke three years earlier.

I still wish that I could have done more for my friend. And while I may not have been able to instantly cure him, I still to this day carry the lessons that Mike imparted: don't feel sorry for yourself; live like it's your last day and mentor whenever and wherever you can.

I took this advice seriously.

To refer back to my time in Boston, 1999: I wrote bang-up live performance and CD reviews (within the word count!) on a dime and on deadline, started circulating, and met Tad Overbaugh (singer/guitarist of the alt-country band The Kickbacks), and, not long after, I auditioned on bass and joined the band (which also included current Nashville hotshot Shawn Byrne). I also met Tad's cousin Max Heinegg, leader of The High Ceilings (I once heard our sound described as Pink Floyd meets Smashing Pumpkins by way of Neil Young. I approve of this description), for which I also auditioned and got in. With Max, Chris Blackburn, and John Woods, the Ceilings recorded two EPs produced by Boston legend Sir David Minehan (The Neighborhoods; Aerosmith; The Replacements).

I had the *That Thing You Do!* moment of hearing myself on the radio ("I am Spartacus!"), graduated from The Middle East's Upstairs Room (for up-and-comers) to the Downstairs Room (for the likes of Morphine, Guided by Voices, and Smashing Pumpkins), and sold out the original House of Blues (2,000 tickets on a Tuesday night!).

Dreams do come true—but only when you allow yourself to go for them.

So, by this time, I happily accepted the realization that I had, in fact, fulfilled my dreams, as I happily set those dreams aside for my new life of "responsibility". I landed a temp job at my grocery chain in July 2002, just after moving home, and started my permanent job in February 2003. Andrea worked a few temp jobs, and then landed a permanent job with a real estate title company. We loved our life in Portland and the fact that we could walk everywhere, including to the magnificent Portland Museum of Art, where we frequently partook of the free Friday nights. We walked and ate out and made our rent, even if things were a bit tight. Life was good. But we wanted something a bit more permanent. So, in early 2005, we started looking at houses. We saw something like 18 before finally walking into ours in April—and when we did, we made an offer and had our offer accepted almost immediately.

With that, we were officially grownups!

We moved north in May 2005. Our house was relatively small—something like 1,300 square feet—with two (officially three) bedrooms, two baths, a basement ready to be finished, a lovely sunporch, and a decent backyard. The house was covered in cheap wall-to-wall carpet with a gaudy lighthouse wallpaper border, but we saw the potential.

Not long after moving in, we started tugging at the corners of the carpets—that whole "What's underneath *this*?" vibe—and after a few weekends, we had uncovered gorgeous hardwood throughout. From there, we started scraping off 75 years' worth of wallpaper layers... and quickly became disillusioned with the task. We scraped one wall of the living room, the logic being that we weren't going to want to stare at a half-scraped wall for very long.

Hmm.

12 years later, and you can guess how much progress we've made.

So, yes, we soon discovered that we would never be featured on any HGTV shows, or whatever, but we were in our house, we were making our mortgage payments, and life was good.

Starting in May 2005, we drove together 45 minutes each morning Monday through Friday, dropped each other off at work, worked, picked each other up, drove together 45 minutes each evening, arrived home, ate, watched the tube, and went to bed. We took a few amazing trips, cooked some amazing meals, forayed out into the outside world occasionally, visited my parents at the Homestead, and flew out to Seattle to visit the in-laws... but that's about it.

Then, in November 2013, Andrea's father died.

(Yes, I realize that timeline-wise, there's a huge gap in the narrative here, but there really isn't much to expand on. This period is the vast desert of my life: I was very happy being married to my best friend and living a quiet domestic life, but that was the extent of my existence during these years, and I never conceived of having any other life. End of story... or so I thought.)

This was a horrible shock to our systems; our first loss.

I loved Andy: he was a huge, burly guy—intimidating at first—who had been a bus mechanic at Seattle Metro and a fierce Union guy with an outsized presence. Once you got past the gruff exterior, however, you were in, and you saw his incredible depth, wicked sense of humor, and intellectual curiosity. Not to mention the fact that he had a lovely spread in Buckley, WA, with an amazing view of Mt. Rainier on his property and a massive garage with his race cars, etc. inside, and it was always lovely to visit and partake in his fierce wit.

He retired seven months before his death, so he never got the chance to do anything he'd wanted to do in retirement. This was a hideous punch to the gut, and we were reeling. That said, he left us a decent inheritance, and with that, we were able to pay off our debts and, because of that, buy our dream Maine lakefront camp in 2014.

Buying our camp—"The Loon's Nest"—was absolutely a dream come true. Many Friday mornings before work, Andrea and I would stop at the store for provisions for the day, and we always stood in the parking lot on those gorgeous summer mornings and said, "Wouldn't it be amazing to get out of work and drive to our lakefront camp for the weekend?" For years, this routine went on, and it was always just a pipe dream. No conception that it could actually happen.

Well, the cost was steep—losing Andy was a terrible thing to deal with—but our inheritance was just enough that we were able to pay off all our debts, save for the house mortgage. Andrea found herself searching online for lakefront camps, and one day, out of nowhere, she sent me a listing. It was only an hour from our house and not on a "popular" lake, so it was absolutely reasonable and realistic. We scheduled a viewing—*Just to take a look. No obligation*—and made an offer immediately. And with that, we became owners of a Maine lakefront camp. Dreams do come true... when you allow yourself to go for them.

Basically, in 2014, we were totally and completely solvent for the first time in our lives. It was a wonderland year, and we constantly joked about our sudden fortune. One common gallows-humor joke revolved around the days when we were behind on our cable bill, during which one of us would pick up the phone with a debit card in hand and type in the numbers while the other turned the TV onto a black screen. When the delinquent payment was registered, we'd both watch our cable return on a dime. Magic!

Not all was to stay rosy, however: in July 2014, there was a monsoon rainstorm that caused our upstairs guest bedroom to suddenly host an internal water feature. The contractors we hired informed us that we'd need a new roof and asbestos removal—as in, the removal of *all* the asbestos upstairs—and insurance would only cover the room in which the geyser appeared. So, we plunked down a very large check and spent a week plus with the area next to our bedroom encased in plastic and framing and industrial vacuums removing the sludge until the room was dry enough for the abatement team to remove the asbestos, which had to be completed before the roofing crew could come out. And while we're doing that, why not install a new furnace (our furnace was original to the 1940-built house, with a motor from the 1960s)? Sure! And new landscaping? Why the fuck not?

Many thousands of dollars later, our house was safe, new, and beautiful, with scalding hot water, and our bottom line wasn't hurt.

Basically, in 2014 and early 2015, we were flush, and life was good.

Then, as we know, I got shitcanned out of a job due to a missed timeclock punch. So, in the summer of 2015, I decided to take advantage of our situation and return to the University of Maine at Augusta to complete the bachelor's degree I'd come so close to earning two decades earlier. The thought of finishing my degree had been in the back of my mind during those 20 years—but then again, in a way, it also seemed somewhat superfluous: I'd already *made* it in my field, so what was the point of getting a piece of parchment in order to prove it? A BA in music is essentially worthless. No offense to anyone who, like me, has worked their ass off to earn it; it just has no bearing on how well you can navigate the music business. A college course can teach you all the music theory in the world, but it can't teach you what to do when you're two songs into a showcase gig at Bill's Bar and your bass amp suddenly blows up (run your bass through the house PA and nobody will know the difference), or how to draw an audience (never play the same club more than twice a month), or how it feels to hear yourself on the radio (elation).

Sure, the consummation of my educational path would've been nice, but I'd already consummated my art.

On the other hand, I needed to eat and pay the mortgage and have beer money for camp, and I suspected that earning a college degree would help me land another (better), higher-paying corporate job while I explored other creative outlets. So, I took the plunge and returned to Augusta.

We were in Seattle visiting the in-laws when I saw my class schedule and realized that my first class, in recording, was Monday, August 31, the day of our return flight. Panicked, I immediately rebooked my flight to the day before, leaving Andrea to return on August 31 (as planned).

24 hours after tripping around the lovely town of La Connor, WA, eating oysters and antique hunting with the in-laws, I was suddenly hurtling 3,000 miles toward my first day of education in 20 years.

Surreal.

That first morning, I arrived on-campus an hour early and spent 40 minutes sitting in the car in the parking lot. One theme of my life is the challenge of getting through the first five minutes of something that feels difficult or out of my comfort zone. After that, I'm fine, but until then, I'm an utter wreck. So, I spent that time in the car meditating and trying to send myself positive vibes so I could get through those first five minutes—and then preferably the rest of the two semesters.

During that (second) first semester, I was learning new technologies while simultaneously (re)learning how to record and play music, and in the second semester, I was constantly working on my senior project: to create, score, record, and present a 30-minute film.

Shit.

In truth, returning to the University of Maine at Augusta was one of the most utterly surreal experiences of my life. The campus was the same (although expanded), but I was 20 years older. I walked through the same classrooms I'd known 20 years earlier to get to the auxiliary trailers (the classroom assignment schedule posted on the front door was wrong, as it turns out), where, in 1995, I'd cheekily added *LARRY* to the *BIRD LIVES* graffiti tributes to Charlie Parker on the supporting joists. I returned to the same recording studio I'd known 20 years earlier—the studio where I'd learned how to record music—and found that the control room was now all digital, the reel-to-reel tape machine replaced by an iMac and ProTools (now the industry standard in digital recording software). I'd never used ProTools in my life! Clearly, I still had a lot to learn.

It was a surreal experience, and I felt myself getting seriously overwhelmed and depressed due to my ever-prevalent fear of failure (sound familiar?), collapsing under the weight of the pressure, running through our inheritance (legit, as it turned out!)... everything, really.

Not fun.

My shrink at the time proffered that what I was doing was comparable to learning Greek while being expected to deliver the results in Greek. True enough—but that still didn't earn me any free passes.

Naturally, I bumped up my student loans and invested in an iMac, ProTools, studio monitors, etc. so I could build a fully functioning home studio, and I utilized that for my endeavors in addition to the campus studio.

It was the challenge of my life.

I've never dedicated more blood, sweat, and tears to anything more than I did on that senior project (clearly time not misspent; I ended up getting an A-minus on it! Whoop!). The film was called *Life in a Day*, and it was a montage of clips found on Shutterstock and such other sites with a soundtrack (poorly) recorded at home by me.

For my senior concert, I was expected to show the film and also play so I could "demonstrate my musical talent". I hadn't played music in 20 years, but I found a fellow guitar student to sit in with, and we whipped through versions of *Autumn Leaves* and Herbie Hancock's *Maiden Voyage*. I nearly sweated through my new suit, but I pulled it off.

Finally, I got my paper, and I was free.

So, what next?

Well, I thought I'd go for an "easy" return to the working world while I worked on my next soundtrack or film or whatever, so I returned to the wonderful world of temping for the first time in 14 years.

Wonderful? Yeah, not so much.

My first temp job was in July 2016 at Maine Public, our NPR and PBS station. Perfect! I landed in the membership department, and nobody interacted with me at all, so I figured I was just "the temp" and that I'd just keep my head down and work my ass off. So, I went right ahead and did mail-merge projects, printing out hundreds of personalized "thank you for your donation" letters and envelopes for my boss to sign before I sealed and sent off every envelope. I'd also research and reach out to other stations to inquire about their membership software, and would compile their answers into a spreadsheet; I'd travel out to visit members and get their signatures on pledge documents, and proofread and edit grant proposals.

I was killing it, and I was loved by my boss' boss (my own boss, not so much, as I would learn).

Later down the line, I interviewed for the position, and didn't get the job because the winning candidate had much more direct fundraising experience than I did. No way I could kick at that—and now here I was, after just three months, unemployed again.

In January 2017, my temp agency sent me to a position where I'd be groomed to be a product manager... or so I was told. In actuality, I was sent into a frigid garage and put to work assembling industrial toolkits—ostensibly to learn the operation from the ground up. Now, I knew nothing about industrial tools, and it showed immediately—and to make matters worse, the owner of the company only allowed the station with Rush Limbaugh to be played during work, and in his office, he had a phrenology skull with a self-styled Hitler mustache and *OBAMA* hand-scrawled on the base.

I kinda didn't like him very much.

Plus, his dog ran amok around the office, turfing me in the balls and sniffing me while I attempted to assemble my toolboxes.

As if I wasn't already on the verge of quitting, once I arrived home on the Friday after my first week, I got a call from my temp agency informing me that they weren't bringing me back because I "wasn't picking things up fast enough". No shit!

So, in February 2017, my temp agency sent me to a proofreading job.

Okay, I can handle this!

I interviewed with a sweet elderly Grandma Wolf Spirit type lady who, I felt, loved me immediately, and I was hired on the spot.

Yes!

I started editing medical papers, educational textbooks, white papers, etc., and thought I was doing okay.

Now, the office was shared with an insurance company, which had a Keurig in the shared cafeteria. The coffee in our area was shit, so occasionally, I strolled to the café to get good coffee from the Keurig—when one day, Grandma Wolf Spirit cornered me and observed that I "spent a lot of time walking around". She also stated that the insurance company's Keurig was off-limits.

Okay, then.

Not much later, I messed up a project and, salt-meet-wound, Grandma Wolf Spirit informed me in front of the entire staff that I "never did anything she told me correctly".

Last day on that temp job! And nothing like a little public humiliation on the way out.

Two months later, I was sent to an architectural firm to cover for a young lady who was facing chemotherapy. Lo and behold, I loved the office, team, and work, and was nailing it... until I messed up the formatting on a project. After that, the young lady going through chemotherapy suddenly decided she felt well enough to work part-time, and I was informed by my temp agency that they didn't feel they needed a temp anymore.

I then interviewed with a payroll company in Portland, and I killed it. They loved me and wanted me, but had to go with another candidate who had a bit more experience. Fine, I totally get that. I then interviewed with a medical billing company in Portland and killed it again, and was told that they were waiting on official word from corporate on when offers could be made, but that things looked real good.

I waited. And waited. And waited a bit more.

The woman I interviewed with, who I absolutely loved and who apparently loved me, then emailed me and said she could now make offers, and was I still interested?

Does a bear shit in the woods? I instantly shot back my affirmative answer, and I waited.

And waited. And waited a bit more.

I never heard back. No explanation. No sorry. Nothing.

I *then* interviewed for (another) proofreading job in Freeport. On the phone pre-interview, my prospective boss asked if I had any questions about the position. My temp agency had only sent me the position an hour beforehand, so I said something along the lines of, "Well, I just received the posting and am still studying it, but I'm sure I'll have a bunch of questions tomorrow." Prospective boss paused for a second, said, "Gotcha!" and confirmed our appointment.

Awkward interview in which I knew I had no shot.

Afterwards, Prospective Boss asked to speak to me alone, and then informed me, "You didn't have any good questions! You need to be *prepared* for interviews!"

So now, I'm not only incompetent and unhireable, but also a total virgin to the workforce. Okay, gotcha!

On the Friday of the July 4 weekend, I was sent to a job to cover for a woman who was about to undergo brain surgery. A three-month position. No future, but I was desperate. I arrived, the woman showed me around and made the introductions, and I got to it. They originally wanted me in for a half-day just to feel me out, but they loved me, and couldn't wait to get me started. "And," they said, "maybe something will open up after the woman returns from her surgery."

On the Monday after the Independence Day weekend, I got in early and went to work. And one hour in, who should appear but Brain Surgery Woman? She was practically crying as she informed me that over the weekend, she got hit in the head with her grandson's frisbee and so had to postpone her surgery due to possible complications from the blow—and while her surgery was postponed, she was returning to work.

I'm not making this up.

They insisted on paying me for the full day, and I walked out to my car and another day of unemployment, thinking to myself, *I literally just lost a job because of a frisbee injury.*

You couldn't make this shit up.

To summarize this time, my hopes felt as though they had been sickeningly dashed on sharp rocks, and the old familiar abyss of frustration and depression was swallowing me whole yet again. This was honestly one of the lowest times of my life, and while I knew everything would eventually even out, I had no clue when or how I'd get to that point—and in the meantime, there was nothing I could do but try to keep my fading hopes up.

I honestly don't even remember all the other temp positions I went through before I finally landed at the bank (finally, a permanent job), but they all sucked and were short-lived. During one of these positions, however, I received the greatest gift anyone could ever hope for: validation and redemption. The head of HR happened to be someone who used to be in the legal department of my old grocery chain. (You know, the one I'd been fired from.) I knew the name, but we'd never actually met. Well, on the first day of the job, we were introduced and went through the usual awkward, "Oh, yeah, from the grocery chain!" pleasantries.

A few weeks later, this individual called me in for a meeting, "just to see how the position was going, are you liking it, are you getting what you need", blah, blah, blah. Well, during this meeting, we started talking about our former employer, and this individual revealed that they'd also had their contract terminated by said former employer. How did they know this? They'd accidentally received their own termination package via email.

Oops!

With this revelation, I felt comfortable enough to tell my story. This individual listened with full-bodied attention, paused in thought, looked me directly in the eye, and said, "If I were still there, I would have never approved your termination."

A former legal counsel with my company had received the same treatment I had and confirmed that I'd done nothing wrong. *It wasn't my fault.* Goddamn.

I left their office in an extremely emotional but

hopeful state.

And this brings us to the climax of this book and, accordingly, my previous life.

Because at this point—after this conversation—a switch flipped, and I knew I could do whatever I set my mind to; and I knew I needed to do something big. Something manageable, yet incredibly out of my comfort zone.

And I know exactly what that something should be.

On Tuesday, March 5, 2019, I interviewed to go permanent in my temp job of four weeks, a fantastic and hard-to-get position in the anti-money laundering department of a major east coast bank. The offer came that afternoon, and I accepted immediately. Four years and ten days after being fired for a missed timeclock punch at my job of 12 years, I'd landed a permanent full-time job once again! (Fun fact: I wore the same pants—Frank And Oak chinos— on both days. They went from my firin' pants to my hirin' pants. Victory is mine!) And while I dreamed of self-sufficiency through creative endeavors, I did enjoy paying my home and camp mortgages and, y'know, eating. Accordingly, I was ecstatic about this development—and, yes, unspeakably proud of myself. I'd put in the work, got my degree, and *earned* this position. After almost four years of sometimes-bewildering bad breaks as a temp, I finally had a job—and one that, as it turned out, I actually loved! Great team, fun work, five-minute commute, awesome benefits... and the pride and joy that came from being part of the contributing class.

I was overjoyed and overwhelmed—and, importantly, felt so much more equipped to take on my dreams.

And now we backtrack two months to 11:26 AM on Friday, January 18, 2019: 110 days until the start of this Route 66 odyssey.

A light snow was falling, and a spectacular blizzard was on the way for Sunday, the day of the AFC Championship Game: New England at Kansas City. My lawn was buried under ice-encrusted snow, and my driveway was a skating rink fraught with peril. The house furnace was set at 67 (I was dreaming of 72, but I was also trying to conserve heating oil), and I was wearing half-calf slipper-socks and crafting a shopping list for chili for the penultimate football Sunday of 2019. We were planning on visiting my parents at the Homestead briefly the next day and then getting our trading done (to quote my grandmother) before the stores were utterly mobbed and ransacked by snowpocalypse raiders (*Must get bread! Must get milk!*)—but for now, I was at home thinking about what I was getting myself into by doing this proposed trip.

Truth be told, I was scared shitless: the magnitude of the trip, the impossibility of it all... 2,278 miles through eight states was one long-ass haul. Yes, Andrea and I had once driven from Seattle to Boston in a ten-foot Ryder, but that was the two of us; the longest *solo* drives I'd taken had been from Portland to Boston. Route 66 was another beast entirely—longer (by far), wider in scope and breadth (by far), and more than I'd ever taken on; more than I'd ever believed possible.

Could I handle it?

I turned once again to the Bible (a.k.a., John Steinbeck's *Travels with Charley*):

> Once a journey is designed, equipped, and put in process, a new factor enters and takes over. A trip, a safari, an exploration, is an entity, different from all other journeys. It has personality, temperament, individuality, uniqueness. A journey is a person in itself; no two are alike. And all plans, safeguards, policing, and coercion are fruitless. We find after years of struggle that we do not take a trip; a trip takes us. Tour masters, schedules, reservations, brass-bound and inevitable, dash themselves to wreckage on the personality of the trip. Only when this is recognized can the blown-in-the-glass bum relax and go along with it. Only then do the frustrations fall away. In this a journey is like a marriage. The certain way to be wrong is to think you control it.

Yeah, that.

DAY EIGHT

MAY 15, 2019

Los Angeles.
Time Out: Late morning.
Time In: Late evening.

FIRST ORDER OF BUSINESS: PUTTING the *Do Not Disturb* sign on the door. I could live without housekeeping for a day.

Today was about to be my first day in seven without driving 300-plus miles, so I wanted to sleep in a bit; linger a bit; take my time.

I mapped out the drive to Sunset Strip, but when I got to Rose, I felt like cruising a bit, though *not* on interstates—so I headed for Route 1 (a.k.a., PCH, the Pacific Coast Highway, which runs the entire length of the California coast). My favorite drives in the world are on Route 1—*my* Route 1, which runs from Key West, FL to Fort

Kent, ME. My Route 1 is quintessential New England: Starting in Portsmouth, NH, north into Maine; Kittery, York, Ogunquit, Wells, Kennebunk, Old Orchard Beach, Portland, the Atlantic stretching out endlessly on the right, with two-hundred-year-old churches, village greens, and seaside towns that look like Sandra Dee and/or Robert McCloskey could show up at any minute, popping up on all sides.

On through Brunswick and Bath and Wiscasset, the route I traveled with my grandparents to the Homestead. Camden, Rockland, Rockport, and onto Trenton, where one gets onto Route 3 to leave the mainland for Mount Desert Isle and Acadia National Park and Bar Harbor. I cherish this route because I've spent so much of my life on it, and because it was traveled so often by my literary god E.B. White, who immortalized the drive in his timeless 1955 essay *Home-Coming*:

> What happens to me when I cross the Piscataqua and plunge rapidly into Maine at a cost of seventy-five cents in tolls? I cannot describe it. I do not ordinarily spy a partridge in a pear tree, or three French hens, but I do have the sensation of having received a gift from a true love.

This is, and ever will be, my Route 1—but I'd also dreamed of driving the *other* Route 1 for years, and here was my chance (yeah, another picture I had long had in my head).

Thus, I caught PCH in Manhattan Beach and kept on driving north, KXLU still rocking out on the juke. El Segundo (A Tribe Called Quest stuck in my head, of course: *I left my wallet in El Segundo... I gotta get it, I got-got-ta get it*) to Santa Monica, Pacific Palisades to Topanga Canyon, and onto Malibu.

The ocean was on the wrong side, and the landscape was utterly foreign, but I loved it.

I passed a sign for Laurel Canyon and thought of Joni Mitchell and David Crosby. I gasped at the mansions on the Malibu hillsides. I watched surfers paddling out and dreamed of ripping a few curls myself (I should probably learn how to swim first, though). The vibe; the feel... In spite of the traffic, I was experiencing an extreme mellow feeling, and loving it. Gray, heavy clouds, but still SoCal. Southern California chill. Happy place. And what were the odds that I would pull off at the exact spot where Jim Rockford's trailer was set on *The Rockford Files*? Life falls out of the sky...

I'd pulled off for a taste of the beach at Paradise Cove, the restaurant which was "The Sandcastle" on the show. I kicked off my Vans and stepped onto the sand, and instantly, there in the pacific climes of Malibu, I was six years old and at the Homestead in Whitefield, Maine, all over again, the smell of the woodstove and Jiffy Pop and my grandfather's cigars melding around that fantastic *Rockford Files* theme song blasting from the Zenith of a cold winter night.

Cue the big, dumbass grin!

With that, I got back in Rose, headed back south for the Strip, got off onto Wilshire, and the noon traffic was relentless. I realized I'd be stuck for hours, and I wasn't feeling it at all.

I got back to the room and laid low for the rest of the afternoon, writing and decompressing from LA traffic. Not my world, not my thing. I then headed back out for a small cheese from PizzaRev a few blocks away, and then returned to resume laying low so I could go back out again for the grand finale: Dodger Stadium. The true end of the line; the end of the trip; the last dream realized. One last stretch on I-10, with the grand prize at the end.

I arrived into downtown, and it took about 40 minutes to crawl three miles past the Staples Center. I then pulled off and cruised through Silver Lake, which was an interesting meld: equal parts bodega and Whole Foods. Then, I took a left onto Vin Scully Way.

This was it.

Driving into Dodger Stadium on Vin Scully Way reminded me of driving into Disney World: the lanes leading to the parking gates, the endless parking lots...

I parked, making a vague mental note of the location. (As it would turn out, my vague mental note was just that. But more on that later.)

I got out and followed the teeming masses bedecked in Dodger Blue, heading toward the light towers. I went up a flight of stairs and an escalator, the park landscaping magnificent and fragrant in the LA sun, and passed through the gate. My seats were in the upper deck, but I'd entered the park on level five, and didn't know I'd have to take an elevator up to level nine. Oops!

I navigated up to the Dodger Dog stand and had a total Maine-boy-lost-in-the-big-city moment; I didn't see right away how the thing worked—that the 'dogs and fries, etc. were all laid out on shelves, like at 7-Eleven or a cafeteria, and one serves oneself. I almost ordered from the guys in the kitchen behind the shelves.

Oh.

Eventually, I figured it out—but now, I was carrying a tray with two mustard-sodden Dodger Dogs, an extremely large Coke, a program, and a Max Muncy bobblehead doll into a full elevator to get up to my level.

Good thing nobody was wearing white!

I finally got to my seat just before the anthem, finally took in the view... and (say it with me!) finally put myself in a picture I'd held in my head for nearly 40 years. And God, it was beautiful: the sun, the palm trees, the San Gabriels in the distance... just stunning.

The crowd was knowledgeable and into the game, and it was an amazing baseball experience—as well as a great experience for the senses! Manny Machado, making his second appearance at Dodger Stadium after leaving the Dodgers and signing a ridiculous free-agent contract with San Diego, was booed mercilessly, and it was fantastic, and

I was *loving* hearing that Angelino accent all around me. It was then that I got that sense of wonder again: *someone sat in this very spot and watched Kofax's perfect game in '65. Someone sat in this very spot and saw Fernando pitch in '81. Someone sat in this very spot and watched Kirk Gibson's pinch-hit homer off Eckersley in Game One of the '88 Series.*

Yeah, I was digging it.

I sat up there, in my element, mowing down my Dodger Dogs (not the be-all-end-all they're made out to be, but very tasty, and yet another check off the bucket list) and thinking of six-year-old me collecting baseball cards. And I thought of Holden Caufield, getting his goodbye to Pency Prep at the football game (in *The Catcher in the Rye*, duh)—and with that, I got my goodbye to this amazing journey in the lights of the San Gabriel Mountains.

I found myself staring at a couple of lights at the top of the mountains, wondering what they were—and that brought it all home: I love driving down the Maine backroads at twilight on a winter evening, when the roads are gauzed by woodsmoke and kitchen lights start coming on, each one a story. A kitchen light snapping on in the cold carries endless stories: the days of the inhabitants, their dreams and plans and conversations... Anyway, I love driving by and speculating, and as I sat in the upper deck of Dodger Stadium staring at lights on a far distant mountain range, wondering what stories those lights told, it felt like Endless Summer California and Dead-Of-Winter Maine were one and the same. Home again.

Once again, I left after a few innings (long drive, plus early flight. Legit excuse this time) and headed back for Rose. I paid for parking ahead of time, and was assigned to Lot E, I think—but when I handed my pass to be scanned, nobody said anything, so I just followed all the other cars.

I didn't notice at the time that there were no lot signs on parking lot lights, like at Disney or the mall. Perhaps I didn't notice this because I also didn't notice that there were no parking lot lights—like at Disney or the mall.

Yes, there were *no parking lot lights* at Dodger Stadium.

Thus, I spent a good 30 minutes in the dark in the general vicinity of where I thought Rose was, going row by row, trying to read license plates in the foreboding dark chill and hitting "unlock" on my fob. *57 years and they haven't installed parking lot lights yet?! The fuck...?* As I wandered the dark, forlorn Dodger Stadium parking lot, desperately searching for my car in a foreign land, I found myself thinking of when I got lost in Grand City when I was six—my earliest memory—and of running from the "hippies" on my road; that feeling of *I might... not... make it...*

It wasn't as dramatic as that this time, though: eventually, I found Rose, crawled in, hugged the steering wheel, and cranked the heat. On the way back, I filled her up with $4.99 gas for the last time (thank God) at a Union on Sepulveda (or maybe La Cienega) and crawled back into bed under the landing flightpath.

LAX is a nightmare, and I did well to get there at 5AM for my 8AM flight. It was raining with authority, and I was horribly sad to turn Rose in.

To conclude:

Odometer out in Chicago: 2,832.

Odometer in in LA: 5,371.

Total miles: 2,539.

Seven days, eight states, 2,539.

Goddamn.

I managed to sleep for a few good stretches of my flight to Philly, even in the middle of a three-seat-aisle-four-seat-aisle-three-seat Airbus (left to right; I was seat five of ten). We had a quick, uneventful layover in Philly, landed at PWM around 7PM, and then Andrea drove me home.

I made a peanut butter sandwich and crawled into my own bed around 8:30PM.

And that was it.

AFTERWORD
SUMMER 2019

As I write this, I've have been off the road for several weeks, and the frame is developing.

I stated earlier that the thing about a journey is that it takes very little time for you to be utterly catapulted into it—and, by the same token, it takes very little time for you to be utterly catapulted *out* of it and back into your day-to-day life, too. I crawled into my own bed with a peanut butter sandwich around 8:30PM on Thursday, May 16, and ten hours later, I was back at my desk. I was thrilled to be back (it's generally not very good form to say during a job interview, "Hey, hire me! And oh, by the way, one month into my new position, I'm going to be taking seven business days off to drive across the country. That's cool, right?" Goddamn, I got lucky), but still... bit of a shock to the system.

And that wouldn't be my first shock upon returning home.

On Saturday, May 25, a tornado ripped through El Reno, Oklahoma, destroying a hotel off of I-40 with two fatalities.

El Reno, Oklahoma.

Being an HSP, I of course think about these things deeply, anyway—but this felt *super*-personal: two weeks before (to the day), I'd been *in* El Reno, Oklahoma, at the Love's Station off of I-40, grabbing a Dr. Pepper with a cherry shot and pondering the fact that this was the spot where the west had begun. Perhaps I even rubbed elbows with one of the fatalities. I'll never know.

The Arkansas River had also flooded, and on Monday, June 3, 2019, I heard the horrifying story of Michael Zimmerman and Linda Merrill on *All Things Considered* on NPR: the couple had bought their first house in Sand Springs, OK, a town just outside of Tulsa that I'd actually passed by... and their house was then flooded from the river 22 days after they moved in. They had no flood insurance because (according to a letter from FEMA) they weren't in a flood zone and thus didn't need flood insurance—and this is personal for me, because Andrea and I have been back and forth with FEMA regarding flood insurance for our Maine lakefront camp and just what level of flood zone it's in. The difference is that we have flood insurance, and, critically, haven't lost everything after 22 days of our residence.

My heart completely goes out to Mr. Zimmerman and Ms. Merrill.

My point is, I was shaken to the core by these stories: I've come to love Oklahoma deeply, and any tragedy that befalls her path now befalls mine. A horrible reality check for a dream trip.

To add insult to injury: I'd spent Sunday, May 12, 2019, with Alex—and on July 12, Andrea flew out to Albuquerque, and they drove to Vegas together. Just after Andrea returned, we learned that Alex would be leaving her job and entering hospice. On August 27, she lost her battle to cancer. This period was horrific; a slow-motion train wreck where you *know* the gruesome end is coming, but have no idea how long you have until the final impact and no way to stop it.

My wife lost her best friend, and I ache for her. As for me, I also lost a dear friend, not to mention a critical participant in this transformative narrative and journey.

Natural disasters and fleeting mortality aside, the frame has been developing rapidly, and I now see that this trip is one of the best things I ever did for myself.

I guess the first question I should ask is: how did I do in terms of my Route 66 To Do Checklist (see the Appendix for my planning)?

Let's find out!

- I did pretty well in Illinois. I walked one of the swinging bridges, saw all the Walldog murals, and drove the

Brick 66. I decided to skip on the IL Route 66 Association Hall of Fame and the Welcome Center, but those were maybes, anyway. I blew the Chain of Rocks Bridge, but not by choice: my GPS failed me here, remember. And I didn't originally have them on my list, but I made The Launching Pad, the Gemini Giant, and the Hot Dog Muffler Man, and I had the ADD stops with the Bluesmobile in Joliet and the Dixie Travel Plaza. First day on the road, and I got in most of what I wanted and a lot that I hadn't planned on. So, all in all, pretty solid. I'll give myself an A-minus for Illinois.

- Missouri: one for five in the Show-Me State. Got my Cards game in and missed the rest (maybe I'm one and a half for five, considering the view of the Gateway Arch from my suite. I didn't make it down there, but I sat in my living room staring at it, so there's that). Timing was against me in terms of the Arch, and I just straight up forgot about Hooker Cut and Devil's Elbow. But I had a lovely drive on the Mother Road through the Ozarks, and I feel enriched by that experience. One and a half for five in terms of the actual list; five for five in terms of spiritual fulfillment. I'll give myself a B for MO.

- I scored a 100 for Kansas! I made Cars on the Route *and* bought merch! *And* I made the Eisler Bros' Old Riverton Store as an ADD stop. I'm giving myself a Ralphie here: A-plus, -plus, -plus!

- For Oklahoma: two and a half out of three! I made Commerce and Picher and hit the "other" Route 66 museum in Elk City. I will definitely be returning to Oklahoma, so I'll be hitting up the Oklahoma Route 66 Museum in Clinton eventually. And I made ADD stops at the Meadow Gold sign, downtown Tulsa, and El Reno. Giving myself a solid A for OK.

- 50-50 for Texas. I missed Palo Duro because I wasn't sure about the timing, weather, and fatigue level, and I forgot about the Cadillac Ranch. But I got the U-Drop Inn and Midpoint Café, even though it was closed at that time of the morning. And I did laundry and got boxers, so I think that raises my score just a smidge. I'll go with a B for Texas.

- 50-50 again for New Mexico: made Tucumcari and missed The Musical Road of Tijeras, but seeing the landscape, being with Alex, hitting up the Sandia Tramway, and staying at El Rancho count as extra credit. Thus, I'm going A-plus for NM. (Hey, I never proclaimed to be a professional grader!)

- Four for five for Arizona. I hit the Painted Desert/Petrified Forest, Jack Rabbit Trading Post, Standin' on the Corner Park, and the wild burros of Oatman. I missed the meteor crater, but that was basic expediency, and I could never replace my tour of the Painted Desert/Petrified Forest. Gotta go A for AZ.

- Yeah, I pretty much nailed Cali. I skipped Elmer's Bottle Tree Ranch due to timing, but I hit Roy's Motel Café (after thinking I wouldn't make it) and Dodger Stadium, and I saw the Amboy Crater from Roy's. And I saw The Forum and the LAX Theme Building, drove PCH, listened to KXLU, saw the spot of Jim Rockford's trailer in Malibu, and drove downtown without a scratch. Gotta go A-plus for the Golden State.

So, how did my grub list fare?

- Kicking off with Illinois: no Portillo's or Lou Malnati's. Instead, I had a lousy Wrigley Field Chi-dog and an okay Wrigley Field Giordano's. That would normally make for a less-than-stellar grade, except The Berghoff made up for it all. Lou Mitchell's was the perfect kickoff, "World's Finest Coffee" aside, and Ariston Café was one of the most memorable experiences of my life. All things being equal and the pros outweighing the cons, I'm going for an A for IL.

- Pretty much a total culinary fail for Missouri. I was too crazy-full after lunch for St. Louis ribs, Ted Drewes wasn't an option, and I forgot about the Elbow Inn. My queso and rice at Gringo was good, but nothing worth writing home about. I didn't even have anything good in MO on the way to Tulsa except for my very large Dr. Pepper from the Kum & Go (still can't get over that name). Eh, whatever. As the great pitcher Catfish Hunter once said after getting shelled in a game, "The sun don't shine on the same dog's ass every day." E for MO.

- I had no "musts" for Kansas—so I guess I ticked all criteria! A-plus!

- For Oklahoma: Tulsa was the site of my greatest

culinary disappointment *and* my happiest culinary redemption. I made it to Waylan's Ku-Ku Burger, but because I'd had a burger the day before, I got a pork sandwich. Theoretically, kind of a failure, but it was a decision of practicality. The sandwich and tots were very tasty, and I made my desired lunch spot. I also made Pops, and it was amazing (ADD tangent: not sure why I put Pops on my to-eat list, since I never planned on eating there, but it's too late now). And though I was denied Ike's Chili, I discovered the Mother Road Market and fell in love over a major slice from Andolini's. And my French press at 918 Coffee was fantastic. Plus, Dr. Pepper with cherry shot at Love's. Plus, Oklahoma, which is love. A for OK.

- Texas. Yep, I made The Big Texan, and it was spot-on in all the right ways: delicious and kitschy as hell. Other than my serviceable burrito at Taco Villa, that's the extent of my culinary experience of Amarillo, but that's enough for me. A for TX.

- I had no musts for New Mexico, but what I ended up with was amazing on eleven: my first green Chile tortilla soup with beans at The Owl with Alex, and my steak with Christmas Chile and fresh tortillas at El Rancho. Amazing. Utterly memorable. I got everything out of nothing, and that doesn't happen every day. A-plus for NM.

- Stopping off now at Arizona, Delgadillo's was delicious and hilarious. Safeway sushi was... Safeway sushi. But

Delgadillo's. A for AZ.

- Finally, in California, I got my musts and my maybes in, *and* so much more. Yeah, the Dodger Dog is, at the end of the day, a standard ballpark hot dog, but it's a Dodger Dog at Dodger Stadium. Thus, its import goes way beyond taste, delicious as that taste is. I also got to In-N-Out, and it was pretty damn good. PizzaRev was fine; no great shakes, but fine. And I had the joy of Damon's brisket and pork with a dear friend 3,000 miles away from home. Yeah, A for CA.

So, I hit much more than I missed in terms of what I wanted to see, do, and eat. Not bad, considering I had no idea what I was getting into, what to expect, and how to plan. I always roll with it on the road: you're going to plan stuff and miss stuff, and fuckups will happen, thus ensuring that you miss other stuff, but you also end up seeing other stuff that you weren't expecting, and that's just as (if not more) memorable—and at the end of the day, it's still all about the adventure and finding your way out after getting lost (and epic run-on sentences like this one!). I allowed that going in, and I think I made it out spectacularly unscathed. I may have missed Palo Duro, but I'll be back, and I unexpectedly took the Sandia Tramway instead. I didn't get to the top of the Gateway Arch, but I'll be back, and I saw Tucumcari Mountain instead.

Door closes; window opens. Life falls out of the sky and into our laps.

Next question (yes, I'm interviewing myself here): what was the most memorable experience?

Cliché to say, but all of it. This trip was like a concept album, like *Sgt. Pepper* or Yes' *Tales from Topographic Oceans* or Marvin Gaye's *What's Going On*: each song on those albums carries the narrative, and each stop on this trip carried this narrative in the same way. Chicago was just as memorable as Los Angeles. Tulsa was just as memorable as Gallup. And the entire trip would have been lesser without any of those experiences.

Yeah, that is a twee cop-out answer. I fell in love with Tulsa and Oklahoma, but I felt slightly indifferent about Amarillo and Kingman, only because I kind of blew them off, and hated LA traffic (though I love LA; just not necessarily in a Randy Newman kind of way).

If I absolutely had to make a list of most memorable experiences, however, it would probably be:

1. Pulling off onto Rt. 66 for the first time in Joliet, IL.
2. The sun rising over I-40 through Texas and New Mexico.
3. Dodger Stadium.
4. Tulsa, Tulsa, Tulsa.
5. Connecting with my new friends Juan and Gregory in Chicago, Holly and Tully at the Launching Pad in Wilmington, IL, and Jennifer in Tulsa.
6. Meeting my old friends Alex in Albuquerque and Jess in Glendale.
7. The Mojave.

8. The Berghoff, El Rancho, Damon's, and Delgadillo's.
9. The Painted Desert and Petrified Forest, California.

That list is in no particular order and subject to change any minute now. But for now (because I had to take a moment to consider this):

...what was the *worst* experience?

Easy: arriving at a closed Ike's Chili. And the fact that that was the worst thing that happened should tell you it was a pretty goddamn good trip. Actually, the worst experience was LA traffic, and that's a qualified "worst experience" because it wouldn't have been so bad if I'd known where I was going ahead of time. Really, though, there was no "worst experience" because there was nothing even approaching bad on this trip.

Next.

What did I do, see, and eat from my lists that I can live without doing, seeing, and eating next time?

Great question, self! Well, I do want to jigger the route a bit for next time—which technically isn't really fair, since the places I'd bypass next time were the ones I really didn't give a fair shake to—specifically, Kingman, Arizona. Nice Safeway (as Safeways go), and I liked Beale Street Brews, but I didn't see much else, aside from driving aimlessly through town. It was nice, though.

I do want to see a bit more of Amarillo, and I will

because I'll be visiting Palo Duro eventually (and if I just happen to end up at The Big Texan again, well...). I can live without returning to the National Route 66 Museum in Elk City, OK, and I want to hit up the Oklahoma Route 66 Museum in Clinton instead. I liked The Owl in Albuquerque, but I want to explore other culinary options in New Mexico because I didn't get enough of a taste, if you will. No Posole, Calabacitas, or Sopaipillas this time, but that changes next time!

The Sandia Tramway was amazing, but I've done it. I saw one burro in Oatman, Arizona, and that's enough (besides, I am *not* driving Sitgreaves Pass again). I also don't need to return to Winslow, Arizona, or the Jack Rabbit Trading Post. I've seen the Hot Dog Muffler Man once, so that's good enough (I will absolutely be returning to see the Gemini Giant and Launching Pad again, though). I stopped at The Dixie Travel Plaza and Clines Corner, so if I don't hit those again, fine. I've seen the ghost town of Picher, Oklahoma, and the Eisler Brothers' Old Riverton Store in Kansas, so no need to retrace those steps. Really, though, I don't have any absolute never-again candidates.

What did I miss out on my lists that I must do the next time?

This is a much longer list! Start with Ike's Chili in Tulsa; continue with Palo Duro and the Cadillac Ranch and eating at Midpoint Café in Texas. The Chain of Rocks Bridge, Hooker Cut, Devil's Elbow, and Ted Drewes Frozen

Custard in Missouri. Elmer's Bottle Ranch in California and the meteor crater in Winslow, Arizona. St. Louis ribs. Portillo's and Lou Malnati's in Chicago (and never again a Chi-dog at Wrigley). And obviously next time I'll plan my visit to the Gateway Arch and museum better... y'know, like, plan *a* visit. And *much* more time in St. Louis: I really liked what I saw. Sunset Strip. Griffith Observatory. I saw the Hollywood sign for about 20 seconds from a great distance on I-10; that needs to change. More time on the beach and more time exploring the Santa Monica Pier, now that I know where to take a leak. Further on PCH: I've yet to see Ventura, not that it was really a thought or an option this time. More time for more ADD stops; I blew past a ton on the way.

What did I do, see, and eat that I will do, see, and eat over and over again?

I will return to The Berghoff every time I'm in Chicago. I will absolutely return to Ariston Café every time I'm in downstate Illinois. The Mother Road Market and 918 Coffee in Tulsa. I will stay at The Campbell Hotel every time in Tulsa. More time in downtown Tulsa; more art deco. I'll eat and stay at El Rancho in Gallup, New Mexico, again for sure (even if I get the Claude Akins room!). Pops 66 was awesome, and I'll have to eat there next time. Dodger Dogs forever, Dodger Stadium as often as I can. Wrigley and Busch Stadium. Delgadillo's Snow Cap was a blast. The Painted Desert and Petrified Forest will be a go-to for the rest of my days. The Launching Pad.

What do I want to do, see, and eat that was not on my list this time?

I totally didn't even think of the Tulsa Golden Driller statue and Cyrus Avery Centennial Plaza (Cyrus Avery is the Father of Route 66)! Um, yeah, I need to return to Tulsa! More of Illinois. Springfield, the Land of Lincoln. Carlinville, and the City Hall that saw a Boss Tweed-like series of cost overruns and general corruption. Dell Rhea's Chicken Basket and the Cozy Dog. More of Missouri, for sure. Springfield I just plowed through—don't even recall seeing the skyline. Much more of Oklahoma: more museums; Oklahoma City. I didn't experience any of Norman, nor see any of the Trail of Tears. More of Texas, although to be fair, that's many more trips. Santa Fe: I had the Georgia O'Keeffe museum on my mind but couldn't pull it off with lunch plans. Seeing the Sango de Cristos as the backdrop of Santa Fe.

This is a very short list, and I can't really continue it right now without starting plans for another swing. (Seriously, don't tempt me.)

What did I learn about America?

I should preface this question by stating that a lot of what I "learned" were things I already knew, or at least suspected, that were just reinforced along the way. I can't honestly say that I had any "ah-*ha*!" lightbulb moments, but I did have many "oh, *yeah*" moments in which I revisited concepts and ruminations with a new, fresh slant, and my thoughts have evolved as a result. Next best thing, I guess.

First of all...

1.   I "learned" about the impossible vastness of America.
I knew that America was a huge land, of course, and I'd already driven coast-to-coast once before in seven days, but having the luxury to take six days to cross to the other side of the continent from my previous venture (and only half of said continent, at that) was revelatory. As soon as I sat at my desk at my day job at 6:30AM on May 17 after logging in for the first time in ten days, I looked at my National Parks Service Route 66 map on my office wall and gasped audibly. *Seeing* what I had just done, what I had just accomplished, hit me like a sucker punch. I looked at how far Chicago was from LA on paper, how far Chicago was from St. Louis on paper, how far St. Louis was from Tulsa on paper, and I almost started shaking. I guess I hadn't quite appreciated it as I was planning it, but having done it, it really hit me. *I drove Route 66. Not the whole way, but still... I saw America.*

And I saw a completely foreign America for sure. I saw the country change before my very eyes. The change in topography I witnessed along I-90 from Seattle to Boston in 2001 is not nearly as dramatic as it is from the Midwest to the southwest along Route 66 (yes, and I-55, I-44, I-40,

I-15, and I-10). Montana and North Dakota were about the only states along that earlier drive that felt completely separate and distinct from the east coast world I'd always known. Seattle is very relatable to Maine, only on a greatly exaggerated scale: Maine's highest peak, Mt. Katahdin, is 5,267'; Washington State's Mount Rainier is 14,410'. The Maine coast is not dissimilar to the Washington coast— different, but not dissimilar. Minneapolis feels like a smaller-scale New York. I experienced the vastness of America on that trip from Seattle to Boston, but there were few points along the way that felt like a foreign America. And yet this trip presented nearly an *entirely* foreign America, and I'm forever changed for having seen it. Having six two-state days in a row presented six separate and unique microcosms of the country, and one doesn't get an opportunity like that very often. I keep thinking of how in a mere 24-hour period I went from rural central Oklahoma to utterly southwestern Albuquerque, NM. Never before had I had such a drastic change in scenery and perspective as this.

I haven't hit up Iowa or Nebraska, etc. yet, but now that I've driven through Downstate Illinois and Missouri, I feel like I've seen the true Heartland. "Flyover Country", they call it. (Goddamn, that term pisses me off. An utterly bullshit canard, designed to divide us, rather than unite us. But I digress.)

2. I "learned" how much we're all invested in our shared

experiences as Americans, even if we don't realize it and even if our end goals differ.

Seeing the same guy driving the same route from Santa Rosa to Clines Corner, New Mexico, reminded me of this: same place, same route, different mission. We all rely on each other on that route to make the same safe navigations; to ensure we all get to our destination in one piece. And if that ain't American democracy, I don't know what is. We all have an equal stake, and we all want and deserve a fair shake.

3. I "learned" that Americans are Americans all over America.

I think it's far too easy to lose sight of this. We live in insular bubbles, and we rarely get the chance to break out and see what the other guy is thinking. In our bubbles, it's so easy to think that foreigners—even foreign Americans— are inherently different creatures; it's easy to think that people on the other side of the country or the other side of the world are utterly different *beings*, like the Italians pee lavender or the Alaskans are part whale, or that it can't possibly be snowy winter in Berlin and New York at the same time because they're separated by 3,000 miles of ocean, or whatever. It's easy to think that because it's winter in Australia while it's summer in America, or whatever. But nope: the human genome is the same in Maine, Texas, California, Quito, Barcelona... Farts stink in Laredo and London alike. (Tangent: I can attest to this fact from our first visit to London in 2013 when, in the middle of the 5:30PM Evensong at Westminster Abbey, one of the grandest churches in the world, a fetid cloud enveloped me and Andrea. Naturally, she suspected me right away, but when she peeked over and didn't see my shoulders shaking in a stifled giggle at my own prowess, she knew I wasn't the culprit. Go me! You're welcome.) Farmhands sitting around a table at a gas station in Oklahoma are just as passionate about local issues as lobstermen sitting around a pot-bellied stove in Maine. Kids in Seligman, AZ, dream of getting out of their "nowhere" town and making it big just like kids in Bozeman, MT. The farmer in Illinois has just as much skin in the game as the farmer in Idaho when it comes to subsidies and tariffs and weather. One guy in Chicago swears by Lou Malnati's while his best buddy swears by Giordano's. And they're both right.

I found people in Texas to be earnest and honest and people in New Mexico to be warm and welcoming, but those are generalities. What I found across the country as a whole is that Americans are *real*; absolutely utterly real and passionate and proud. I found people from all over coming *to* all over and making a go of it, living out dreams and welcoming strangers along for the ride. The guy I met in the parking lot of the Eisler Bros' Old Riverton Store in Riverton, KS? He was doing the same thing I was doing, but on a slightly different course. And yet we were both in it together. We're all on the same path. Same place, different mission, but same place, same route. I'll do well to remember that and make decisions that impact my fellow travelers favorably.

I learned (from here on out, "learned" will be in air-quotes) that despite the noxious climate we're living in, we're *all* Americans. I'm sick to death of hearing jeremiads about how those who live in "flyover country" are the *real* Americans and "coastal elites" are not (amazing how these screeds are always delivered by pundits on the coasts with elite media platforms, no?). I'm sick to death of "other-ism", the dog-whistles that imply that sinister "others" are coming along to steal our jobs and way of life. My sweet elderly server with the heavy Chicano accent at El Rancho? I didn't for one second fear that she was going to take my job (an anti-money laundering investigator); instead, I thought she was American as fuck for her kindness and work ethic. And I suspect I shared the route with many people of different background and sexual orientation and ethnicity to me, and I didn't for a second think that the resale value of my house had gone down because of it. They're all Americans, too.

I learned that America is truly the Great Melting Pot, and that we *all* have skin in the game. We're *all* immigrants, and we're all here looking to cast our stones and improve our lot. I learned that none of us own America or Americanism, nor do any of us own patriotism. We all have the right to believe that our version of America is the greatest ever—but none of us have the right to ascribe our version upon the entire populace. This worldview leads to nothing but division and hate, and that is *not* America. America is all about the *freedom* to believe that our America is the greatest, while *not* having to live somebody *else's* "greatest version of America".

We split from England because we wanted to be able to worship as we saw fit—or to not worship at all. And that, right there, is the greatness of America: we *all* have the liberty to live in the America that we most believe in. And we're all right! The America we love is the greatest America ever, and none of us have any right to point a finger and cry "bullshit" at somebody else's America.

That is democracy in action, and it's a beautiful thing.

The homogenization of America is spreading more rapidly than ever, and is killing its individuality in its wake. National chain stores, national food franchises, national television standardizing national speech. But get past that and you discover the joy of regionalism and individuality, and that's where the *real* America lies. Sure, I could go to a Burger King and get the same exact cheeseburger I could get at tens of thousands of Burger Kings anywhere else in the country—or I could go to Waylan's Ku-Ku Burger and get a cheeseburger only available at Waylan's Ku-Ku Burger in Miami, OK (next time!). Yes, I could buy a Richard Russo novel at any Barnes & Noble in the country (and I do love Barnes & Noble), but I'd rather get that Russo at Crowe Bookshop, Burlington, VT, where I get the creak of the old wooden floors and the old brick and beams and the joy of being in a cozy place where literature and reading and knowledge are cherished. Absolutely, I can get a pack of strings at any Guitar Center in the country, but give me Buckdancer's Choice Music, Portland, ME, any day: a local institution still holding on against the corporate behemoth.

America offers the same choice everywhere one goes, but one can often find even better—and certainly more unique—choices in their own backyards.

(BTW, before you start sending hate mail, I cannot emphasize this enough: I am *not* knocking chains, and I am *not* saying that anybody who shops at a chain store or eats at a chain restaurant is a fool. I shop and eat at plenty of chains myself, and there's nothing wrong with that. I'm only saying—and this is just me—that if/when I have a choice, I choose small, local, and unique over large, national, and standardized. And who cares what I think or do. End of PSA.)

4. I learned that we all have *so much more in common than not*.

We all have our points of pride and, to be sure, our points of contention, but the pride wins out, every time. The towns we live in are *all* the greatest places in the world, and we can't possibly conceive of living anywhere else—and we're all absolutely right.

5. I learned that America is what you make of it.

If you can get to this country and try to make a better life for yourself, whether by scrubbing toilets, serving burritos, or ringing up Dr. Peppers with cherry shots, you're living the American Dream—the Dream that beckoned *all* our forefathers, whether Irish or Italian or Jewish or Japanese or Bangladeshi. If you can get here and go for it, then God bless your ass.

6. I learned that travel, in America and abroad, is so much better when you go in with an open mind and a proper respect.

I knew that my experience in Paris would be infinitely smoother and more rewarding if I went in with a respectful attitude and made a humble effort, so I revisited my two years of high school French and bought a Rick Steves translation book, and with that, I was able to order *steak frites au vin rouge, s'il vous plaît.* My waiter knew I was struggling and switched to English, and he might not have done so, had I not shown that humble bit of respect and effort. He *definitely* would not have done so had I sauntered in wearing a stars-and-stripes cowboy hat and assless chaps, bellowing, "*I speak American, goddammit!*" And on this trip, I also went in with an open mind and proper respect, and I was rewarded with extreme kindness and warmth. The random conversations I had with Juan the Bartender, Greg the Crime Writer, Tina the Waitress, Jen the Bartender, the Iowa Cattle Rustlers, and the front desk lady at El Trovatore, stay with me, and they came from keeping an open mind and being open to the moment. As the great American philosopher Clark Griswold once said, "This isn't Wally World, Russ, this is a country!"

7. I learned that as Americans, we are an interconnected people in an interconnected world.

And this lesson was brought home by my spiritual guide on this journey, Anthony Bourdain. Bourdain has been gone for just over a year, and I don't know if I will ever get over his loss, and I don't know if a time will come when it won't be too painful to watch his shows again, but the wisdom he imparted on me will remain, nonetheless. Anthony Bourdain was truly a hero to me. It's not *just* that he found success later in life with writing after years of struggling as, basically, a line cook. It's not *just* that he overcame demons. It's not *just* that he was a great writer and, if his on-air persona was any hint, a fucking cool guy. It's that Tony *got it*. He got that, like it or not, we are an interconnected world, and we all need each other. And that we all have so much more in common than not.

Early Bourdain shows are great: travel, eat, drink, puerile double-entendres, lather, rinse, repeat. *But*, while filming an episode of *No Reservations* for the Travel Channel in Beirut in 2006, Tony and his crew were suddenly caught in the middle of the Lebanon War. This experience changed his worldview, and he realized that life is bigger, and that real people are out there experiencing real life. *Parts Unknown* premiered on CNN in 2013, and it was a completely different slant—and it changed my world. Sure, there was still plenty of travel, eat, drink, and puerile double-entendres, but now, Tony was much more engaged, and he got the most amazing, thought-provoking dialogue out of the most basic questions: "What do you like to eat?" "What's life like for you in Turkey under Erdogan?" "How do you live?"

I remember bingeing *Parts Unknown* one day, and in every episode, Bourdain visited a local family for a homecooked meal. Whether in Colombia, Morocco, Libya, Peru, Spain, it was *always* a homecooked meal, with plenty of close-ups of food prep in the kitchen. Tomatoes, onions, garlic...

Wait, a second, what?

It dawned on me (this *was* an "ah-*ha*!" lightbulb moment) that while the locales are drastically different, the fundamentals are the same. With a tomato, an onion, and some garlic (plus cilantro), I can make a good Tex-Mex salsa. With a tomato, an onion, and some garlic (plus more tomato and oregano), I can make an Italian marinara. With a tomato, an onion, and some garlic (plus olives and raisins), I can make a Cuban Picadillo. With a tomato, an onion, and some garlic (plus curry paste and seasoning), I can make an Indian chicken curry. The people are different, but the ingredients are the same.

The message: we all have so much more in common than not, across the world and across the country.

That's the biggest thing I learned about America: we're all fundamentally different, but we're all fundamentally the same, and the same base ingredients connect us all. We share these basic ingredients over a meal and conversation, and we discover other points of commonality. We bridge gaps, and we find connection points, and we become closer to one another. This is the gift of America: it allows us (if we go in with an open mind) to find common connection and purpose, and it allows us to learn and grow through these discoveries. America is the Great Melting Pot, and the ingredients are the same, even if the presentation differs. And, like most good meals, it gets better when the flavors marinate together.

8. Ultimately, though, I learned that America is beautiful. Stunningly, achingly beautiful. The Painted Canyon/Petrified Forest is one of the most breathtaking natural sights I've ever beheld; the mesas and steppes of Arizona are stunning; the lush Ozarks welcome one in and invite one to slow down and take it all in. The architecture of Chicago; the frantic pace of New York; the idyllic beaches of Florida; the foreboding grasslands of North Dakota; the chill vibe of Southern California; the rocky coast of Maine... these are all indescribably beautiful, and they are *all* America. America is a beautiful place.

So, what did I learn about Route 66?

Earlier, I stated, "The facts were, Route 66 was, for all

I knew, mostly gone, and the superhighway had won out fair and square"—and I've since learned that in this I was completely, absolutely, totally, wonderfully wrong: Route 66 is alive, and remains as vibrant and necessary as ever; maybe even *more* so than ever. Yes, I spent far more time on the interstates than the Mother Road itself, but I spent enough time on the Double Six to see that it is still an essential American artery; still a vital thread through the country and our dreams. Route 66 is still the Great American Touchstone; still a cultural talisman whose import still spreads far beyond its 2,278 physical miles. It is still the road of dreams; the road that still leads to a better place—or so we think. Millions are still inspired by this stretch of American macadam, and now, I know why.

Route 66 still matters because it still matters to *people*. Every mile I spent on (and along) Route 66, I was enveloped by it—enveloped in the pride of being located along Route 66; pride in surviving the downturns after the interstate system diverted traffic away; in staying in business for 50, 60, 70, 80 years; in merely being associated with such a great American symbol. Route 66 just *matters* in a way that no other routes or highways do (and yes, this is a gross oversimplification, as all routes and highways matter when they're *your* routes and highways and you care about their upkeep, but go with it).

I mean, can you imagine an I-80 Diner? Jersey Turnpike Fudge? I-90 soda or I-5 Chile sauce? I've never seen anyone wearing an I-70 t-shirt; have you?

Nope. It's nearly unthinkable. The above roads matter and are critical, for sure, but none have become as emblematic of America as Route 66. No songs have praised I-94; no books have been written about all the magical stops along I-10; no poems have been dedicated to the Vince Lombardi Travel Plaza on the New Jersey Turnpike (and for the record, I'm *not* knocking Jersey or the Pike; I genuinely love both). Route 66 doesn't even exist as an official highway designation number anymore, and hasn't for nearly 35 years, yet it's still Route 66. And without it, we'd all be somehow less.

I saw pride of place along Route 66 more than most places I've ever been. People *care* and go to great lengths to maintain what they have along Route 66. The Launching Pad and the Gemini Giant, the Meadow Gold sign and The Campbell Hotel, the Blue Swallow and the Motel Safari, the Burma-Shave jingle, the *HERE IT IS* sign... these things were all on the verge of destruction, done in by apathy, but their location on Route 66 saved them all, thanks to the groundswell of nostalgia and care for the Mother Road. And now, they're all restored and thriving, symbols of America and the importance of place, ready to inspire new generations.

I believe in preservation because I know that self-preservation has saved my life—that is, caring just enough about myself to keep going, and reminding myself that things (truly) will get better. And I saw self-preservation all along Route 66, and this renewed my passion for saving and holding onto what's important.

I learned that for many decades, our American city planners have gotten it all wrong. And Route 66 made me realize this all the more.

Urban planning is another fascination for me, and it all started with those drives to visit my grandmother in Brooklyn: I fell in love with design elements on these visits—the masonry of the West Rock Tunnel; the keystone arches in the window frames across the courtyard; the lights of the bridges; filigrees on a building façade; *THE BAY SHORE* etched above the front door of the apartment. Water towers, streetlamps, the fences around Central Park...

I remember my grandmother had a copy of Robert Caro's epic tome *The Power Broker*, the story of master builder Robert Moses. The image on the cover (Robert Moses on a golden pedestal) captivated me. In the fall of 1999, Ric Burns' *New York* premiered on PBS, and Robert Caro frequently discussed Robert Moses and his impact. From there, I became captivated and later read *The Power Broker*... and my life was changed forever. Robert Moses was New York City Parks Commissioner from 1924 to 1968—which sounds like a sleepy, low-level bureaucratic gig, but over the course of his career, Moses was able to wrest and consolidate unprecedented power—and New York City, America, and the world as a whole, haven't been the same since. Here is a short, highly incomplete list of things that came into existence in New York under Moses' reign:

- 1939 World's Fair.
- 1964 World's Fair.
- Jones Beach.
- Triborough Bridge.
- Verrazzano Narrows Bridge.
- Throgs Neck Bridge.
- Bronx-Whitestone Bridge.
- Restoration of Bryant Park.
- Restoration of Central Park.
- Northern State Parkway.
- Southern State Parkway.
- Henry Hudson Parkway.
- Taconic Parkway.
- Lincoln Center.
- Shea Stadium.
- Astoria Park.
- Crotona Park.
- Cross-Bronx Expressway.
- Whitestone Expressway.
- Brooklyn-Queens Expressway.
- Stuyvesant Town apartments.
- Peter Cooper Village apartments.
- Co-op City apartments.
- United Nations Headquarters.

You get the idea.

This building came at great cost, however: estimates

are impossible, but conservative scholarly guesses put the number of people displaced by Robert Moses' projects in the high six figures. Neighborhoods were destroyed in exchange for highways (my dad watched his Bay Ridge neighborhood nearly destroyed for the on-ramps to the Verrazzano), Moses favored highways over public transportation, and upkeep and maintenance on New York City's subways—the primary mode of transportation for the working class—was shortchanged for generations. And some projects Moses tried to build would have been especially disastrous. One such project was the Lower Manhattan Expressway, which would have connected the Williamsburg Bridge and the Holland Tunnel via a six-lane highway running through the heart of SoHo, Little Italy, and Greenwich Village.

This plan was thwarted by Jane Jacobs.

I found a new hero when I found Jane Jacobs. Born in 1916 in Scranton, PA, Jacobs was a writer for *Architectural Forum* magazine living at 555 Hudson St. in Greenwich Village. Her keen powers of observation led her to reject the 1950s wave of Urban Renewal, in which the federal government tried to fight "blight" by investing in the razing of "blighted" neighborhoods, a.k.a., "slums", a.k.a., "ghettos" (read between the lines there), in favor of commercial redevelopment, and championed the *neighborhood* (a few blocks in which one has all one needs for daily existence—from the corner store to the local school to the dry-cleaner to a doctor making house calls—

and a street constantly populated with pedestrians observing the block and maintaining safety) as a healthy ecosystem for urban life. Her book *The Death and Life of Great American Cities* was published in 1961, and it remains a touchstone for thought about what makes a city work.

Jane Jacobs took on Robert Moses over the Lower Manhattan Expressway, and she won.

Unfortunately, however, the Urban Renewal ethos held, and from the 1950s on, the Homogenization of America spread: highways, shopping malls, franchise restaurants, all populating the idea that one can have the same meal and stay in the same hotel in Providence as one could in Houston.

Yet Route 66 reminded me that the greatness of America lies in its singularities: along every stretch of Route 66, I found stores, restaurants, tourist traps, institutions, and architectural features that exist nowhere else in the world. And I *loved* it. The town square of Pontiac, IL, exists nowhere else but Pontiac, IL. There is no Staples in the town square of Pontiac, IL, and why should there be? Why would I want to go to Pontiac, IL, just to shop at the same Staples I could shop at in Jersey City? Similarly, Ariston Café exists nowhere but on Route 66 in Litchfield, IL, as it should: why would I want to eat at a copycat version of Ariston in Tucson? El Rancho Hotel exists nowhere but on Route 66 in Gallup, NM—and why would I want to stay at a perfect clone in Charlotte where none of the celebrities who stayed at the original stayed?

Case in point: have you seen the CBGB's Cafe at Newark Airport? I've seen few more laughable ventures in my life. Trying to recreate CB's at EWR? Please. CBGB's was a dump. It was a Bowery dive; a biker bar under a single-room-occupancy hotel on Skid Row in Manhattan. And it was the *only* place where a scrappy quartet from Queens called The Ramones could get a gig in 1974. The floor was a minefield of dogshit, the bathrooms were malarial cesspools, and no businessman ever popped in for a perky chardonnay. But The Ramones, Television, Blondie, Talking Heads, and other great bands gravitated there because it was the only place they could get a gig— and from there, a singular movement was launched.

You *cannot* recreate that with a $30 cheeseburger at CBGB's Newark while waiting for your connecting flight to San Antonio.

Sure, there's something to be said for convenience, and I'm fine with being able to pick up the same Apple charger at Best Buy regardless of whether I'm in St. Louis or Santa Fe, or the same venti red eye at Starbucks in Albuquerque and Atlanta, but the homogenization of America is a slippery slope because *it values sameness and convenience over localism.*

Route 66 is the antithesis of this ethos, and that's the land I want to live in. I don't care that I can only eat at Lou Mitchell's once every few years; that makes it even better when I get there. And I don't care that I can only visit the Painted Canyon/Petrified Forest once every few years; that makes me appreciate my excursions to Acadia National Park even more.

Route 66 is the celebration of American individuality, and there's nothing more American than that.

On my trip, I also learned that (contrary to what I thought while planning) Route 66 is an American calling, and that I *want* to do it all: I *want* to bust my ass detouring 40 miles to see a two-by-five-foot slab of original Route 66 concrete accessible only by walking 20 yards over barbed-wire fences into a cow pasture; I *want* to hit every single lovingly restored gas station on the route; I *want* to gorge at every fried chicken and corndog shack and visit the site where Mickey Mantle had his first lay and where Will Rogers once took a dump, and where all bits of arcane Americana happened. Hell, I now want to drive on Route 66 (or what's left of it) for *all* of the trip. I want experience *and* cult-like authenticity—and Route 66 offers the best of both.

So, what has this trip meant to me?

Obvious Answer I: it was the trip of a lifetime.

Obvious Answer II: I'm better off.

But the trip was supposed to be a midlife crisis salve, right? A chance to (re)discover America and myself along Route 66?

Well, the midlife crisis isn't *solved* per se, but I do feel that it is more at bay now—and now that I've largely removed myself from it, I can step back and observe it with some distance and in the past tense. I see that the lessons I've learned about myself, my America, and Route 66 while on the road will guide the rest of my days on multiple levels.

I see that having a tangible goal in mind means I have to get to work to make it happen, and that this is a good thing. For too much of my recent life, I've had nothing fixed that I've been working towards: I haven't had gig calendars and publication deadlines like I did in my late twenties, nor anything else tangible to accomplish. So now, I see that I need to have goals and ideas and dreams and plans in physical existence in order to kick up my discipline (which I thankfully already have) and make it happen. I see that once a plan is in a fixed form, this is as good as a written contract—that is, it had goddamn well better happen. And the work that goes into executing the plan is often as much fun as the plan itself.

I see that plans are great as far as they go, but it's important to leave plenty of space for improvisation, because things *will* go sideways, and you'd better be ready to go along with it. Plus, often, the biggest "calamities" are the most memorable, fun, and life changing. (See Samuel Beckett: "Try again. Fail again. Fail better.")

I see that it's vitally important to have a mental compass on any journey—that is, some vague thought or goal or expectation or notion to guide your path. On this journey, it was the goal of (re)discovering my America and myself that urged me to absorb and appreciate every mile and compare this America I didn't know to the America I'd always known and the self that I'd lost to the self that I'd been. In this way, I found that that this trip could barely be compared to my past travels: the six states I visited for the first time on this trip presented six entirely new worlds to me, and, in turn, six new entities to contemplate. Illinois, Missouri, Kansas, and, to an extent, Oklahoma, share similarities to the world I've always known and were thus relatable, whereas the rest of Oklahoma and all of Texas, New Mexico, Arizona, and California were nearly foreign planets to me, and, now having seen them, my worldview is completely expanded. This is the gift of travel: seeing foreign lands (even "local" foreign lands) changes everything, and you'll never be the same for it.

Now I know how quiet life must be in Galena, Kansas, and how the kids in that town must love its ethereal beauty, but still long for someplace else.

Now I know how wonderful Tulsa, Oklahoma, is, and how the young must love its vibrancy, hipness, and neon American opportunities.

Now I know how far the land stretches out on the Texas Panhandle, the scrub-grass rolling for incalculable miles between the road and any sign of water or civilization. Now I know what a desolate life a rancher in McLean or Wildorado must lead.

Now I know how stunning and primordial the landscape of New Mexico is, and why artists have flocked to its rugged individualistic landscape for years.

Now I know how American Arizona is; how close the landscape remains to that known by the *real* Native Americans—the Navajo.

Now I know what it's like to cross the Mojave, and I can only imagine how difficult the trip must have been in the days of early American automotive travel, without the luxury of air-conditioning, cruise-control, gas gauges, and convenience stores selling potable water every other exit.

Now I know what it is to see glorious restored neon and to stay at hotels saved from demolition and restored with love; to eat at institutions beloved by locals for generations and to travel on roads maintained for decades and for posterity.

Now I know what it is like to hear local morning news in eight states and to peruse the "local" section in bookstores across the land for foreign (to me) American fare and find new literary treasures and see the world change before my very eyes.

Now I know a little more about what America truly is.

Further, revisiting my journals has reminded me that I have a gift for notation, which served me very well on this trip. My passion for documentation—for holding onto everything—made this trip a critical exercise in observation, and I'd like to think I did it justice.

Driving through downstate Illinois reminded me of driving from Vermont to Montreal, and that made me remember and appreciate that long-ago trip.

Driving through the Ozarks reminded me of The Berkshires, and I thought fondly of trips through western Massachusetts and upstate New York.

Stopping at the buffalo statue in El Reno, Oklahoma, reminded me of the Fisherman's Memorial statue at Land's End, Bailey Island, Maine, and I thought of myself as a kid playing on that statue and reveling in the natural beauty of the Maine coast.

Stopping at Midpoint Café in Adrian, Texas, I thought of myself at that moment and all the moments before; all that I'd been through and overcome. And then, like always, I kept going.

Driving through New Mexico reminded me of my unstoppable sense of wonder; my partiality to taking time to breathe in a world that was utterly foreign to me and letting the change in perspective guide me. Allowing myself to be inspired again; be alive with life.

Seeing the Painted Desert and Petrified Forest reminded me that life is beautiful and that it takes a long time (millions of years versus my own lifespan, but still) to distill and create this beauty.

Life is a work in progress, and so am I.

All of the moments of this trip are imprinted on the memory card of my mind, and they will linger, mingling with all the memories of my life, until the whole of my existence is purely a mélange of experience and lessons learned.

I will never be the same for this—I can say that with

certainty. And I'm grateful for this fact.

So, what did I learn about myself while on this trip?

I need to take my time with this one, because I have so much to unpack.

To grossly oversimplify: I'm alive.

To oversimplify slightly less (but still oversimplify): I am, and have been, doing pretty well for myself.

I learned that I can shut off the demon screams and go for it, and that I won't necessarily fail by doing so—and that if I *do* take a few missteps along the way, I can learn from them and grow, and that they need not be fatal.

I learned that I've lived with depression and anxiety my whole life, and yet I'm still here. When I was in my twenties, I thought I'd never overcome my demons; never have friends or a steady job; never make anything of myself. My journal tells all: "I'm heading for a life unresolved." Yet I overcame all of that and found unimaginable success—and then "settled" into quiet stability. In my thirties, I thought that I'd never have anything but domestic stability again—and I overcame that (not by choice, but by taking advantage of a second chance after my termination). And in my forties, I thought that I'd never recover from my termination and never again emerge from the chasm of my all-encompassing depression—and yet, here I am, telling the tale.

I learned that I'm very comfortable living my life in negative space (not negative as in the opposite of positive, but... well, you'll see). Being a creative type, I tend to order my thoughts around concepts of music, art, and architecture. Music: rhythm is not the notes; it's the spaces in between the notes. A dotted quarter-note with an eighth-note rest; it's the rest that pulls you into the next note. The negative space in between. Art: think of a Japanese print of a pagoda on a fog-shrouded mountain. It's not the pagoda that draws you in; it's the fog—the negative white space—which pulls your eye to the mountain and the pagoda. Architecture: the Doric columns on the Lincoln Memorial. The negative space in between the columns is what pulls your eye to the columns themselves. And driving six-plus hours between Chicago and St. Louis is the negative space; the space that draws me on to St. Louis. Driving six-plus hours between St. Louis and Tulsa is the negative space; the space that draws me on to Tulsa. The negative space allows me to look back and look ahead. The negative space gives me time to reflect on the journey; the journey that is this trip; the journey that is my life.

And, needless to say, driving six hours plus six days in a row gave me a lot of time to think.

Since the goal of this journey and book is (re)discovering myself, I spent a lot of time ruminating on that subject. Again, no real "ah-*ha!*" moments, but plenty of "oh *yeah*" realizations, for the good and the bad. To summarize:

The Bad

- Depression and anxiety. The effect these demons have had on my life have been fairly well-documented, but ultimately, these are the root cause of all the bad. After acknowledging this and working on it over the last decade, however, I'm much more aware of how I'm affected, and as such, I can work to do better.

- I can be very judgmental and impatient. This trip reminded me to relax and go in with an open mind, which mitigates my judgmental qualities. Problem solved... ish. The lesson: always relax and go in with an open mind. And don't judge or jump to conclusions.

- I can be too sarcastic for my own good, especially in print. Nothing wrong with sarcasm, but the problem is it often doesn't translate well in print: if I make a social media post in which, to me, I'm clearly laughing at the absurdity of a situation, it makes me look like an asshole. In my mind, it seems obvious that I don't *really* want to run over the woman who parked across two parking spaces with her own car, but in print, it looks like I *really* did, and, as such, I look like a petty dick who can't get over such an insignificant first-world crisis. This is a valuable lesson in perspective, and I don't really care to present myself in this way.

- I can honestly say I've never felt self-loathing, because my self-preservation streak (see The Good below) has always won out—but I *have* lost many years of my life to self-aversion (i.e., the demon screams; the *what-if-I-*

fail mentality). I've spent years kicking myself over the most minor things. (Yes, this does tie into depression and anxiety, and I'm aware of that now.) So, this is a good time for a shift in self-perspective—from self-aversion to self-approval. This can only do me good going forward.

- Tangential to both of the above, but I care too much. I *do* care what you think about me, and I *do* want to be loved and respected and appreciated and cared about—and after all those years of never feeling like I fit in anywhere, I do struggle with that. I want to make a good impression and belong and be loved and validated. I'm scabbed over from those days, but the skin is still pretty thin. I'm working on it.

- I don't know how to let go; how to give up. All too often, I make things worse by trying to defend myself; trying too hard to explain; justify; absolve. Classic HSP at work—and I need to let that shit go. It's like the one thread on the sleeve of your sweater: you pull it and eventually the whole sleeve falls off. I need to keep this visual in mind: *don't rip off the entire sleeve just to save one thread.*

- Far too often, I don't give to myself what I give to others. I always make myself available to my nearest and dearest and make it a point to know that I am there for them, but reaching out to them when *I'm* struggling? Nope. It's hard to be vulnerable; to be low; to be human. But I also deserve what I give, and it's a two-way street.

I should do better to openly receive what I give.

- I've spent years of my life not standing up for myself; not being able to express myself or say what I want and what I don't want. I think this is mostly rooted in the fear of causing hurt: it's so much easier to take the pain than to inflict the pain. I have hurt people in my life, don't get me wrong, and I would rather rip out my own heart and stomp on it than hurt people again. But life is hurt, and it's inevitable. I *will* hurt people again, and people *will* hurt me again, and there's nothing that can be done about it. I'm close to fifty, and I don't have much time left (comparatively speaking), so I'll do well to realize this and accept that I have needs and desires, and that sometimes, they will be incompatible with the needs and desires of others. And this is not necessarily a failure on my part: compatibility is a two-way street, and sometimes incompatibility just happens.

- I've lost years of my life to negativity. Being in negative environments, being around negative people, absorbing it, living it. And the thing about negativity is that it's so much more difficult than positivity. It takes so much more effort and maintenance to see the bad side of people and things. People and things are inherently good, and if you go in with that premise, you won't be disappointed. If you go on the premise that people and things are bad, you expend so much more effort *looking* for things to be disappointed about. And then you have to expend that much more effort to fuel the negativity around you and in yourself.

- Tangential and related to my thoughts on sarcasm above, as I stated earlier, I often laugh at what scares me in order to try to take the fear away, but often, when laughing at myself, it comes off self-depreciatory. Not how I care to present myself anymore.

The Good

- First off, I'm pretty goddamn talented. Yeah, I said it—and it's true. I can do a number of things pretty well, and some things *very* well: I've learned that I can paint a scene accurately, and that I can take mental notes and flesh them out into spot-on, coherent narratives after the fact; I'm a good musician, a decent home-recording engineer, and filmmaker; I can cook up some deliciousness; I can take care of myself after years of not doing such a great job at the same.

- I know a lot about music, art, pop culture, history, baseball, etc. I'm often a walking trivia napkin of useless crap—as you can probably tell from our many tangents in this book!

- If you're in my inner circle, I'm loyal as fuck. I'll take a bullet for you.

- I do my best to be kind and make a difference.

- I am (despite initially not realizing it) quite disciplined. I make the bed in the morning, do the dishes after dinner, clean and vacuum the house, do laundry... I can't stand having stuff hanging over my head: shit needs to get done, whether I want to do it or not—and since I usually *don't* want to do it, I'd rather just do it and get it over with so... well, so it's over with.

- I'm a total optimist and I always look for the best in any situation and any person. And I can always find it and laugh at the absurdity or embrace the positive.
- I'm still here because of my self-protective streak. It's always been there, and it's always saved me from stepping over the edge. And it's encouraged me to never quit...
- I believe in people and the inherent goodness of people. I believe in our interconnected world, and I know I can learn something of worth from anybody. I want to bring *everybody* in the world together for a global group hug!
- I appreciate things and I'm grateful for all experiences, good and bad.
- I am incredibly self-reflective, constantly (re)evaluating where I am against where I've been and how I can do better, connecting the dots, finding a common narrative thread, and editing as necessary. Many positive changes have arisen as a result.

So, again: I'm alive; I am (and have been) doing pretty well for myself; and I love my life and where I am in it. I'm in the negative space now, years away from the lows of my twenties and with many more highs to come.

Balance and repose. The spaces in between.

Everything is now so much better—so much clearer—and I've learned that I can still dream big and accomplish big. I've learned how far I've come in life and that when I need them, I've got a serious brass pair.

When I was twenty-six, I was struggling to find temp jobs and I had one box of rice, one box of mac and cheese, one loaf of bread, and about five dollars to my name—and now, at forty-six, I have a permanent job, a house with a new roof and furnace, a lakefront camp, and two paid-off cars... and I spent eight days driving across the country in a rental car, staying at hotels and eating out every day, without sweating about money. This trip would have been utterly unimaginable to myself at twenty-six—fantastical, even. Yet it happened.

When I was twenty-six, I fucked up dough-in-a-can—and now, at forty-six, I have some decent game in the kitchen and can take care of myself without resorting to $0.39 cheeseburgers. When I was twenty-six, I slept on the floor because I didn't have a bed—and now, at forty-six, I have a house full of furniture. When I was twenty-six, I had undiagnosed depression because I didn't have insurance—and now, at forty-six, my insurance pays for my meds and therapy, and I'm managing my life well. When I was twenty-six, I'd never even thought of writing professionally—and now, at forty-six, I've been a music critic and had articles published in *Elephant Journal*, *Reverb Press*, and other prestigious publications. I was ballsy enough to think I might be able to be a music critic with absolutely no experience, and I made it happen. When I was twenty-six, I thought I'd never play music again—and now, at forty-six, I know what it's like to play for 2,000-plus people and hear myself on commercial radio. I was ballsy enough to think I might be able to get in a band and play originals in Boston, and I made it happen. And now, at forty-six, I'm ballsy enough to think that I can write a book. And here we are. This fearlessness comes from turning off the demon screams and forcing myself out into the world, to hang my shingle in the town square.

On this trip, I learned that whatever I am in life, I'm pretty much self-taught. I am the product of many bad decisions caused by a lack of essential tools in my arsenal (social skills, the ability to read signals, knowledge of how to cope with depression and anxiety, etc.)—yet I figured all these things out along the way, usually after learning the hard way and suffering the consequences. I learned that I *can* learn about myself and learn how to do better, and I have.

On this trip, I learned that I can find joy *and* hold onto joy. As I type this, I'm thinking of the girl at Delgadillo's offering me the option of a small milkshake in a ketchup cup ("You get free refills!"), and I'm cracking up yet again. I think of all those big dumbass grin moments along the Mother Road: seeing the *Wrigley* building in Chicago; crossing into Kansas; passing a Burma-Shave jingle... These moments of joy remind me of all the elements of found-

and-sustained joy that are part of my present life: kayaking; building a fire and listening to the loons on the lake at camp; Vermont Coffee Company, extra dark, black, in my favorite cup in the morning; autumn foliage in New England; winter sunsets; Dave O'Brien, Jerry Remy, and Dennis Eckersley in the Red Sox booth, Dave Sims, Mike Blowers, and Dan Wilson in the Mariners booth (just like I'm visiting my in-laws in Seattle!), and Gary Cohen, Keith Hernandez, and Ron Darling in the Mets booth; Sarah Vaughan, Ella Fitzgerald, Billie Holiday, Frank Sinatra, Mel Torme, and Johnny Hartman; Sonny Rollins and Coleman Hawkins; McCoy Tyner and Herbie Hancock; Miles Davis and Lee Morgan; Buffalo Springfield, Neil Young, Crosby Stills & Nash, The Byrds, and The Rolling Stones; The Ramones and Television, Hüsker Dü and The Feelies; Faye Webster, Molly Tuttle, and Margo Price; Crumb and FOAMM and The Marias and Japanese Breakfast; paintings from the masters of the Hudson Valley School (Thomas Cole, Albert Bierstad, Frederic Edwin Church, and Jasper Cropsey); Scorsese and De Niro films; Ken Burns documentaries; Richard Russo, Robert B. Parker, E.B. White, Chris Bohjalian, Paul Doiron, Jonathan Franzen; cooking up a big pot of gumbo; stacking a perfect row of firwood to season for the summer; my mom's apple pie; my mother-in-law and stepfather-in-law grilling; my wife and sister-in-law together and hyperventilaughing just outside of Seattle; timing myself every day on the New York Times crossword on paper and in pencil; woodsmoke. When one is in the worst of a depression, finding and holding onto joy is critically important—and this trip reminded me that I have a penchant for doing so.

On this trip, I learned how every point of my life has connected and led me to where I am now. I see myself at six, seeing the Thompsons' house burning to the ground and fearing the same would happen to my house. I see myself passing the abandoned buildings that I was sure were hideouts for robbers and running from the "hippies". I see my visions of P-3 Orions crashing on the runway and getting lost in Grand City. I see myself uprooted to Florida and having my entire world altered. I see myself struggling, not feeling like I belonged, feeling completely lost and alone. I see myself starting over six times in four years and still not fitting in at any point. I see myself at fourteen returning to Maine, enduring trauma, and triumphing with music. I see myself thriving with music in my early twenties and drifting through my mid-twenties. I see undiagnosed depression taking over and nearly destroying me in the process. I see myself recovering in my late twenties, pushing myself and reaching heights I never thought I would. I see myself settling into a quiet, relatively happy domestic life: a life of pleasant existence, occasional Big Adventures, and no dreams on the horizon. I see myself at forty-two, when my world was shattered. I see the depression return and commandeer my life with a ferocity I hadn't experienced in two decades. I see myself making the choice to settle old scores, earn old degrees, and explore new avenues of creative joy. I see myself struggling through a hideous period of unemployment, broken down on the side of the road, totally lost and terrified. And I see myself at forty-six, gainfully employed after years of turmoil and basking in the glow of the greatest road trip—the greatest Big Adventure—of my life. I see that I have overcome enough trials and tribulations for a lifetime and have made my dreams come true.

I've learned that I've survived a lot of traumas, and (critically) I've turned each one into triumph. I see that I can survive pretty much anything and go on to turn the experience into something good. I see what a gift this is, and I see that I want to share this gift and help others to overcome their battles. Because we *can* all overcome our battles. I've overcome a lot, and I will overcome much more. I'm battling... but I'm battling.

As a whole, this trip formed an amazing part of the process of overcoming myself. I drove 2,359 miles across eight states in six days by myself, with no serious conception of what I was doing—and I made it. I traveled across a completely foreign America and found my way home. No, I didn't cure cancer, but I *did* live out a number of dreams in the process and put myself in a number of pictures I held in my head along the way. And I learned a hell of a lot about my country and myself... and with that, I've set myself up to do greater things from here on out—and who knows what else I'll be able to accomplish by doing so?

I see even more clearly now who I am and how I got here. I still don't quite see where I'm going yet, but it's a great start.

I still see me.

I still see that I can challenge myself and achieve great new heights.

And I have.

And now that I have, I see that I am forever changed for the better. And maybe I'll do it all again; see what else I can learn...

ACKNOWLEDGMENTS

Dear George:-
Remember <u>no</u> man is a failure who has <u>friends</u>.
Thanks for the wings!
Love
Clarence

Yes, I'm turning into George Bailey in *It's a Wonderful Life*, but I appreciate the sentiment all the more having finished this tome and seeing where I am *vis-a-vis* where I've been. Or, to quote another pop culture icon, Sam "Mayday" Malone (from the last episode of *Cheers*), "I'm the luckiest son-of-a-bitch on Earth."

I need to start with the bloodlines first: my parents, Eric and Eleanor Westbye, and my brother, Eric. Without you a) I wouldn't be here, and b) I wouldn't have been able to do this. Thank you for the DNA and the love.

Tammy Townsend Westbye: a great sis-in-law, a great influence, and an *amazing* stacker of firewood, scallion dicer, and bringer of delicious Buffalo chicken dip.

Departed bloodlines: William Glidden and Edna Glidden. Thank you for having the Homestead and remaining there still every time I visit. Swanhild Westbye: thank you for living in The Bay Shore in Bay Ridge, Brooklyn, and hosting this eager Maine boy. Hans Westbye: I've never met you, but thank you for being there. Without you, there would be no Eric Westbye!

Next, the (non-)bloodlines: Mary Fuzzell, Clayton Fuzzell, Jessica Gilmore English (sissy!), Chris English, and Lauryn English. My second family; my second home. I love you all more than I can say.

Seattle (non-)bloodlines (but bloodlines nevertheless): Jenni Sandler, Brian Sandler, Avery and Holden Sandler, Amy Wheeler, George Wheeler, Rachel and Charlie Wheeler, Audry Henniger, Chuck Henniger, Debbie Henniger, Angie Henniger Elmore, Julie Henniger Nelson, Brandy Burns, Maggie Szymanowski, Magen Lang Queen (Magen Queen from the West Coast!), Joe Queen, and Lauren Rojas. You're all my family.

Leonard, Donna, Rick, and Scott Moreau: you are also truly family, and I love you as such.

Kristin Letrud: holding down the Norse bloodline in Italia! And Gretchen Elliot Regan: doing the same in RI!

Lisbon peeps: Lori Dineen and Corey St. Pierre: I love

you both dearly. Thank you for being there and helping me get over myself. Traci Austin, you are an inspiration. Travis and Kelly Crafts: hosts of the greatest Christmas (and other) parties ever and deliverers of balls in all forms! Ed Judd, Brenda Card-Burmeister, Karen Durisko, Angel Broadwater, Angel Tibbetts, Tyson Curtis, Libby Poulin, Angie Dickinson Booker, Audra Martel, Beth Jones Earle, Bobbie Freve, Cameron Thomas, Chandra Dione, Charmer Miller, Coral Sunshine Woodbridge, Dain Stephens, Darcy Wilcox, Darrin Barschdorf, Leanne Barschdorf, Elizabeth Collins Luddington, Elizabeth Hartmann-Rogers, Eric James Roy (Rook!), Erin Kamke, Heather Cronin, Stephanie Doyon, Jacquie Harris, Jamie Hoar, Jen Waters Fuller, Jeremy Allen, Jason Allen, Jessica Herling Bailey, Kelly Austin, Kelly Fortin, Kevin Beaulier, Kevin Davis, Kristina Eastman, Lisa Robbins, Mark Koza (Cube!), Norm Albert (ooooh yeah!), Dean Hall, Staci Stanley, Tim Biron, and Yolanda Jellison. Thank you.

U Maine Round I: Marshall Moody, Jerry Perron, Walt Craven, Justin Crouse, Gary Clancy, Bob Thompson. Dan Corbett, Eleanor Healy, Art McConnell, Benjamin Logan, Bill Moseley, Christopher Scott Poulin, Gary Wittner, Gregg Hoover, Steve Grover, and Mark Polishook. Thank you, thank you, thank you.

Boston: first and Foremost, T-Max, for taking a chance on a young punk who had never written before, but was ballsy enough to submit a few bogus writing samples. Second and equally foremost, The High Ceilings: Max

Heinegg, Chris Blackburn, John Woods, and Alex Polemeropoulos. With you, we saw the world (or at least Boston to the Cape) and rocked it fiercely. And with you, I realized dreams I never thought I would achieve. Thank you. Much love.

Now, to backtrack to Berklee: Leigh Hasan, Jason Anderson, Christan Cambas, Ajda Snyder, and Sarah Scarletta. *Mass Ave fo' life!*

More Boston pals and co-conspirators: Kier Byrnes, Will Dailey, Ed Valauskas, Corin Ashley, Cynthia Von Buhler, Linda Bean Pardee, Melissa Gibbs, Meredith Lyn, Ad Frank, Adam Lewis, Dawn Kamerling, Angelle Wood, Brian Charles, Tad Overbaugh, Shawn Byrne, Carmalita Yarbles, Cat Wilson, Chad Rousseau, David Thompson, Dave Minehan, Eleanor Ramsay, Mick Mondo, Mary Ricciardi, Tina Bugara, Jess Finn, Lexi Kahn, Michelle DiPoala, Michelle Poppleton Chumase, Joe Kowalski, Michelle Yvette Paulhus, Paul Hilcoff, Joanne Robinson, John Surette, Joel Simches, Julie Chadwick, Justin Tibbetts, Julie LeBlanc Pampinella (all my love, darlin' inspiration), Karen Martakos, Linda Jung, Sean O'Brien, Linda Viens, Lynette Estes, Matt Hutton, Patrick MacDonald, Matt York, Mike Piehl, Scott Janovitz, Peter Moore, Rick Berlin, Rob Cushing, Shilo McDonald, Tim Mungenast, Tom Kielty, and Meredith Cooper Mascolo.

U-Maine Round II: Bryant Sirois: your friendship got me through the first five minutes of my return after 20 years, and we graduated together. And Anthony

Lopatosky: you presented my senior concert. Thank you both for being there.

Friends from along the way: Mike Tolen, Cindy Tolen, Jenn "The Fabulous" Cooper, Jessica Beebe (Westbeebe!), Jenny Paquette, Rebecca Rinaldi (Mary!), Lorna Paige, Jenny Lou, Scott Morgan, Cedar Barnett, Bonny Smith, Jana Eklund, Jenna Brooks, Joanne Robinson, Tori Leigh, Megan La Londe, Melissa Rivera, Ed Kern, Amy Royse Kern, Amy Wengler, Keeley Milne, Renee Picard, Jessica Yergin, and Derek Dorr.

Hayley Paige and all at Notebook Publishing for giving birth to the only baby I'll ever have: this book baby. You took a "not quite a turd, but..." and polished it into a diamond. My eternal gratitude and love.

And I saved the best for last: Andrea Westbye. My best friend and life partner. Thank you for being there and putting up with me. I love you. Goodnight.

I lied about the book being the only baby I'll ever have! My cat babies, Noodle and Nestle! Daddy loves you both!

Goddamn. Did I ever think I'd have this many people on my thank-you list? No way. But there are so many more, most of whom I haven't met. Thank *you*, everyone who has read this book. Every one of you who has battled Depression/Anxiety and have kept going. Every one of you who has ever dreamed of, or accomplished, Route 66. You are my tribe, and I am with you always.

APPENDIX: ROUTE 66 PRE-DEPARTURE PLAN

SPRING 2019

Illinois

Must

- Swinging Bridges, Pontiac.
- Walldog Murals, Pontiac.
- Brick 66, Auburn.
- Chain of Rocks Bridge, Madison.

Maybe

- IL Route 66 Association Hall of Fame, Pontiac.
- Route 66 Welcome Center, Litchfield.

Chicago

I've been to Chicago, and it's one of my favorite cities I've visited. Hence, I'm planning an early flight out of Portland for a leisurely day in the Windy City—no agenda, save for a pilgrimage to magical Wrigley Field. Maybe I'll pay a return call to Edward Hopper's masterpiece *Nighthawks* and Grant Wood's *American Gothic* at the Art Institute of Chicago, and I'll perhaps have a cigar at Ditka's. And I'll *definitely* have a Chicago hotdog.

Downstate

Pontiac, Illinois, creates a problem! It's 303 miles and almost six hours from Chicago to St. Louis, and I'd *like* to make it in time to walk the Chain of Rocks bridge, visit the Jefferson National Memorial (I'm a Lewis and Clark fiend), take the tram to the top of the Gateway Arch, and gorge on ribs before the Cardinals host the Pittsburgh Pirates. Damn you, Pontiac, with your Walldog murals, swinging bridges, Illinois Rt. 66 Association Hall of Fame, and apparent smalltown Heartland quaintness!

Okay, I could theoretically hold off on the Jefferson Memorial/Arch until the next morning. Day Two is St. Louis to Tulsa (?) with no absolute musts on the way. I think that just might work, because I think I just might have to spend a little bit of time in Pontiac. There's the museum and the murals, and I'm a sucker for relics of our American industrial past—and the swinging bridges are right in my strike zone. Three footbridges spanning the Vermilion River built for the shoe manufacturing industry in the early 20th century and restored for pedestrian pleasure? Win! My office at the day job is in a former textile mill that once produced shoes and, earlier, uniforms for the Union forces during the Civil War, and I often walk the repurposed rail trestles in my town—so this is a huge point of interest for me.

Pontiac, I think I just might love you already.

The Brick 66 in Auburn, meanwhile, is a 1.4-mile stretch of original brick pavement on the original 1926-1930 alignment that's still drivable, *and* it isn't too much of a detour. Hell. Yes.

Finally, the Chain of Rocks Bridge in Madison: a must. The Mississippi. A classic steel-truss bridge with a 30-degree turn over a nasty point of the river and views of the Gateway Arch. Pedestrian repurposing. Sign me up. I'm definitely walking this one, one mile each way.

That's about it for Illinois. And no, I won't be getting my Lincoln on during this trip. My admiration for The Great Emancipator is endless, but this trip isn't meant to be a historical deep dive. Thus, no Lincoln's Home, Lincoln-Herndon Law Offices, Lincoln Depot, or Lincoln's Tomb. Maybe next time.

Missouri

Must
- Cardinals game, Busch Stadium.
- Jefferson National Memorial, St. Louis.
- Gateway Arch, St. Louis.

Maybe
- Hooker Cut, Devil's Elbow.
- Devil's Elbow Bridge, Devil's Elbow.

St. Louis

I've seen the Mississippi, but from Minneapolis, not the spiritual epicenter of St. Louis. I've read *The Journals of Lewis and Clark* and inhaled Ken Burns' *Lewis and Clark* and *Thomas Jefferson,* but I've never seen where the Corps of Discovery launched their unimaginable journey (okay, it was St. Charles, not St. Louis, and the Missouri River, not the Mississippi, but close enough). Westward Expansion, Manifest Destiny, the Cradle of the New America, for the good and the bad. I've never touched the silvery skin of Eero Saarinen's magnificent Gateway Arch, nor taken the tram to the top; never stood on the steps of the Old Courthouse, where America's Great Shame, slavery, stained the air; never had St. Louis ribs in St. Louis.
All of that changes during this trip.

And I'm finally seeing a game at Busch Stadium.

The St. Louis Cardinals have always held a place in my heart, for good and for bad. By birth, I'm a Boston Red Sox lifer, a card-carrying member of Red Sox Nation—and the Cards crushed my ancestors in the 1946 and 1967 World Series (though we finally exacted revenge in 2004 and 2013). My dad grew up with Jackie Robinson and the Brooklyn Dodgers, who seemingly never had a chance against Stan "The Man" Musial and the Redbirds, and on clear Maine nights, I'd tweak the dial and the antenna and get Jack Buck calling the Cards on KMOX St. Louis, and his magnificent voice (like a sack full of gravel) and signature calls ("Go crazy, folks!") are deeply rooted in my very being.

More broadly, as a lover of history, the Cardinals are a fascinating case study of race relations in America. In 1947, St. Louis was, like many towns across America, confronting issues of race, and the Cardinals were all white. In 1967, St. Louis was, like many towns across America, still confronting issues of race. But, a mere two decades later, the Cardinals were a fiercely integrated team.

1947: only eight teams in the National League, only eight teams in the American League. No teams further west or south than St. Louis. The American League St. Louis Browns were a hapless joke, totally off the radar (they would move to Baltimore in 1953, reborn as the Orioles). The National League St. Louis Cardinals were the original America's Team. KMOX's 50,000-watt signal was the most powerful in the country, thus large swaths of America were able to hear Harry Caray, long before he became Mr. Cub on WGN TV Chicago, calling the play-by-play.

The 1947 Cardinals have been broad-brushed as a team of racists. Many of these stories (like that of the team organizing a boycott against Jackie Robinson) have unfortunately been distorted and/or overblown. History is complicated. But there were incidents. Outfielder Enos Slaughter famously spiked Robinson that season, as did catcher Joe Garagiola, who spent his years as a beloved morning fixture on *The Today Show* playing down and changing the storyline of the incident. It was a toxic atmosphere, and the Cardinals were in the middle of it.

But by 1967, the team looked very different. Tim McCarver caught the great pitcher Bob Gibson. Roger Maris shared the outfield with Curt Flood and Orlando "Cha Cha" Cepeda. The Cardinals integrated in 1954, seven years after Brooklyn and five years before the Red Sox. The '67 Cards were a beloved integrated team, and I can only imagine how far-fetched that might have seemed only 20 years earlier.

That, to me, is a goddamn great American story.

Downstate
The Ozarks. The Gasconade and the Big Piney. Devil's Elbow and Hooker Cut. Rolla and Cuba, Joplin, and Eureka. Not much really calling me about the rest of Missouri, to be honest, but those names brew up a big cup of Americana

in my mind. I can't imagine the beauty of the Ozarks: the vast rolling farmland, the gentle flow of the Gasconade, Osage, and Big Piney rivers; and I've read of Hooker Cut, the massive trench blasted out to widen the 1940s alignment of Rt. 66 from two lanes to four to accommodate travel from nearby Fort Leonard Wood for the war effort: the largest man-made cut in the world at the time. I've also seen "before and after" photos of Devil's Elbow Bridge, and I want to walk it. And maybe a little more BBQ at the adjacent Elbow Inn... Otherwise, downstate Missouri looks to be just a pleasant, long drive through the Heartland with minimal distractions, and I'm cool with that.

Kansas

Must
- Cars on the Route, Galena.

And...well, there's only 13 miles of Rt. 66 in Kansas, so I want to spend a few minutes at Cars on the Route in Galena, the old Kan-O-Tex Service Station which houses the trucks that inspired the Disney smash *Cars*. But really, that's about it. Sorry, Kansas. It's not your fault.

Oklahoma

Must

- Mickey Mantle's Childhood Home, Commerce.
- The Ghost Town of Picher.
- Oklahoma Route 66 Museum, Clinton.

Man, Oklahoma is going to be tough, because there's a *lot* of amazing stuff that I'll probably be blowing past. I admire Woody Guthrie, and the Woody Guthrie Center looks like a fantastic museum. I know there are some top-notch museums dedicated to Oklahoma's Native American heritage, oil-boom past, and Civil War significance, and I've also heard that OK City is a surprise art deco lover's dreamscape. All the above resonates with me, but again, this is not a deep dive history tour, and honestly, I don't know if it's all enough to warrant any extensive time off the road. I might have to stop in Commerce to see where one of my idols, Mickey Mantle, came from, as well as take a gander at Picher (a town nearly destroyed by mining pollution) and the grand Coleman Theater in Miami (pronounced Mi-*am*-uh), but beyond that, as of right now, I plan on laying down for the evening around Tulsa and then swiftly moving on. I'm keeping an open mind, though.

Okay, actually, I lied: I'll need to hit up the Oklahoma Route 66 Museum in Clinton. Knowing that the flags of all eight Route 66 states fly outside the museum is enough:

this isn't just a bit of esoteric local memorabilia! And yeah, it's in Oklahoma, starting point of the Joads. The exhibits sound amazing: an interactive wonderland of big band sounds, diner stools, and Dust Bowl ephemera. Fat pitch in my strike zone right there!

Texas

Must
- U-Drop Inn, Shamrock.
- Palo Duro Canyon, Canyon.
- Cadillac Ranch, Amarillo.
- Midpoint Café, Adrian.

I definitely need to drop in at the U-Drop Inn in Shamrock. This magnificent 1936 art-deco Conoco station calls to me like an American siren song. It's a typical Route 66 story: business boomed with the birth of the Mother Road, and then the Eisenhower Interstate Highway system took traffic away, and the U-Drop Inn accordingly fell into disrepair. The station was refurbished thanks to a federal grant in 2003, and is now owned by the town of Shamrock, TX—and it looks to be a magnificent place to get out, stretch the legs, and take in some vintage neon Americana.

Bring it.

Meanwhile, Palo Duro Canyon, the "Grand Canyon of

Texas". Georgia O'Keeffe called it a "seething cauldron, filled with dramatic light and color", and Georgia O'Keeffe knew what the hell she was talking about! Not to mention the fact that Palo Duro looks to me like the part of the trip where the topography really starts to change; where the west really begins. I can't wait to see the mesa walls and rock towers; the mesquite, cactus, and wildflower. I'll have to set aside a little time here, either for a hike or just a long drive through.

The Cadillac Ranch in Amarillo. Sure, it's cheesy as hell, but why not? What's more American than ten Cadillacs stuck in the parched earth ready to be spraypainted? A fun little side trip—one where I can leave my mark. Literally.

And the beloved Midpoint Café in Adrian: halfway there! Adrian, TX, is the geographic middle-of-the-Mother-Road: 1,139 miles from Chicago, 1,139 miles to Santa Monica. Midpoint Café's slogan is, *When you're here, you're halfway there.* And they got that goddamn right! Plus, they're famous for their "ugly crust" pies, and I love the outcasts in life... and that certainly applies to pies, too. I don't discriminate.

New Mexico

Must
- Tucumcari.

- The Musical Road of Tijeras, Tijeras.

I *really* want to stay at the Blue Swallow Motel in Tucumcari, but the timing will be against me. Even still, Blue Swallow, to me, is *the* quintessential Route 66 icon: this 12-room gem has the most magnificent neon sign out front, and there's an attached garage for each room. Seriously.

Next time, for sure.

While the timing might not work for a stay at the Blue Swallow, I still must spend a little time walking around Tucumcari so I can enter the images in my head: Better Than Ezra's *Deluxe* album was on heavy rotation in my Boston of 1998, and the song *Coyote* mentions Tucumcari. I'd never heard of it before that point, but instantly, the mental snapshots appeared: flat plains of cactus; mountains spreading out, 66 a thinning arrow pointing toward them. Plus, according to the lore, the Apache chief Wautonomah decided to choose his heir via a knife fight between the braves Tonopah and Tocom on a mountain just outside of town. Tocom got shanked, and Wautonomah's daughter, Kari, who was in love with Tocom, grabbed the blade and killed herself. The heartbroken chief then grabbed the knife, screamed, "Tocom-Kari!" and did himself in. Very likely an apocryphal story, but I love it, and I'm going with it. It just adds to my images of Tucumcari, and I can't wait to insert myself in that frame. I also plan on spending a bit of time walking the strip, probably hitting Tee Pee Curios (the business is listed as Tee Pee, but their own sign out front spells out "TePee". Curious!) and maybe taking a spin to the mountain, if possible.

I rarely use cruise control, but I'll be setting it at 45 for The Musical Road of Tijeras. The rumble strips on the road have been positioned such that if you're hitting it at exactly 45 miles per hour, the road plays *America The Beautiful*. The New Mexico Department of Transportation selected this quarter-mile stretch for this because it's beautiful, but also because too many cars were blasting through like bank robbers in a high-speed pursuit. Now *that's* what I call public planning!

Arizona

Must
- Painted Desert/Petrified Forest National Park, Petrified Forest.
- Jack Rabbit Trading Post, Joseph City.
- Meteor Crater, Winslow.
- Standin' on the Corner Park, Winslow.
- The Wild Burros of Oatman.

Painted Desert/Petrified Forest National Park. Um, yeah? Totally in my wheelhouse. Another mini Grand Canyon, since I won't be hitting the actual Grand Canyon this time around. This is the west as I've seen it in my mind's eye, and I'm going to put myself in this frame. The mesas... The buttes... Oh, yes.

Jack Rabbit Trading Post. The famous *HERE IT IS* sign. Well, what is "*IT*"? I must find out! I love that this sign was erected in 1949 and has since been lovingly restored, and that the store has been run by the same family for generations. A quick little diversion; a chance to stretch the legs and buy some memorabilia.

Meteor Crater, Winslow. Okay, how often does one get to see an actual meteor crater dating back 50,000 years? Cool! Its circumference is 2.4 miles, and it's 560' deep. I can only imagine the intensity of a chunk of an asteroid hitting Earth at 26,000 miles per hour and creating this monstrosity. Nature rules.

Standin' on the Corner Park. I either love or loathe The Eagles, depending on my mood and the hour of the day. But, of course, I will have to follow Jackson Browne and Glen Frye and find myself standin' on a corner in Winslow, Arizona. Jackson Browne wrote *Take It Easy* after having car trouble in Winslow, and thus, a 1970s soft rock anthem and dentist office staple was born. The park features the requisite flatbed Ford (*with a girl, my Lord...* Lord help me, now it's stuck in my head) statue with a full-size Route 66 road sign painted in the intersection, and I do have a soft spot for intersection art (such as the giant seashells painted between the crosswalks in Daytona). And dammit, that's America.

Finally, Oatman is a town ruled by asses. No, really. It was a serious boomtown, and when the bust came, the town's prospectors scrammed out of town, leaving their burros behind. The town is now populated by wild burros roaming the streets, and stores sell feed ("Burro Chow") for their maned overlords—and that's the goddamndest thing I've ever heard! I must investigate. If I come back missing a hand, you'll know why and where.

California

Must
- Roy's Motel & Café, Amboy.
- Dodger Stadium.

Maybe
- Amboy Crater, Amboy.
- Elmer's Bottle Tree Ranch, Helendale.

Roy's Motel & Café. It doesn't get more 66 than this! That amazing iconic arrow sign in the middle of nowhere, Mojave; the ghost town Amboy. Ghosts of the past, spectral presences in the California dust, where the world looks like a *CHiPS* episode. Really looking forward to this one.

Amboy Crater. Could be kinda nifty. A 250'-high, 1,500'-diameter ash heap formed in one of the youngest volcanic fields in the U.S. (with my in-laws in Seattle, fault lines are a major background narrative in my life) with a little picnic area. Looks like an extremely miniature Mount St. Helens. Might be nice to grab a seat and ponder the power of magma, or something.

Elmer's Bottle Tree Ranch. Twinkling Americana Kitsch in the Mojave! Elmer Long sounds like my kind of eccentric: a guy who's dedicated his life to building sculptures festooned with old bottles. He's built over 200 bottle trees in his home, and sounds like a guy who loves his work. And I have a feeling I will, too.

LA, baby. I'll likely allow enough time for a taste of the City of Angels. Not much more than a taste, but it'll be a delicious nip. I'll end the trip at the Santa Monica Pier, of course, and plan to spend a bit of time frolicking in the Pacific before turning the rental in and checking in to my hotel. From there, I want to walk the Sunset Strip, past the landmark Whisky a Go Go, and the Rainbow Room. If I have time to hit up the Griffith Observatory, I shall. Same for loitering around Echo Lake. A casual end to a whirlwind.

And finally, the Grand Prize: Dodger Stadium. A lifelong dream for a lifelong baseball fan. I got swept up in Fernando Mania in 1981 when I was eight, when the great pitcher Fernando Valenzuela became a sensation, and I've dreamed of catching a game at Chavez Ravine ever since. Obviously, I didn't know at that age that I was supposed to hate the Dodgers; that these were the same Dodgers that my dad had loved when they'd played in

Brooklyn and the same Dodgers who'd broken his heart when they left after the 1957 season. I just saw that beautiful baby-blue park with the big Union 76 gas sign above the outfield and the San Gabriel mountains looming over the wall, and I fell in love. Not necessarily with the team—they beat my Yankees (I didn't hate the Yanks yet) in the '81 World Series—but with the park; the setting; the image of sitting in the warm California sun with Vin Scully on my transistor, a Dodger Dog in hand, and paradise on the horizon. I've always seen myself at Dodger Stadium in my mind's eye. And now, it's going to happen.

Now, what about food?

I'm coming into this trip with only one hard and fast rule: *no* chains. But, of course, there are some gray areas in this rule (such is life). For example, Portillo's Chicago: a chain, yes, but not a chain readily available to me in Maine. Therefore, we must amend this rule to no chains that I can easily access at home. Who says I'm not flexible? Basically, it's go local—and *no* golden arches.

Dietary side note: in my everyday life, I try to be more vegetarian than not for a myriad of reasons—namely environmental, health, and (especially) humanitarian. But I'm not gonna preach to you; we all need to make our own choices, and who gives a shit what I think, anyway? Even still, over the last few years, I've felt more and more strongly about animal rights. I mean, who am I (especially after crying my way through *Babe* or *squee*ing my way through baby animal pictures and videos) to say that I can take a sweet little piggy, have him butchered and cooked for my benefit, and turn him into nothing more than a delicious memory and a big deuce presented to my sewer system? Who am I to sign a death warrant to another beautiful living creature? Animals are sentient beings, just like me; they feel fear and pain just like I do, and they deserve the best quality of life possible, just like I do.

But goddamn, St. Louis ribs and Texas steaks and New Mexican fare...

I was raised on meat, and I'm not fully a vegetarian. So, what can I do? Like everything in my life, I try to split the difference: I do the best I can to make the best decisions I can. It's not perfect, but it's better than it could be. That's what I try for, at least. At home, I do my best to be meat-benevolent: I personally think that factory farming is barbaric, so I do my best to source my meat carefully, find humane vendors, and avoid the big processing firms. And on the road... well, I do my best and try to atone when I get back home.

I mean, goddamn, *St. Louis ribs and Texas steaks and New Mexican fare.*

I'm going to be eating a shit-ton of meat on this trip, and I'm fine with that. Thus, I want the best of the best local. And so, I present to you my dining list:

Illinois

Must
- Portillo's, Chicago.
- Lou Mitchell's, Chicago.
- Ariston Café, Litchfield.

Maybe
- The Berghoff, Chicago.
- Lou Malnati's, Chicago.

Portillo's. Damn, I love me a Chicago hotdog. There used to be a Chicago Dogs restaurant by my former office, but I got fired, and then it closed, so any opportunity I can get for a 'dog dragged through the garden I'm all in for. In fact, I would posit that the Chicago hotdog may just be the epitome of American foodstuff perfection: it was born of the Depression, when a man, having only a nickel for food for an entire day, could fill up on a Vienna beef dog with all his requisite veggies (pickles, tomatoes, sport peppers, onions, neon relish, mustard, and celery salt), all on a steamed poppyseed bun. Everything you need in one fell swoop. Deliciousness and historical import. God bless you, Depression-era hobos!

Lou Malnati's. Another chain not readily accessible to me, so all bets are off. There's an Uno's about an hour away from my house, but Lou Malnati's is the real deal: Chi deep-dish pizza *in* Chi. I think there may be a place for this experience. They do have individual si—wait, hold the goddamn phone: there's a Giordano's stand at Wrigley! Sorry, Lou Malnati's!

The Berghoff. I was recently at a gate at O'Hare across from that branch of the Chicago institution, and I was salivating at the smell wafting across the terminal. Alsatian classics served in the same building since 1898 = one amazing-sounding Chicago experience. Definitely, probably.

Lou Mitchell's. The traditional starting meal for a Route 66 trip, so they say, and who am I to argue tradition? We'll just have to see about this "World's Finest Coffee" claim, now, won't we?

Downstate

Downstate Illinois is tough because there are some serious Route 66 icons that I'll likely be bypassing—this time around, anyway. Dell Rhea's Chicken Basket in Willowbrook and the Cozy Dog Drive-In in Springfield are legendary: magnificent American neon beacons to artery-clogging, nostalgic greatness. But I'll be blasting through in the morning hours, and I can't hit 'em all. I definitely need to set aside half an hour for Ariston Café in Litchfield, though. In the picture in my mind (largely based off those images from *Route 66 Lost & Found: Ruins and Relics Revisited*), I imagine wrought iron and Astroturf, rickety chairs, and huge homemade pies. My research since then tells me that Ariston is renowned for its Baklava. Either way, I need this in my life.

Missouri

Must
- Pappy's Smokehouse, St. Louis
- Ted Drewes Frozen Custard, St. Louis.

Maybe
- Elbow Inn Bar & BBQ, Devil's Elbow.

St. Louis

St. Louis ribs. Period. I've heard good things about Pappy's Smokehouse on Olive, and it's not too far off from Busch. A pre-game sup and walk it off on the way to the stadium.

Ted Drewes Frozen Custard. Custard is addictive, and Ted Drewes is world-renowned. I may have to settle for one at Busch, though, as I'll probably be heading by the original too early in the morning on my way to Tulsa. Sacrifices must be made.

Downstate
Elbow Inn Bar & BBQ. Another joint that got me in *Route 66 Lost & Found: Ruins and Relics Revisited.* An old shack

next to a classic truss bridge. Perfect. It's the old Munger Moss Café, which dates to 1929, and I'm not about to argue with 90 years of deliciousness! Then again, my stomach certainly will, but fuck it: I'm packing Imodium.

Kansas

I got nothing. Not enough of Kansas to even think about. Onto Oklahoma!

Oklahoma

Must
- Waylan's Ku-Ku Burger, Miami.
- Ike's Chili, Tulsa.
- Pops 66, Arcadia.

Waylan's Ku-Ku Burger. Have I mentioned that I'm a sucker for cheesy Americana and great signs? I have? Oh. Well, that crazy classic neon sign with the chef's-hat-wearing cuckoo bird sucked me in immediately. And the burgers look like sloppy American perfection; like a Heartland Shake Shack. And tots! Yes! And it's three-plus hours from the Elbow Inn, so I might be getting a bit hungry again by then...

Ike's Chili. The same top-secret family recipe since

1908. A small chili mac (chili with mac and cheese) for $4.79. Oh, yes, we'll be having a bit of that! I love, love, *love* places like this—joints that are institutions beloved by locals for generations. For one night, I want that experience. Get me a bib and get out of my way!

Pops 66. The soda ranch to top all soda ranches. I'm not much of a soda drinker, actually, save for the semi-occasional mini (eight-ounce can) ginger ale. If I have two Dr. Peppers in a month, it's a binge month. I just don't like the heaviness in my stomach and the feel of battery acid lingering on my teeth. *But* I do love me a unique soda experience (again, nothing I can readily access at home), and Pops has over 700 varieties *and* one of the greatest signs I've ever seen: a 66' (clever!) neon soda bottle with a straw glowing across the plains like the Beacon of Carbonated Freedom. Raise the bunting!

Texas

Must
- The Big Texan Steak Ranch, Amarillo.

The Big Texan Steak Ranch. My God, there is *no way* that I'm doing the 72oz steak challenge. Just... nope. One hour to down a 72oz steak, shrimp cocktail, salad with a roll and butter, and a baked potato. I know everything is bigger in Texas, but... nope. Naturally, Adam Richman, host of the

Travel Channel show *Man V. Food*, completed the challenge in 29 minutes, though I always had a problem with that show: in an age of such desperate food insecurity for so many Americans and such draconian cuts in aid to the needy, it seems distasteful at best to me to glorify such gluttony. Then again, me ordering a 12oz (max) steak for myself is benevolent gluttony, right? Yes! And dammit, I love American kitsch. That glorious cowboy sign; the giant cow out front; steer heads and lanterns and wagon wheels, oh my! Yeah, I'll be stopping in and settin' for a spell. And there's a hotel on the premises with a Texas-shaped pool. Yeehaw!

New Mexico

Nada. I don't really have any specific dining musts in New Mexico, other than authentic New Mexican fare. I plan on keeping an open mind and looking out for mom-and-pop dives, preferably in strip malls. I've found across the country that the best food is usually found in a mom-and-pop dive in a strip mall—small hole-in-the-wall, family-run joints. That's where you find family tradition—recipes crafted from motor memory. I want Chile sauce and fry-bread. I'll be looking for big lines, not websites. And the chips (and salsa) will fall where they may. I have no doubt I'll end up ahead in the game.

Arizona

Must

- Delgadillo's Snow Cap, Seligman.

Delgadillo's Snow Cap Drive-In: my only must in Arizona. I've read about the menu ("dead chicken") and the "pranks" that may greet visitors, and that's enough for me. Delgadillo's, you're on my list.

California

Must

- A Dodger Dog.

Maybe

- In-N-Out Burger.

Dodger Dogs. That's it. I've dreamed my whole life, as a baseball fan, of a Dodger Dog at Dodger Stadium. That's a big check off the old bucket list right there. I've heard that they're not even all that great, but I don't care: I've dreamed of having a Dodger Dog at Dodger Stadium ever since I was collecting Ron Cey and Steve Garvey baseball cards when I was eight. Time to make good on that dream. And, finally: no In-N-Out Burger anywhere close to me, but not a huge priority. If I get my Animal Style on, great; if not, next time. Because there *will* be a next time.

ABOUT THE AUTHOR

Brian Westbye is a certified dreamer. By day, he is an anti-money laundering investigator for a major East coast bank, and by night, he makes music and fills blank pages.

Westbye has battled depression/anxiety, childhood trauma, and a hideous midlife crisis, and has mostly won. Accordingly, he wrote *Driving Toward Clarity: (Re)Discovering America and Myself Along Route 66*, his first book: so he could help others overcome the same demons.

Westbye lives in Maine with his wife and two cat babies, and frequently visits his second family and home in Seattle.

www.brianwestbye.com